TOTAL HEALTH

TALKING ABOUT LIFE'S CHANGES

TOTAL HEALTH

TALKING ABOUT LIFE'S CHANGES

SUSAN BOE

purposeful design®
publications
A Division of ACSI

Colorado Springs, Colorado

Purposeful Design Publications is the publishing division of the Association of Christian Schools International (ACSI) and is committed to the ministry of Christian school education, to enable Christian educators and schools worldwide to effectively prepare students for life. As the publisher of textbooks, trade books, and other educational resources within ACSI, Purposeful Design Publications strives to produce biblically sound materials that reflect Christian scholarship and stewardship and that address the identified needs of Christian schools around the world.

References to books, computer software, and other ancillary resources in this series are not endorsements by ACSI. These materials were selected to provide teachers with additional resources appropriate to the concepts being taught and to promote student understanding and enjoyment.

Printed in the United States of America
16 15 14 13 12 11 10 09 08   2 3 4 5 6 7 8

Boe, Susan
   Total health: Talking about life's changes
   Second edition
   Total Health series
   ISBN 978-1-58331-229-2   Student textbook (hardcover)   Catalog #7603
   ISBN 978-1-58331-230-8   Student textbook (softcover)   Catalog #7604

Cover design: Sarah E. Schultz

Purposeful Design Publications
A Division of ACSI
PO Box 65130 • Colorado Springs, CO 80962-5130
Customer Service: 800-367-0798 • www.acsi.org

SPECIAL THANKS

This book could not have been published without the contribution and expertise of many people. I wish to give special thanks to the following for their involvement.

David G. Mackin.

Thank you for the many hours of writing and editing this manuscript. Your knowledge, insight, and experience have given this book its professional as well as personal touch.

The 1998-1999 junior high students and teachers from the following schools:
Jackie Ford with Santiam Christian School, Kathy Williams with Tualatin Community Christian School, Diana Scoville with Eugene Christian School, Steve & Chelan Powlison, and Phil Zedwick with City Bible School, Joy Felt with Willamette Christian School, and Linda Moxley representing the homeschool community.

Thank you for your availability to me during my research. Talking on the phone, attending the brainstorming luncheon, and taking the time out of your teaching schedules to allow your students to participate in the lengthy interview process made this project what it is today. Your students' honest responses and genuine questions will touch many teens across the country.

City Bible School, Portland, Oregon.
Administrators Bruce Paulson and Janice Dorszynski.

Thank you for your continued willingness to support *Total Health*. I appreciate your flexibility, encouragement, and willingness to allow me to disrupt your daily schedules. A special thank-you to the 1998-99 junior high class for their cooperation in the photo shoot.

Chad Ellars.

Thank you for your insight and expertise in the mountain climbing analogy used throughout Chapter 7. May you find true success and fulfillment as you pursue your goals.

John and Christina Mackin.

Thank you for your thoughtful answers to my sometimes difficult questions.

My Family.

Special thanks to my husband, Scott, and our two boys, Steven and Christopher. Your patience, love, and encouragement kept me going even during the most stressful days! I love you guys.

John and Martha Bryan.

Thank you once again for the opportunity to serve the Christian educational community. Your generosity and support is evident in every publication.

Glenda Malmin, Tisha Rayson, Kathy Mackin, Ann Finley, David Mackin, and Rosemary Long.

Thank you for your prayers and words of encouragement during this production. God bless you for your faithfulness.

CREDITS

Art Credits

Cover design by Susan Carrington of Susan Carrington Design.

Cover photos by Fred Wilson with junior high teacher Steve Powlison, art director Susan Carrington and the students from City Bible School, Portland, Oregon.

Layout and graphic design by Adam Forrest of Forrest Creative, Lisa Million of Million Graphics, and Susan Carrington of Susan Carrington Design.

Anatomical illustrations on the following pages are original and copyright 1995 by Lisa Million and are used with permission: pages 16 (Total Health Wheel), 21 (Life of a Cell), 25 (Flow of Blood Through the Heart), 26 (Circulatory System), 31 (Respiratory System), 35 (Skeletal System), 38 (Muscular System), 40 (Digestive and Excretory Systems), 49 (Endocrine System), 61 (Food Guide Pyramid), 90 (How "Fit" Are You?), 202 (The Skin), 213 (Teeth in the Mouth), 214 (Tooth), 216 (Brushing/Flossing Teeth), 219 (The Eye), 221 (The Ear), 243 (Alcohol Related Problems), 259 (The Harmful Effects of Tobacco).

Illustration of The Two Trees on page 7 is by Susan Carrington of Susan Carrington Design.

All other line art illustrations throughout text are from Dynamic Graphics, Inc. and are used with permission.

Personal photos of the author's are on the following pages: pages 201 (teen shaving), 284 (girl in car), 302 (Father and son laughing).

Photos from Dynamic Graphics, Inc. are on the following pages and are used with permission: 273 (Two girls reading), 286 (Girl standing at ocean edge), 298 (Girl in pool).

Photos from Fred Wilson Photography are on the following pages and are used with permission: pages 127 (Girl at tree with teens behind), 128 (Mother/daughter sitting at swings), 282 (Father and son at bench), 310 (Group of teens on bleachers).

Photos from Corbis are on the following pages and are used with permission: pages 2 (Two trees), 146 (Mountain climber), 228 (Man reaching for sky), 283 (Father/daughter at bike).

Photos from Tony Stone are on the following pages and are used with permission: pages 176 (Mother/daughters arguing), 299 (Girl encircled by teens).

A photo from Adobe, Inc. is on the following page and is used with permission: page 74 (Sad girl with teens teasing).

All remaining photos are from Photo Disc, Inc. and are used with permission.

Text Credits

Baker Encyclopedia of Psychology edited by David G. Benner. Copyright © 1985 by Baker Book House.

"Blasting Away at Body Fat" by Roger Rapoport. *Running* (March/April 1982).

Dake's Annotated Reference Bible by F.J. Dake. Copyright © 1961.

"The Ultimate Child Abuse" by Dr. James Dobson. Copyright © March, 1999. *Dr. James Dobson's Bulletin*. Focus on the Family.

Fearfully and Wonderfully Made by Dr. Paul Brand and Philip Yancey. Copyright © 1980 Zondervan Publishing House, Grand Rapids.

"I'm Living With Cancer", Kristen Drenten as told to Michelle Sullivan. Copyright © January, 1998 by *Teen*.

Prescription for Nutritional Healing. 2nd Edition by Dr. James F and Phyllis A. Balch. Copyright © 1990 by C.N.C. Avery Publishing Group.

RIGHT FROM WRONG: What You Need To Know To Help Youth Make Right Choices by Josh McDowell and Bob Hostetler. Copyright © 1994 by Word Publishing.

Stretching by Bob Anderson. Copyright © 1980 by Shelter Publications.

The Plug-in Drug by Marie Winn. Copyright © 1985 Penguin Books, New York.

The Three Battlegrounds by Francis Frangipane. Copyright © 1996 by Arrow Publications, Cedar Rapids, Iowa.

There Were Two Trees in the Garden by Rick Joyner. Copyright © 1992 by Whitaker House and Morning Star Publications, Pineville, North Carolina.

Total Health: Choices for a Winning Lifestyle by Susan Boe. Copyright © 1995 by RiversEdge Publishing Company, West Linn, Oregon.

"What is Fit?" by Karen Catchpole. Copyright © April, 1998 by *Jump*.

"Why are Hamburgers called Hamburgers?" Copyright © February 28, 1999 by *Parade*.

Word Pictures in the New Testament by A.T. Robertson. Copyright © 1930 by Broadman Press, Nashville.

TABLE OF CONTENTS

A MESSAGE FROM THE AUTHOR

Dear Students of Total Health,

I felt that no one really understood me, when I was in middle school. I didn't have anyone to talk to. Besides wondering who my real friends were and struggling with my parents, I also doubted if people liked me. I asked myself what the purpose of my new-found faith in Jesus Christ actually meant. If you can relate to any of these feelings, I can really understand how you feel. Having felt this way before I entered high school, I've written a text for students your age that would be different from any other text-book that you've ever read. I've entitled the book, *Total Health: Talking About Life's Changes* because I know that what I needed the most when I was in middle school was someone to tell me that all of the changes in my life were okay and that God totally understood. Before I wrote the book, I interviewed over 350 students your same age to find out what issues were the most important to them. I've changed the students' names, but their stories, feelings, and questions are very real.

When I look back at what meant the most to me, it was not just a bunch of scientific facts or memorizing a long list of Bible verses. It was experiencing how much God loved and cared for me—as someone unique and different from everyone else. A verse that still means a lot to me is in *Jeremiah*: "For I know the thoughts that I think toward you, says the Lord, thoughts of peace and not of evil, to give you a future and a hope. Then you will call upon Me and go and pray to Me, and I will listen to you. And you will seek Me and find Me, when you search for Me with all your heart."

These verses meant a lot to me because I felt that God was telling me that He even knew my nickname (which is "Sooney"); that He had very good plans for my future, and that He wasn't hiding from me. I hope that this text is more than just another textbook to you. I hope that you will feel in its pages the very love and care that both God and I have for each one of you. May God draw you closer to Him as you read.

Sincerely,

Susan

Susan Boe
5/19/99

Unit 1 • Physical Health

"The tree of life was also in the midst of the garden, and the tree of the knowledge of good and evil."

Genesis 2:9

THE POWER OF CHOICE 1

1•1   Facing a Choice

. . . .

Imagine...

The stage is set, the script is written, and the actors are cast. The main character walks onto the stage where the props resemble a beautiful garden. Carefree in attitude, she strolls among the flowers and stops to rest beneath a fruit tree. She hears a soft and intriguing voice. She glances upward to see a serpent perched on a limb of the tree. She remembers seeing him in the garden before, but she never really noticed him until now. They begin to chat. Their conversation seems harmless at first; until the serpent begins to isolate her from the person she trusted the most by questioning one of the laws of the garden.

"Did God really say, 'You can't eat the fruit of every tree of the garden'?" asked the serpent. Eve answered, "We may eat the fruit of any of the trees of the garden; except of the tree in the

middle of the garden, God said that if we ate of it, we would die." Then the serpent said to Eve, "God knows you won't die. He's just keeping you from trying something that's really good." Pausing for a moment, Eve turned to go and ask Adam what he felt about the issue. When the serpent noticed that Eve was leaving to talk to someone else, he quickly inserted, "No need to talk to anyone else. Aren't you mature enough to have a mind of your own? Besides, look at this big, red, juicy apple." With that remark, the serpent dropped the most succulent piece of fruit into Eve's hand. She looked at it. There was something different about this fruit that made her want to try it. The **temptation** seemed more than she could resist. "This is the best fruit of the whole garden," he continued, "just take one bite, and you'll see. It won't hurt you. As a matter of fact, it'll make you a better person: more attractive, more intelligent, and much more powerful. Go ahead and give it a try. No one else will find out…" (Genesis 3:1–10, paraphrased)

Choosing the right person to talk to about your feelings is very important. Can you think of qualities you look for in a person you can trust?

How many times have you heard this story? You recognize the characters: Adam, Eve, and the serpent (Satan). You remember the setting: the Garden of Eden, the most beautiful place on earth at the time. You recall how the serpent's deceptive words caused Eve to question God's commandment. And, you know the end of the story. Eve fell into temptation and ate the forbidden fruit. You're also aware of the **consequences** of her decision. You've been personally observing as well as experiencing the pain and devastation ever since.

Take a moment and ask yourself an interesting question. What might have happened if Eve had decided not to handle the temptation *alone* but had gone to someone whom she could trust? What might have occurred if she had talked to someone else about her inner struggle; someone who could have understood exactly how she was thinking and feeling? Imagine Eve talking with Adam before she

ate the apple. What if they had talked it over, prayed about it, and recognized together that the serpent was bad news. What might have been the outcome? Keeping this in our imagination, let's pick up the story where we left off...

The temptation seemed more than Eve could resist, but then she remembered Adam. She felt that he might be able to help her with this decision. Before the serpent could say another word, Eve ran off to find him. This made the serpent furious. He knew that if she talked to Adam, his plan would be ruined.

When Eve found Adam, she was almost out of breath. "Where have you been and why were you running?" Adam asked. "Adam," Eve replied, "I've just come from the tree in the middle of the garden. The serpent began to talk to me about the fruit of the tree. I almost grabbed an apple. I really became worried when the temptation got so strong. I ran away from the serpent to try to find you, and—" Adam interrupted, "What were you doing in that part of the garden? Don't you remember how God told us that it wasn't a good idea to hang around that tree?" "I'm very confused," Eve continued, "and I don't know what to do. The serpent began to talk to me about things I've never thought about before. He said that God is jealously trying to keep us from something that is really good for us; some experience that will make us just like Him. That sounded good to me. I'm so curious about that tree! What do you think that I should do?"

Sometimes you may feel afraid of sharing your strong feelings for fear of the other person's reaction. But sharing with your parent(s), for example, often brings you closer together.

"Eve, I understand exactly how you feel," Adam responded, "I've felt the same curiosity as you as I've walked by that part of the garden. Just like you, I don't always understand why God has told us not to eat from that tree. I feel puzzled sometimes, but then I tell myself that there must be a very good reason why He's said "No." God has been so good to us. He's given us so many other trees from which to eat. To avoid the temptation altogether, I've decided not even to go near the forbidden

tree again. If I were you, I'd totally avoid talking with the serpent—no matter how sweet his words sound. He really gives me the creeps."

With that, Eve never went back to the tree to finish her conversation with the serpent. Instead, both she and Adam prayed and asked God for strength to overcome the temptation that they both had felt. After talking it over with each other, and with the Lord, Adam and Eve both experienced less and less of a curiosity for the forbidden fruit. With a renewed desire to do what God had asked them to do, they never went back to that tree.

Growing Up: The Desire for Independence

Oh, how you probably wish that the imaginative version of this story were the real case. Unfortunately, it's not. Everyday you're faced with the consequences of Eve's independent decision. Often, you're tempted to say and do things that you know aren't the best. What specific painful struggle does the forbidden tree represent to you? In his book, *There Were Two Trees in the Garden*, Rick Joyner describes it this way:

A driver's license and a car means more freedom and independence, but also requires more responsibility.

> There were two trees in the Garden of Eden that challenged the course of the entire human race—the Tree of the Knowledge of Good and Evil [or, the Tree of Death] and the Tree of Life. These same two "trees" continue to challenge us. When we become Christians, these challenges don't end—they may well increase. Many times we have to choose between the fruit of these two trees… [which] represent the fundamental conflict between the kingdoms of this world and the kingdom of God.[1]

We'll never know how life may have turned out in the Garden, if Eve would have gone to Adam instead of eating the fruit. But, what we do know is that Eve listened to the tempter and yielded to the temptation by making an independent decision. She made a choice without the input of anyone else. She didn't seek out a person she could trust, a person with a different perspective, someone who could pray with her for strength.

You may not realize it, but you answer this inner question every-day: "Do I face my battles alone, or do I talk to someone else about them?" As a younger person, you rely upon others to make many of your decisions. You ask your parents' permission to spend the night at a friend's house. You need to get an "okay" from your Dad or Mom to watch a certain movie.

As you get older, the problems in your life seem to get a lot bigger, don't they? Several years ago, the temptations were less danger-ous than they are now. Your choices are still less deadly than they will be in the future. However, as you make right decisions, you'll earn a growing sense of independence. But, with your in-creasing independence, you'll be facing your own "serpents" and will be tempted by your own "forbidden trees."

The Two Trees

- Dependent on God
- Needing others
- Involved
- Talking with safe adults
- Telling the truth
- Open and transparent

TREE OF LIFE

- Independent from God
- Not needing others
- Isolated
- Not talking with safe adults
- Covering up
- Closed and afraid

TREE OF DEATH

I'm drifting further away from God. Actually, I go back and forth. But, either way, I don't know what to do. There's no one I want to talk to.

Mary

Can you relate to Mary's feelings? Many people feel they have no one to talk to. Our culture says that as you get older and more mature, you should become totally independent from everyone

You may not realize it, but you answer this inner question everyday: "Do I face my battles alone, or do I talk to someone else about them?"

else in life. It encourages you to make your own decisions without getting anyone else's input. It claims that you don't need anyone else. This concept of independence has a seed of truth in it. God does want you to find His unique will for your life.

But, there's a subtle danger here. The danger is that you will equate growing up with being totally independent, thinking that you don't need anyone else anymore. The hazard is in feeling that in order to be an adult, you should be able to solve all of the challenges in your life without ever having to talk to anyone else. God does want you to be mature and responsible. He doesn't, however, want you to be totally independent and isolated. God wants you to recognize your need for others. The benefit to you is that God can really use others to bring many blessings into your life. It's also important to know that other people need you, too! God has made life in such a way that you never outgrow your need to talk to others about the questions you're facing. Even the most "independent" person in the world is still very dependent in many ways upon other people. Even the richest person in the world, for example, still needs many financial advisors to counsel him.

The Power of Influences

Everyday, you are faced with choices. Some are more difficult than others. Many you make without a second thought. When you get up in the morning, you may shift into "autopilot" as you go through your daily routine. You may automatically brush your teeth, eat breakfast, and choose what clothes you want to wear. You might have an argument with your brother, snap at your Mom, and head out the door in a huff. Throughout your day, you're bombarded with **influences** which are all trying to affect your choices. These influences may seem innocent at first, but many can be very

Even the strongest athlete sometimes gets injured and needs help on the field.

destructive to your life. King Solomon wrote, "There is a way that seems right to a man, but its end is the way of death." (Proverbs 14:12) Can you think of both positive and negative influences affecting your decisions today? Think about how the following areas influence your choices about God, yourself, and others.

- *Media/entertainment*: images of sex and violence, profanity, commercials ("You're not cool unless you buy this!"), magazines, advertisements, television, computer/video games, star/celebrity lifestyles, the Internet, movies, videos

- *Music*: lyrics, tunes, moods, sounds, MTV

- *Friends*: what you talk about, jokes, clothes, habits, what you do to have fun, comparing yourself with others, copying others

- *Family*: the tone in your voice, topics of conversation, daily habit patterns, good and bad examples

Some negative influences can make your life capsize like a raft in rapids.

- *Church*: practical messages, relevant Bible studies, leaders who "walk the talk," feeling accepted as you are, finding genuine friends, having open discussions

- *The Bible*: reading and applying the Word of God to your daily struggles, how much you allow it to influence your life

- *Relationship with God*: how often you talk with Him, how much you want to follow Him, if you obey Him

Not all of the influences in life are negative. In our story, Adam was Eve's positive influence. She thought he might be able to help her with her perspective. How can a person recognize which influences are positive and which are negative? Once you determine if the influence is negative or positive, the conflict lies in how much power you give to it.

I wish that more kids got to know God. Their decisions would be better, and their problems would be less.

Lindsey

The consequences of your choices will become more serious as you get older. What are some of the consequences of your decisions as a young teenager?

In your daily decisions, you're setting patterns of how you'll handle life's challenges. You form **habits** which can be difficult to break.

The serpent has not changed his tactics. He's still lurking around the garden of your life. Even as you're reading this page, he's trying to figure out how he can deceive your mind, cause you to make poor choices, and, eventually, destroy your entire life. He's trying to plant proud, totally independent thoughts in your mind; feelings of despair and hopelessness in your heart. The serpent is attempting to keep you away from the very people who would be able to understand your struggles, strengthen your faith, and help you to succeed. Unwise decisions can make you feel so embarrassed that you want to run away or hide. Fortunately, you can resist wrong influences by sharing your struggles with others. Sharing can prevent you from making poor choices and strengthen you to make better ones. The choice of sharing or not sharing is up to you.

Because of feeling guilty over their sin, Adam and Eve tried to hide from God (Genesis 3:8). What caused Adam to think that he could hide from the Father who knows everything? **Deception** brought this fear and separation into Adam and Eve's hearts. Instead of going to God to admit their mistake, get forgiveness, and gain strength to resist the next time, they thought that they could hide from God and resolve the situation by themselves. Adam and Eve not only hid from God, they also tried to get rid of their guilty feelings by putting on fig leaves for clothes. Instead of going to a loving God who would have forgiven them, they ran away and tried to fix their problem themselves. It just didn't work.

When I make a mistake, I feel like
God is really disappointed in me.

Jan

How many times have you felt like hiding from God? How many times have you felt that God wouldn't know or care, only to find out later that not only did He care, He also knew all about your situation from the very beginning? Your mind knows that your heavenly Father is omnipresent (everywhere at all times), but your heart still tries to hide and cover-up. Why? This is what sin does to you. When you make a poor decision, your independent self says, "God doesn't love me anymore. I'm going to hide. I'm going to do something else to try to get myself to feel better. Unless I'm perfect, God doesn't want to talk to me." These are all untrue thoughts. The truth is that there's nothing that you could ever do to cause your heavenly Father to stop loving you!

And, there's some more good news, too. Someone else totally understands your feelings. The same emotions you have when you disappoint God through your unwise choices in the garden of your life is the same feeling Adam and Eve experienced in their garden. The good news also means that just as God took the initiative to go into the Garden and find Adam and Eve, so will the Holy Spirit come looking for you whenever you hide from Him (Genesis 3:9). Just as God called to Adam and Eve, so God is calling to you. His seeking you out only means that He loves and cares for you. He's showing you a better way to live; a way to get closer to Him and others.

Have you ever felt like hiding from the world and even from God? Contrary to what you may have experienced from other relationships, when God calls you and brings correction, it never means rejection.

1•2   Choosing to Change

I was raised in a home that attended church faithfully every Sunday. Church was a regular routine for us. I didn't really mind it. I also attended a private school that offered a religion class. I knew all the Bible stories. Even though I passed my religion classes with A's, I couldn't say that I had a personal relationship with Jesus. By the end of seventh grade, I had a reputation in the school of being the "teacher's pet" or the "religious one." I got that reputation from answering the questions in religion class and offering to pray for requests when other students didn't want to. Through a series of circumstances, I began to get more and more interested in spiritual things. I specifically remember crying in church during a sermon one Sunday. Something was happening inside of me. As I now look back, God was calling to me. But, like Adam and Eve, I was hiding.

When you choose to surrender your entire life to God, every change God brings into your life will bring you closer to Him.

One night, I attended a Christian concert. I found myself listening very closely to the speaker. He was sharing about how Jesus truly loved us just the way we were. This made me feel good. He also told us that God had a special plan for our lives. He kept talking about having a personal relationship with Jesus. In all of my years in private school, I had never heard anyone talk about God in this way. With tears in my eyes and a heart open for change, I chose to welcome Jesus into my life that night. I surrendered my entire life to Him. I gave Him every poor choice, each painful memory, and all of my sins. Ever since that moment, I've never been the same.

This textbook will probably be unlike any other text you've read. This health class may cause you to re-evaluate your life. You may even make the choice to change in a few areas. You'll learn more about yourself, your fears, and your God. The stories you'll read are true. They're from

real people who have experienced genuine battles. The years before young adulthood are very difficult, even more difficult than a few years ago. But, remember, there's power in your choices—just ask Eve!

1•3   Exploring Design and Purpose

· ·

Just as each invention is designed for a purpose, God has created you with an incredible purpose and plan.

God created everyone and everything with a purpose. When an inventor begins to think creatively about an invention, there's an ultimate intention that the invention must serve. A light bulb, for example, was created to produce light, and not heat. Although heat is a by-product of a light bulb, the heat generated would not be enough to heat a room. If you wanted to communicate with a friend across town, you wouldn't use a hairdryer. You'd use a telephone because it was designed for that specific purpose.

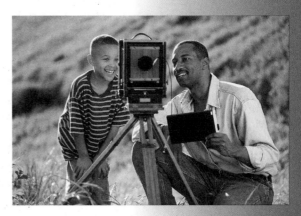

Similarly, when God created you, He had a special purpose in mind. He made plans for you in the future and said, "I see (put your name here) doing this for My kingdom. I will make him/her especially suited for that specific purpose."

For You have formed my inward parts. You have covered me in my mother's womb. I will praise You, for I am fearfully and wonderfully made. Marvelous are Your works, and that my soul knows very well.
Psalm 139:13–14

The Total Health Concept

Immediately after both Adam and his wife made the wrong choice, separation from God and others began to increase. The human race discovered that sin was very self-destructive. But, in God's mercy, He revealed some laws to Moses and the people of Israel that would protect them from hurting and destroying themselves. These laws or principles covered every aspect of life. In *Total Health*, you will see how some of these divine boundary markers

13

apply to you today. You'll discover that these principles are relevant not only to your physical health, but to your mental, social, and spiritual health, too.

When Adam and Eve made the wrong choice, it affected every area of their lives. They damaged more than their relationship with God. The consequences were not just "spiritual." Both of them immediately experienced the negative outcome of their choices in at least four ways: physically, mentally, socially, and spiritually.

Physically, as soon as Adam and Eve disobeyed God, their bodies immediately began to be subject to disease, decay, and death (Genesis 3:19). What once was a perfectly designed human body, now became imperfect. Eve was going to bring children into the world with much physical anguish and pain (Genesis 3:16). Adam would have to exert much energy in manual labor. He would have to struggle to get food for himself and his family (Genesis 3:17–19). Before they chose to eat from the forbidden tree, Adam and Eve were never sick. They were enjoying eternal life right here on earth. After their unwise choice, however, they both became open to sickness and death.

Mentally, Adam would no longer enjoy nature or the animal kingdom as much as he had before he disobeyed God. God cursed both the creation and the animal kingdom because of Adam's sin (Genesis 3:14,17). Even though Adam showed dominion over the animals in the beginning by naming each one (Genesis 2:19), now many of the animals were going to be a lethal danger to him. He was going to experience mental and emotional stress from fear of bad climate and animal attacks.

He was going to experience mental and emotional stress from fear of bad climate and animal attacks.

Socially, sin brought severe conflict between human beings. This conflict would begin at a very young age and continue throughout people's lives. Jealousy, hatred, and violence were going to be experienced—even between family members. Cain murdered

his younger brother Abel because his brother's sacrifice was accepted by God while his was not (Genesis 4:6–8). Cain allowed his anger to turn into rage and murder. Shortly afterwards, the spirit of revenge ("getting even") increased between people (Genesis 4:15, 24).

Spiritually, Adam and his wife walked and talked with God every day in the cool of the Garden before they disobeyed. They had a close friendship with God. After they disobeyed God, however, their spirits, which were once in close union with the Father, were separated from that intimacy. As a consequence, they experienced a lonely, isolated feeling that they had never known before.

Conflict between people begins at an early age— but this was not God's intention when He created mankind.

The strength you feel to overcome your temptations is directly related to your relationship with God. Adam and Eve had an open and honest relationship with God before they ate from the forbidden tree. But, after being thrown out of the garden, they struggled with keeping their relationship with Him so open and close. It took Jesus Christ to come into the world, pay the penalty for sin, and make it possible for you to have a close relationship with God. Adam and Eve didn't get to experience that reunion with God the Father, but you can experience it through His Son, Jesus Christ. All you have to do is choose to surrender your entire life to God. Every change God brings into your life will bring you closer to Him.

God created each part of you according to His unique plan. He designed your body, soul, and spirit to do something for Him that no one else can do! In order for you to fulfill His plan, He must separate (sanctify) you from the sin that would hinder His work

through you. This is the way Paul described God's changing process in a letter to the church of the Thessalonians:

Now may the God of peace Himself sanctify you completely; and may your whole spirit, soul, and body be preserved blameless at the coming of our Lord Jesus Christ. He who calls you is faithful, who also will do it.
I Thessalonians 5:23

How your body functions, how your **soul** (your mind, your will, and your emotions) responds, how you relate to others, and how you communicate with God, all determine what kind of person you are. When all these parts of your being are functioning well, I call it "**Total Health**." Just as Adam and Eve's choice affected each area of their lives, so your choices impact every area of your life. Throughout this course, we will explore choices and their consequences. Some consequences are immediate while others are not. How have your choices already affected your life? What choices do you face today that may positively or negatively influence your future? In the next chapter, we will explore human biology in relationship to your choices and the consequences affecting the physical aspects of your total health.

Chapter 1 Review

Defining the Terms (use the Glossary if necessary)
Temptation
Consequences
Influences
Habits
Deception
Soul
Total Health

Recalling the Facts

1. What caused Eve to begin to question God's laws of the Garden?

2. How did Adam and Eve's decision to eat the apple immediately affect their relationship with God?

3. Explain what is meant by the phrase "forbidden fruit".

4. Compare the Tree of Life with the Tree of Death as it relates to your relationships with others.

5. When Adam and Eve ate from the forbidden tree, and hid from God, how did God respond to them?

6. How has Eve's decision affected all of mankind today? Give one example under each of the following categories: physically, mentally, socially, and spiritually.

Applying the Truth

1. Eve allowed Satan to entice her with his deceptive words and by the sight of the delicious looking fruit (Genesis 3:1-6). Read Proverbs 1:15; 3:7. Discuss how Solomon advised people to handle evil influences. How might this truth apply to your daily life?

2. What painful struggles might the "forbidden fruit" represent to you and many other young teenagers?

3. Evaluate yourself for a moment. Do you face your battles alone, or do you talk to someone else about them? Who would be your first choice to talk to and why would you choose him/her? What makes him/her a positive or negative choice?

4. What choices do you face today that may positively or negatively influence your future?

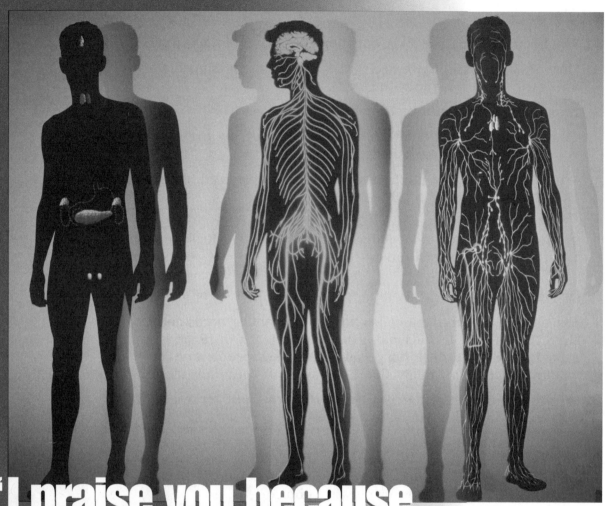

"I praise you because
I am fearfully and
wonderfully made..."
Psalm 139:14

HUMAN BIOLOGY 2

2•1   Exploring Biology and Health

Understanding your body's divine design is an exciting exploration. Even though human beings have been studying their own physical structure for centuries, we're continually being amazed at new discoveries. Scientists have not completely understood this simple yet complex organism called the human body.

Every day, your body is changing. Today, you're not exactly the same person as you were yesterday. Every seven years, for example, your body covers itself with an entirely new layer of skin. Your body works hard for you. It tries to maintain itself with excellent health. However, chemical changes within your body, your exposure to germs, your level of stress, as well as your food choices all affect your body's state of health.

Have you ever told someone, "I feel great today!"? When you say "great"—or healthy—what do you mean? "Good health" to you may seem like poor health to another. As a general definition, being **healthy** can be defined as a state of physical, mental, social, and spiritual well-being. Being in good health is more than not feeling the symptoms of sickness or disease. It means more than simply not feeling a head- or stomachache. As you learn more about the biology of the human body, keep in mind that the whole body is affected by each functioning part. When you stub your toe against a heavy rock in your backyard, your entire body reacts in some way to the pain, even though your toe is a very small part of your body. Furthermore, the condition of each organ inside of your body is really only as healthy as the condition of each of its smaller tissues and cells. Most importantly, every part—each cell, tissue, organ, and muscle—will be affected by the choices you make.

2 • 2   Exploring the Body

As you open the hood of a car, you will notice many parts influencing the ability of the car to run smoothly. In this way, the human body is like a car. Each part, or system, varies in its purpose, but without each piece fulfilling its assigned duty, you couldn't stand up or walk to your friend's house. Your body consists of four main levels. Each level plays an important role in the functioning of your body as a whole. Let's look at each level individually.

Although the human body is an efficiently running system, each individual part has a very unique function.

Cells

Although the human body is an efficiently running system, each individual part has a very unique function. God created the cell as the smallest living unit within the body. The human body is made up entirely of cells. **Cells** are the basic building blocks from which all larger parts are formed.

The following terms describe the life of a single cell:

The Life of a Cell

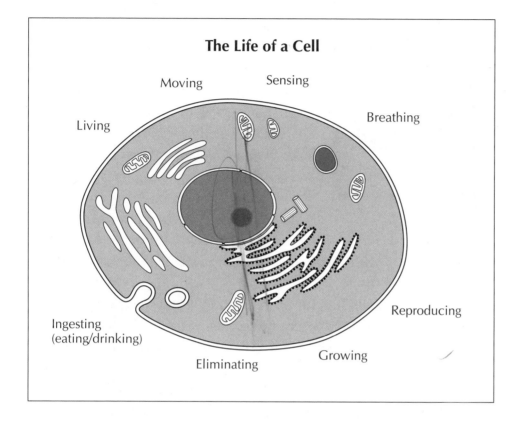

Cells instinctively know their own function and don't try to be something that they were never created to be.

The different sizes and shapes that cells have closely relate to their individual function. Cells instinctively know their own function and don't try to be something that they were never created to be. A muscle cell cannot perform the duties of a nerve cell. How many different kinds of cells do you think that your body has?

...If I parade these cells under the microscope, certain impressions about the body take shape. I am first struck by their variety. Chemically, the cells in my body are almost alike, but visually and functionally they are as different as the animals in a zoo. Red blood cells, discs resembling Lifesaver™ candies, voyage through my blood loaded with oxygen to feed the other cells. Muscle cells, which absorb so much of that nourishment, are sleek and supple, full of coiled energy. Cartilage cells are like shiny

A lab technician prepares a slide for examination under a high-powered microscope.

black-eyed peas glued tightly together for strength. Fat cells seem lazy and leaden, like bulging white plastic garbage bags jammed together. Bone cells live in rigid structures that exude strength. Cut in cross section, bones resemble tree rings, overlapping strength with strength, [and] offering…sturdiness. In contrast, skin cells form undulating patterns of softness and texture that rise and dip, giving shape and beauty to our bodies. The king of cells…the nerve cell…has an aura of wisdom and complexity about it. Spider-like, it branches out and unites the body with a computer network of dazzling sophistication.[1]

As each of your cells has its own special job, so God designed you for a specific function; to carry certain unique responsibilities. You were created for a different purpose than your best friend. If you try to become just like someone else, you'll not fulfill the intention for which God created you. If you do follow the special calling that He has planned for you, however, you'll be very happy and fulfilled.

Tissues

Another incredible part of your body are your tissues. You probably take them for granted. When similar cells are organized into specialized groups to carry out particular functions they're called **tissues**. It's important to understand that all of your body systems rely heavily upon the health of these tissues to keep functioning properly. The human body contains four primary types of tissues:

Epithelial tissues cover all body surfaces inside and out. The *skin* is an example of an epithelial tissue.

Connective tissues bind structures together providing support and protection. *Tendons*, *ligaments* and *cartilage* are examples of connective tissues.

DANGER!

The heart is composed of *cardiac muscle tissue*. Over a period of time, if a person's diet consisted of high levels of saturated fat and cholesterol, the arteries which feed the cardiac muscle would become clogged. The result would be *arteriosclerosis* (hardening of the arteries). The cardiac muscle would become less effective in its specialized function. This would be called *coronary heart disease*. The good news is that coronary heart disease is preventable through healthy lifestyle choices. When people replace a high-risk lifestyle (unhealthy diet/habits → bad fats → blockage → heart attack → death) with a low-risk lifestyle, then they can increase both the quality and longevity of their lives. What other lifestyle choices do you think can affect the health of your heart muscle?

Muscle tissues primarily provide movement. There are three types of muscle tissue: the *skeletal* muscle, the *smooth* muscle, and the *cardiac* muscle.

Nerve tissues receive and transmit impulses to various parts of the body. These highly specialized tissues are located in the *brain*, *spinal cord*, and *nerves*.

LOGON!

Your Body's Incredible Communication System

How many miles of nerves do you think run throughout your body? One mile? Five miles? The answer is almost 45 miles! If you were to line these nerves up end-to-end, it would take you 45 minutes at 45 MPH to drive from one end to the other. This incredible communication system is responsible for controlling all of your body's movements and functions.

Organs

Organs are the next level of organization in the human body. An organ is a more complex structure than a cell or a tissue. Each organ is designed for a highly specialized purpose. An **organ** can be defined as two or more tissues grouped together to perform a singular function. Organs have incredibly important job descriptions. What would your body do, for example, without the proper functioning of your heart, brain, or lungs? If any of your organs wasn't fulfilling its responsibilities, your whole body would eventually break down and stop functioning.

Next, let's explore the different systems of your body; the necessary networks that are made up of your cells, tissues, and organs.

2 • 3 Exploring the Body's Systems

Your body has many "systems" just like the universe does.

The universe which God created is composed of millions and millions of "systems." We usually call the coordinated group of stars and planets in our Milky Way galaxy our "galactic" system. In a similar way, your body is comprised of several different systems. Each of these systems is a divine miracle in itself. Have you ever wondered how the skin on your face could be of a certain texture and then suddenly change to an entirely different type when it comes to form your lip? Each of your *body systems* is a highly complex, well-ordered, and smoothly coordinated group of organs (or, parts of organs) of the same or similar tissues that are concerned with the same function. This chapter will give you a brief overview of eight major body systems. As you learn about the incredible systems of the human body, notice how each system is not only unique and separate in function but also very dependent upon the others.

The Circulatory/Cardiovascular System

The **circulatory system** is the group of body parts that transports the blood throughout the body to keep it functioning properly. This system is like a major road transportation network. This invisible "roadway" performs four main functions in your body. It:

1. transports fuel to your body,

2. carries wastes to your liver and kidneys (where they are eliminated),

3. sends cells to fight disease, and

4. transports hormones throughout your body.

The Flow of Blood through the Heart

4 Blood carrying oxygen is returned to the left atrium through the pulmonary veins

1 Blood from body enters right atrium through superior vena cava and inferior vena cava

5 Blood enters left ventricle through bicuspid valve

2 Blood enters right ventricle through tricuspid valve

6 Heart pumps blood from left ventricle to aorta, which carries blood to the body

3 Heart pumps blood from right ventricle to pulmonary trunk, which carries blood to the lungs where oxygen is absorbed

Septum

The cardiovascular and circulatory systems of the body work together so closely that, oftentimes, their names are used interchangeably. The **cardiovascular system** is the specific portion of the circulatory system that includes the heart (*cardio* means heart) and blood vessels (*vascular* means vessels).

The organs that make these functions possible are the heart, arteries, veins, and capillaries.

Heart: the engine that drives the circulatory system. With every beat, the heart is the muscle that pumps blood throughout the body by way of the *blood vessels.*

Arteries: the largest blood vessels. Arteries carry blood filled with oxygen (*oxygenated blood*) away from the heart. The arteries must be very strong due to the high pressure of blood pumping through them.

Incredible Pumping Machine!

Did you know that your heart beats about 100,000 times a day and pumps blood through 100,000 miles of blood vessels?

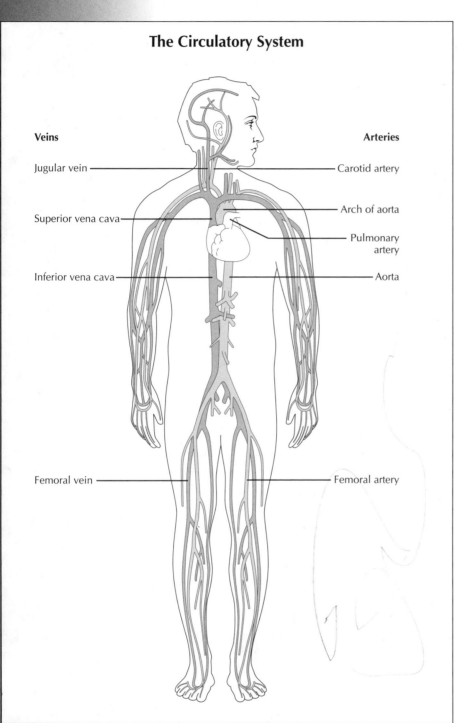

The Circulatory System

Veins

Jugular vein

Superior vena cava

Inferior vena cava

Femoral vein

Arteries

Carotid artery

Arch of aorta

Pulmonary artery

Aorta

Femoral artery

Veins: the blood vessels that take blood that lacks oxygen (*deoxygenated blood*) back to the heart. Veins have thinner walls than arteries because of the lower pressure of blood flowing through them. Veins also have valves to direct the blood flow.

Capillaries: the smallest blood vessels. Capillaries carry blood from the arteries to the body's cells and from those cells to the veins. The capillaries have *semipermeable* walls (allowing certain molecules to pass through) so that nutrients, gases, and wastes can be exchanged between blood and tissues.

Without clean oil, your car's engine would become filled with "gunk." It's the oil that keeps your engine clean and well-lubricated. Auto mechanics say that the most important service that a car owner can do to maintain his car is to change the oil regularly. The blood in your body is similar to the oil in your car. Your *blood* is your life fluid. Have you heard of the biblical statement, "The life is in the blood" (Leviticus 17:11)? Your blood carries all that your body needs to live, heal, and defend itself. When germs and vi-

ruses enter your body, the blood stream is the main battlefield. God made your body's bloodstream with the ability to recognize a foreign invader and destroy it.

Your blood consists of one liquid and three solid portions. The liquid portion is called **plasma.** It carries all of the other parts in it. The solid portion consists of **red blood cells** (carry oxygen), **white blood cells** (fight germs, viruses, and diseases), and **platelets** (help blood to clot).

Your Life Is in Your Blood!

How much blood do you think is in your body? The volume of blood in a person's body varies with body size and several other factors. An average male (about 154 lbs.) will have a blood volume of about 5.2 quarts. An average female has a lower blood volume than an average male. One exception to this is during pregnancy when a woman's blood volume will increase by 3-4 lbs.

Your Blood Pressure

Have you ever heard of someone having high or low blood pressure? Measuring your blood pressure is one way a doctor determines the health of your blood vessels. **Blood pressure** is the force that your blood puts on the inside walls of your blood vessels as it moves throughout your body. Blood pressure is measured with two numbers. During each heartbeat, blood surges out of the heart and back into the arteries. The peak (or highest) pressure caused by this surge is known as the *systolic pressure.* When the heart relaxes, blood flows back into the heart, and the blood pressure drops. This lower pressure is called the *diastolic pressure.* The range for normal blood pressure varies with age. In general for adults, the upper number (systolic pressure) should be less than 140 and the lower number (diastolic

Your Red Blood Cell Count

Red blood cells have limited life spans that average about 120 days. The number of red blood cells in a cubic millimeter of blood is called the *red cell count.* Although this number varies from time to time, the normal average range for an adult male is 4,600,000–6,200,000 cells per cubic millimeter! The average adult female range is 4,200,000–5,400,000 cells per cubic millimeter. The number of red blood cells generally increases after exercise, a large meal, or a rise in body temperature. Why do you think this increase occurs?

pressure) less than 85–90. Blood pressure readings such as 110/70 would be read as "110 over 70."

What Blood Type are You?

Knowing your blood type is an important part of your health history. Would you like to know your blood type? All you have to do is to ask a parent or doctor. People have their blood types in their medical records. To help someone who may need blood, doctors must know the blood type of both the *donor* (the one giving blood) and the *recipient* (the one receiving blood). Because some blood pools have experienced contamination due to AIDS, etc., doctors will sometimes ask patients who are coming into the hospital for surgery to allow their own blood to be drawn ahead of time so that it can be used during their operation. In this way, there's no danger of mislabeled or contaminated blood. Blood type is categorized in two ways: the ABO system and the Rh system. People can be type A, type B, type AB, or type O. People are also either Rh-positive or Rh-negative. Only certain combinations of these categories can share blood without complications.

Blood type is categorized in two ways: the ABO system and the Rh system.

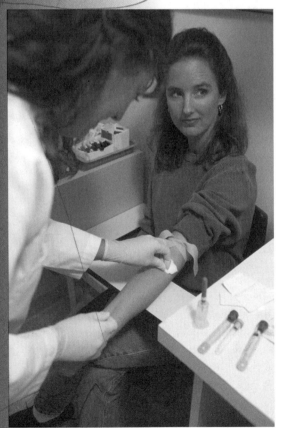

People with type O blood are called *universal donors* because they can give blood to anyone who has the same Rh factor as they do. People with type AB blood are called *universal recipients* because they can receive blood from any of the other types as long as they have the same Rh factor.

Health Alert! Problems in the Circulatory System

Problems that occur in the circulatory system may be directly related to the blood, heart, kidneys, or blood vessels. You may know of someone who has suffered from one of the following conditions: anemia, leukemia, hemophilia, arteriosclerosis, or hypertension.

When a person has an inadequate supply of red blood cells, he's said to be anemic or suffering from **anemia**. There are many causes and types of this

disease, but general anemia is often caused by a lack of proper nutrition resulting in an inadequate amount of iron.

Leukemia is a form of cancer characterized by an uncontrolled increase in the production of white blood cells. This cancer affects both the bones and the blood. Leukemia decreases an individual's resistance to infection. It also lowers the victim's red blood cell count. There are many types of leukemia, and doctors today don't understand what causes it.

You may know a person who is a hemophiliac. **Hemophilia** is a disease in which the blood is lacking one or more of the clotting factors. The hemophiliac's blood lacks the ability to clot when he is cut or injured. As a result, excessive bruising and bleeding occur. There's a medicine available that allows the blood to clot. Hemophilia occurs only in males. Women, however, may carry the disease and pass it on to their male children.

Arteriosclerosis, or hardening of the arteries, is a disease in which certain arteries become hardened or obstructed. These clogged arteries eventually limit or stop the flow of blood to certain organs of the body. Arteriosclerosis is often called the *"silent killer"* because people may have the disease without knowing it. This disease is very common in Western societies like America due to a diet high in saturated fat and cholesterol. If the blood flow to the heart is cut off, and the heart stops working properly, a *heart attack* may result.

Arteriosclerosis is often called the "silent killer" because people may have the disease without knowing it.

A stroke is another disease related to the flow of blood. It occurs when a blood clot forms, detaches itself from a wall in an artery, and travels through the body to the brain. When the blood flow to

DANGER!

What vitamins do you think are necessary for red blood cell production? If your diet consists primarily of hamburgers, french fries, and chocolate shakes, your blood may not be receiving the important nutrients to produce the oxygen-carrying red blood cells your body needs. Make sure you're getting vitamin B_{12}, folic acid, and iron. (The vitamin and mineral chart in the nutrition chapter will show you which foods are high in these essential vitamins.)

one part of the brain is severely restricted or cut off a person is said to have had a **stroke**. Common causes of strokes are blood clots, arteriosclerosis, and untreated high blood pressure.

Hypertension or **high blood pressure** occurs when the pressure on the inside walls of the arteries becomes too high. It's a very common condition in Western societies. Poor diet, little exercise, and high stress can all negatively influence blood pressure. Doctors often prescribe medication to help control this condition.

The Respiratory System

Before body cells can use nutrients as sources of energy, they must be supplied with oxygen. The carbon dioxide that results from the use of this oxygen must be released. The **respiratory system** is the group of passages that exchanges gases in order for the body to function properly. Other roles of the respiratory system include: filtering incoming air, controlling the temperature and water content of the air, producing sounds in speech, and giving the body the sense of smell.

When running a race, your ability to breathe in oxygen efficiently is vital to your performance.

The organs of the respiratory system can be divided into two parts: the *upper respiratory tract* (nose and throat) and the *lower respiratory tract* (lungs). The major organs of this vital system are: the nose, nasal cavity, sinuses, pharynx, larynx, trachea, bronchial tree, and lungs.

Taking a Breath

The act of breathing is both an involuntary as well as a voluntary action. You can choose to hold your breath, but sooner or later your body's need for oxygen will overcome your own ability to resist, and you'll gasp for air.

When air enters your nose, three interesting events occur. First, small hairs filter and trap dirt and particles. Second, the blood vessels which line the inside of your nose warm the incoming air. In this way, your body helps the air to adjust to its own internal tem-

perature. Third, the *mucous membrane* of your nose moistens the air you inhale. Sometimes, the combination of moisture and dirt causes you to sneeze or to feel the need to blow your nose.

When air enters through your mouth, it travels down your throat (**pharynx**) by way of the trachea (windpipe). The windpipe doesn't filter particles as well as the nose does, so it's better to breathe in using your nose instead. When working in areas where the air is filled with dust, a person should wear a mask over his mouth and nose to protect his lungs.

Have you ever choked when you were trying to eat and talk at the same time? After you caught your breath, did anyone ever say to you, "Did you put something down the wrong pipe?" Comments like these make it sound like your throat has two tubes in it. The fact is that because food enters the body by way of the mouth, just as air does, the pharynx splits off into two separate passageways. The front portion, the **trachea**, carries air to the lungs. The back portion, the **esophagus**, takes food to the stomach. To prevent food from entering the trachea, a small flap of skin, the **epiglottis**, closes over the top. If a person laughs or talks while trying to swallow, the epiglottis may not close in time and coughing or choking can result.

In your chest, the trachea also divides into two directions to allow air to reach both lungs, one on each side of your chest. These passageways are called *bronchi*. The *bronchial tree* branches off from the bronchi into several smaller tubes so the air can inflate the lungs.

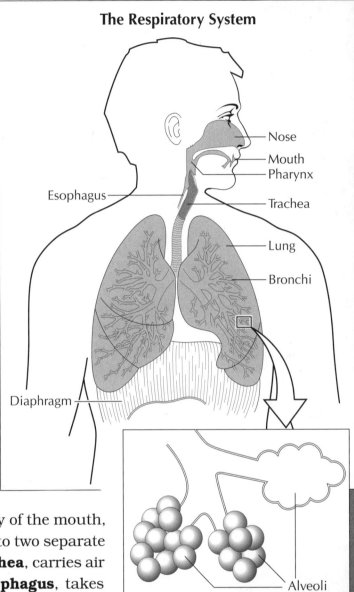

The Respiratory System

Nose
Mouth
Pharynx
Esophagus
Trachea
Lung
Bronchi
Diaphragm
Alveoli

The **lungs** are large, soft, cone-shaped organs, one on each side of your heart. Without healthy lungs, a person's breathing is impaired and the oxygen supply to the body is deficient. The bronchial tree stretches out into the lungs where millions of tiny air sacs called *alveoli* exchange gases with the blood. Take a moment to notice your own breathing. As you inhale (*inspiration*) your chest rises slightly. As you exhale (*expiration*) your chest returns to its normal position. Your intercostal muscles as well as your diaphragm are used for this breathing motion. The **diaphragm** is a large muscle that separates the chest from the abdomen. Learning how to control the diaphragm is an important part of efficient breathing. The diaphragm plays a vital role in the act of producing a full, resonating sound when singing.

Health Alert! Problems in the Respiratory System

The common *cold* is the most frequent illness that affects the respiratory system. Cold viruses cause symptoms such as fever, aching body, runny nose, itchy/watery eyes, and sore throat. A cold may also affect your lower respiratory tract by giving you a cough. If you have a cold, the medications you take only temporarily relieve the symptoms. They don't treat the cause (the virus).

The Common Cold

One reason why doctors can't find a cure for the common cold is because there are over 200 viruses that cause its symptoms. The good news is that you can't catch a cold from the same virus twice.

Pneumonia is a serious disease affecting the lungs. It causes breathing difficulties. It's important to see a doctor who can prescribe certain medications for this infection. **Bronchitis** is a swelling or inflammation of the bronchi. A serious cough, a general feeling of fatigue, or a fever are symptoms. It can last several weeks. Medications can help bronchitis.

You may suffer from asthma or know someone who does. **Asthma** is a fairly common condition in which the bronchi swell and constrict breathing. It can be triggered by an allergic reaction to something, by exercise, or by psychological factors such as intense fear or nervousness.

Have you seen the following billboard? A man and a woman are talking. The man asks, "Do you mind if I smoke?" The woman responds, "Do you mind if I die?" **Emphysema** is a serious disease that affects the alveoli (air sacs) of the lungs. It prevents air from passing in and out of the lungs. The main cause of emphysema is inhaling smoke and/or polluted air. The damage created by this disease cannot be reversed. The result is eventually fatal.

Your lungs are extremely sensitive organs. It's vital that the air you breathe is as clean as possible. Sometimes, you might inhale air pollution or the smoke from cigarettes, cigars, or pipes. **Lung cancer** occurs when cells grow out of control and destroy the alveoli. The most common cause of lung cancer is smoking. The warning, "Smoking May Be Hazardous to Your Health," is really an understatement when it comes to smoking's negative effects. Lung cancer is treated with radiation and chemicals. Often, a diseased lung must be removed. Lung cancer eventually results in death.

Your lungs are extremely sensitive organs. It's vital that the air you breathe is as clean as possible.

The Skeletal System

The 206 bones that make up your frame are the organs of your **skeletal system**. These bones are made of several types of tissues. Each kind of bone has a particular function in your body's structure and design. The combination of all your bones, joints, and connective tissues provides the following benefits to your body:

- Support: Bones help hold your body upright.

- Protection: Bones protect your internal organs.

- Manufacture: Bones manufacture red and white blood cells.

- Storage: Bones store important minerals and substances.

You may think that your bones are just a single mass of hard substance. Actually, they have three uniquely designed layers:

Your bones, joints, and tissues can hold-up under great stress.

1. *Periosteum*: a membrane on the outer portion of the bone filled with nerves and blood vessels; helps in the formation and repair of bone tissue.

2. *Compact bone*: a strong, solid, and dense portion of the bone; so hard that surgeons must use a saw rather than a knife to cut through it.

3. *Spongy bone*: the inner area of the bone in which the bone marrow exists; looks like a honeycomb; has thousands of tiny holes which serve as passageways for nerves and blood vessels.

Your bones are linked together with a very unique design of tissues. These fibrous connective tissues consist of **cartilage** (strong elastic material on the ends of bones), **joints** (points where bones meet), and **ligaments** (strands of tissue that join bones or keep organs in place). Working together, these bone tissues provide you with the flexibility you need everyday. They help to make your movements fluid and coordinated.

DANGER!

Did you know that a lack of exercise can cause your bone tissue to "waste away", or atrophy? The bone becomes weaker and thinner. So, the next time you're exercising, remember that you're not only strengthening your muscles, you're increasing your bone tissue, too.

Health Alert! Problems in the Skeletal System

Have you, or anyone else you've known, ever broken a bone? It doesn't matter what you may have broken—arm, leg, or ankle—it really hurts! Although bones are strong, they can break. Accidents, unnecessary risk-taking, nutritional deficiencies, or disease may cause an injury to a bone.

Scoliosis is a condition when the vertebral column develops an abnormal curvature so that one hip or shoulder is lower than the other. There is no known cause for this condition. The only treatment is to wear a brace that corrects the curvature. Sometimes, physical therapists will recommend certain stretching exercises.

When joints become inflamed, a person may have **arthritis**. This condition can be very painful and may impair movement. Because arthritis is a common problem among adults, you may have a parent or a grandparent who suffers from it. There's no cure for many types of arthritis, but some have found relief using medications and some natural remedies.

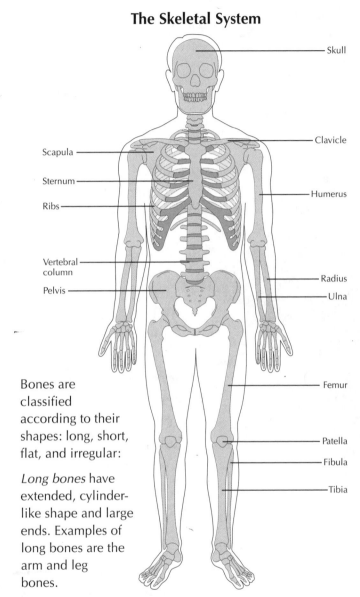

The Skeletal System

Bones are classified according to their shapes: long, short, flat, and irregular:

Long bones have extended, cylinder-like shape and large ends. Examples of long bones are the arm and leg bones.

Short bones are similar in shape to long bones but are smaller and have less prominent ends. Examples of short bones are the wrist and ankle bones.

Flat bones have broad surfaces. They protect the internal organs. The ribs, scapulae, and the bones of the skull are examples of flat bones.

Irregular bones have a variety of shapes and are usually connected to several other bones. Bones of the face and the vertebrae of the backbone are examples of irregular bones.

LOGON!

A Difference in Bone Structure

If you were to discover the remains of two complete human skeletons, do you think that you could tell which one was male and which one was female just by looking at the bones? If you were to compare the pelvis (hip) bones, you would discover that the female's is much wider than the male's. It has a large, round opening at its center for giving birth. Other bones of the female, however, may look slimmer and more petite.

Many years of playing sports can cause excessive stress on one's shoulders. Sometimes, people wake up in the middle of the night from pain and tenderness in one or both of their shoulders. This condition, called **bursitis**, is caused by an inflammation of a bursa (a tiny, fluid-filled sac located between tendons and bone in different parts of the body). Bursa are used to cushion against friction between bones and other tissues. "Tennis elbow," "policeman's heel," or "frozen shoulder" are other names used for bursitis.

Osteoporosis, a loss of bone tissue, can be caused by a lack of calcium in the diet, a lack of exercise, or a low level of certain hormones. Many elderly people suffer from this condition. As a result, bones are easily fractured or broken when a person falls. Eating a healthy diet and maintaining a habit of exercise are good ways to help prevent this condition in your future.

Many years of playing sports can cause excessive stress on one's shoulders.

Injuries

Teens enjoy a high energy level and a carefree attitude that are just normal parts of growing up. Teens, however, will sometimes take some wild and crazy dares that often make their parents worry. Some of your dares can end up causing the following painful injuries to your skeletal system which can give you a permanent disability or weakness in that part of your bone or joint.

LOGON!

Alcohol's Effect on Your Bones

Did you know that drinking alcohol can have a direct effect upon the strength of your bones? Researchers have found that alcohol in large quantities prevents certain body chemicals from doing their jobs. This can result in weak bones that are easily broken.

Fracture: A fracture is a break in a bone. There are six different types of fractures, each named according to its cause and degree of break. The treatment of a broken bone depends upon its severity. A cast is usually used to help in the natural healing process.

Dislocation: A dislocation occurs when the end of a bone is pushed out of its joint. A dislocation is usually the result of vigorous physical activity or a fall. If you've ever experienced a dislocation, you'd agree that it's a very painful injury. The bone must be placed back into its joint and kept still until the area heals.

Sprain: Sprains are the result of stretching or tearing the ligaments at a joint. This can be very agonizing. It should be treated with cold packs on the injured area as soon as possible to keep down the swelling.

Some accidents that you may experience are unavoidable, while other accidents are a result of pushing yourself too hard.

The Muscular System

Did you know that nearly half of your body weight is made up of muscles? Your **muscular system** is the group of tissues that makes body parts move. Were you aware that it takes seventy separate muscles to allow you the wide variety of movement that you enjoy when using your hand? Did you know that your muscles are so strong that if all the muscles in your body pulled together in one direction they could lift 25 tons? Your muscular system makes your body an incredible moving machine!

There are three different types of muscle tissue in the body. Each type of muscle tissue causes movement in a different part of the body.

Skeletal muscle: causes your body to move. These are attached to the bones and joints. Skeletal muscles come in different shapes and sizes based upon function.

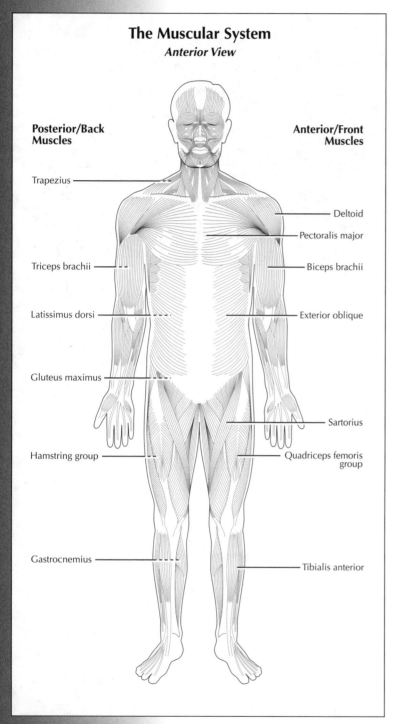

The Muscular System
Anterior View

Posterior/Back Muscles

Anterior/Front Muscles

Trapezius

Triceps brachii

Latissimus dorsi

Gluteus maximus

Hamstring group

Gastrocnemius

Deltoid

Pectoralis major

Biceps brachii

Exterior oblique

Sartorius

Quadriceps femoris group

Tibialis anterior

Smooth muscle: is found in your digestive system and your blood vessels. These muscles allow movement within your body. Your diaphragm, stomach, and intestines are examples of smooth muscle tissue.

Cardiac muscle: is located only in one area in your body—your heart.

A muscle tissue is either *voluntary* (you control its movement) or *involuntary* (you don't control its movement). There are millions of functions within your body over which you have no direct control. The cardiac muscle is an example of an involuntary muscle. Your skeletal muscles, however, are voluntary. You can make your leg or arm move whenever you like. Can you think of other examples of muscles that are involuntary?

Your body has over 600 major muscles that need energy from food and oxygen to produce a wide variety of movement. Although your muscles produce different movements, they all work the same way. When the brain sends a signal by way of the nervous system, a muscle *contracts* (shortens). When another signal is received, the muscle *extends* (lengthens).

Let's look at a common movement to show how your skeletal muscles work in pairs. Imagine a baseball player up to bat. As he holds the bat in proper position, his biceps muscles contract, and his triceps muscles extend. As he swings at the pitch, the biceps muscles extend and his triceps muscles contract. This

cooperation between the muscles allows for a powerful swing that sends the ball over the fence!

To keep your muscles in top working condition, they need to be exercised. Skeletal muscles that are considered "in shape" have good muscle tone (firmness). When a muscle is not exercised, it's considered "out of shape" and weak. If you have good muscle tone, you're less likely to get injured when participating in physical activity. If you're trying to improve your athletic skill or physical endurance, you must work those muscles that relate specifically to your sport.

Health Alert! Problems in the Muscular System

Most problems associated with the muscular system are related to injury. The most common injuries include:

Strain: Overworking a muscle or group of muscles causes a stretching beyond the normal limit. The treatment for a strain is rest and heat applications.

Cramp: A cramp results when a muscle doesn't relax. Applying heat and trying to relax the muscle should relieve the cramp.

Bruise: When a muscle is injured, blood vessels are broken in the area and can create a **hematoma** (bruise). A direct hit to any area of the body can cause a bruise. A cold pack applied to the area may reduce the swelling.

Pulled or torn muscle: A muscle that has been overworked or didn't receive adequate warm-up prior to an activity can result in the muscle pulling away from the bone. This can be a serious injury and might require immediate medical attention.

Muscular fatigue: Muscle exhaustion puts your body at greater risk of injury. When your muscles are tired, they may not withstand the extra strain you place on them. The best idea is to rest and wait until your muscles recover before participating in vigorous physical activity.

Muscles work in pairs. For every action there is an equal and opposite reaction of a muscle.

The Digestive System

Digestion is the process by which food is broken down and made useful for the body. You make the choices of what to feed your body. Your body is responsible to use this food as fuel and energy through your bloodstream. Once food enters your mouth, the process of digestion has begun. The digestive system consists of a long muscular tube called the **alimentary canal** that extends from the mouth to the anus. The different sections of this canal are designed for specific purposes. However, the canal's structure and function (the way it moves food) are similar throughout its length. The alimentary canal doesn't work alone. Other organs that are not considered a part of the canal are also needed in the process of digestion. These include your salivary glands.

Salivary Glands

Digestion begins in your mouth when certain *enzymes* begin to break down your food before it reaches your stomach. Your teeth and tongue help prepare the food for digestion. It's very important to chew (masticate) your food thoroughly before swallowing so that it'll be easier for the rest of your system to digest. *Saliva* is released by the salivary glands in your mouth to moisten the food and begin the digestion of starches. Saliva not only functions in digestion, but it also keeps your mouth moist so that you can speak.

Esophagus, Stomach, Small Intestine

The **esophagus** is a straight tube that functions as a passageway for food from the mouth to the stomach. **Peristaltic** (wave-like) action moves the food down the esophagus into the stomach.

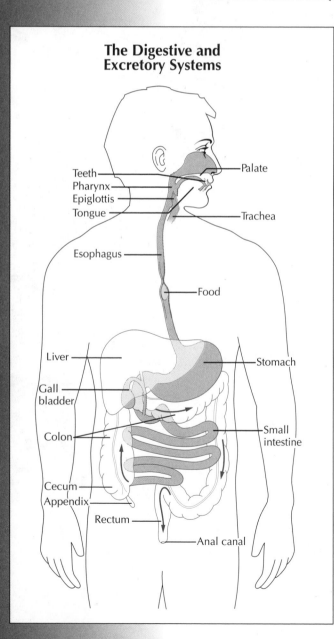

The Digestive and Excretory Systems

Teeth
Pharynx
Epiglottis
Tongue
Palate
Trachea
Esophagus
Food
Liver
Stomach
Gall bladder
Colon
Small intestine
Cecum
Appendix
Rectum
Anal canal

LOGON!

Your Digestive Canal

Your esophagus measures about 10 inches in length; your small intestine 18–23 feet; your large intestine 5 feet. Thus, the alimentary canal that runs from your mouth to your anus is 28–30 feet in length!

Once food enters your stomach, it's mixed with chemicals to continue its chemical breakdown. The main function of your *stomach* is to store the food before it moves on to the **small intestine** for further digestion. The small intestine is the location where the most digestion occurs. Millions of villi line your intestinal wall and act like fingers, grabbing the nutrients for absorption into your bloodstream. Your small intestine, however, couldn't effectively digest your food if it didn't have help from your liver, gallbladder, and pancreas. The following section describes the important roles that these three organs play in proper digestion.

Liver

The **liver** is the largest organ in the body and has many vital functions. The following functions relate to digestion:

- the production of bile, a bitter, alkaline, yellow or greenish liquid that helps to digest fats,

- the conversion of sugar into an energy source or to store it for later use,

- the balance of blood sugar in the body,

- the detoxification of the blood (changing poisonous waste into harmless substances), and

- the storing of fat-soluble vitamins such as A, D, B_{12}, and iron.

When you eat an ice cream cone, your liver is necessary to digest both the fat and the sugar.

Gallbladder

The **gallbladder** is a pear-shaped sac which lies underneath the liver. The liver produces bile which is passed to the gallbladder. The bile is stored in the gallbladder. From there, it's released into the **duodenum**, the first part of the small intestine. In the duodenum, the bile breaks down fats contained in food.

Pancreas

The **pancreas** is an elongated organ that lies in back of the stomach. It's attached to the duodenum by a duct (tube). The pancreas produces a juice that travels through the duct into the small intestine. This pancreatic juice contains enzymes capable of digesting fats, proteins, and carbohydrates. Besides helping the digestive system, the pancreas also helps the endocrine system. The endocrine system of hormones includes the thyroid, adrenal, and pituitary glands.

The Excretory System

Your **excretory system** works very closely with your digestive system. The part of your food that your body can't use builds up toxins (poisons) in your system. The purpose of your excretory system is to provide ways for such waste to be removed from your body. This system is like the exhaust system of a car. Even if a car owner tuned up his engine and put fresh oil into it everyday, if the exhaust from his car was like a cloud of smoke, then something would be wrong inside. No matter how good the outside condition of a car, its exhaust, a waste-product, must be continually released for the car to function properly.

Your excretory system works like the exhaust system of a car.

There are several ways your body rids itself of waste:

- Your lungs expel carbon dioxide (a colorless, odorless, incombustible gas formed during respiration or breathing).

- Your large intestine expels semi-solid waste.

- Your sweat glands expel water and salt.

- Your *urinary tract* expels liquid waste in the form of urine.

After your food has been digested and the nutrients have been absorbed into your bloodstream to give you energy, the leftover waste must be expelled. The large intestine (colon) is the organ whose primary purpose is to expel the waste from your body. In

DANGER!

Each meal you eat takes about 24 hours to be digested and excreted. If you eat 3 balanced meals a day, each meal should pass through your body every 24 hours. If you're not eliminating that waste with a good bowel movement each day, where is it going? What is it doing to your health? If your waste material is not regularly expelled, it can become toxic (poisonous) to your body. In order to keep your large intestine functioning properly, you should drink 8–10 8 fluid oz. glasses of purified water every day. (A pop can is 12 fluid oz.) It's also essential to eat foods that provide you daily with about 25 grams of fiber. Fiber is the part of a plant that cannot be digested. It's found in: popcorn (unbuttered, unsalted), fresh fruits and vegetables, bran, nuts, seeds, beans, lentils, and peas.

the colon, most of the water will be absorbed back into your system. The remaining semi-solid waste (feces) are passed out of your body.

The **large intestine** is made up of the *cecum, colon, rectum,* and *anal canal.* Notice the arrows in the diagram on page 40 which show how waste moves through the large intestine. The primary function of the first half of the colon is the absorption of liquids. The primary function of the second half of the colon is the storage and excretion of waste.

Kidneys

The kidneys are two bean-shaped organs located on either side of your spinal column. The main job of the **kidneys** is to cleanse the blood of impurities and send it back to the bloodstream. The kidneys send waste to the bladder in the form of urine.

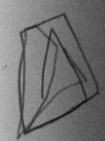

You should drink eight to ten glasses of purified water every day.

It's very important that your body maintains a fairly constant balance of fluids. The kidneys play a vital role in the regulation of water and electrolytes (salts) within your system. Although water is the major component of urine, the amount of water in your urine depends on your health, and the amount of food, water, and other liquids you consume. The amount of exercise you do

If you don't drink enough water to replenish your need for pure fluids, you'll become dehydrated. By the time you feel thirsty, you've already been walking around in a dehydrated state.

also contributes to the concentration of water in your urine. If you get *dehydrated* (lacking water), your body cannot function efficiently.

Health Alert! Problems in the Digestive and Excretory Systems

Indigestion and heartburn: Indigestion occurs when food is not completely digested. Overeating, eating too fast, eating while being upset, or eating the wrong combinations of food can contribute to indigestion. Heartburn occurs when the stomach acid flows back into the esophagus.

Nausea and vomiting: The feeling of being nauseated is often accompanied by a headache or body aches. The vomiting center in your brain can be triggered by motion, certain medications, poisons in food, strong emotions, viruses, or bacteria. When your body vomits, it's trying to cleanse itself by expelling the food.

Halitosis or bad breath: When halitosis is caused by the onions or garlic you just ate, then a strong mint, mouthwash, or fresh lemon juice will probably help. But, when a person has a consistent, offending problem with bad breath, a poor diet and/or poor digestion is often to blame.

Gallstones: Gallstones are formed when the bile stored in the gallbladder hardens into small crystals. These pebble-like solids may block the flow of bile into the small intestine and cause intense pain. The stones can be removed and, oftentimes, the gallbladder is also taken out. Unlike the liver, you can live without your gallbladder.

DANGER!

Did you know that beverages such as cola (pop), tea, and coffee all drain needed water from your body tissues? They act as a diuretic (a substance that increases the amount of urine excreted from the human body). If you don't drink enough water to replenish your need for pure fluids, you'll become dehydrated. By the time you feel thirsty, you've already been walking around in a dehydrated state. So, drink *before* you feel thirsty!

Constipation: Constipation occurs when your feces are hard and dry. This makes a bowel movement very difficult. Some of the causes of constipation include: poor diet (lacking fiber), little or no exercise, ignoring the urge to use the bathroom, lack of water, and the use of certain laxatives that can cause your body to lose its natural ability to eliminate waste.

Diarrhea: Diarrhea is the opposite of constipation. Too much water in the bowels causes loose and watery stools. Some of the causes of diarrhea are: a virus or bacteria that the body needs to cleanse, a change in diet that you may not be used to, food poisoning, or strong emotions. The danger with diarrhea is the possibility of becoming dehydrated. Drink plenty of liquid and, if it persists, see a doctor.

Flatulence or gas: A certain amount of gas in the stomach or intestines is normal. Some of the causes of gas include: a diet which includes gas-producing foods (beans, chocolate, high fiber foods), eating too fast, extra bacteria in the intestines, and foods to which your body is sensitive (e.g., milk and dairy products, wheat, wheat gluten (in breads), and extra rich foods). If you feel that you have excessive gas, modify your diet slightly to see if you experience a change.

Kidney stones: The kidneys can develop "stones" that are composed primarily of calcium. The stones can be small enough to pass out in the flow of urine, or they may be too large and block the passageway. Kidney stones are very painful, but doctors can remove them by breaking them up with sound waves.

Running in a race involves both your muscular and nervous systems.

The Nervous System

Imagine running in a race. When the starter sounds the command, "Ready," you place your feet in the starting blocks. Everything within you is feeling uptight about the race. Your heart is beating quickly. Your hands are shaking. Sweat is dripping from your

face onto the track. As the gun goes off, an automatic response occurs, and you explode toward the finish line.

All these actions are the result of messages sent to and from the brain by your **nervous system**. This complex set of impulses controls and coordinates all of your body parts so that they all work together as one flowing unit. Your network of nerves allows you to respond instantly to changes—even as they arise unexpectedly. Your body works very hard at remaining stable and balanced on the inside, even when the outside environment may be causing you distress. This balance is called **homeostasis** (a stable internal environment).

Your body works very hard at remaining stable and balanced on the inside, even when the outside environment may be causing you distress.

There are two main sections that make up your nervous system: your **central nervous system** (CNS) and your **peripheral nervous system** (PNS). Your CNS includes your brain and spinal cord. This is the main control center of your body. Your PNS includes the nerves that connect the CNS to other body parts.

Masses of neurons, or nerve cells, in the brain and spinal column are specially designed to react to certain physical and chemical changes in your body. Unlike other cells, neurons are very unique in that they cannot repair themselves. Once these nerve cells are damaged, they cannot be replaced.

Your ability to respond to the sound of the gun in a race is controlled by the sensory nerves of your somatic nervous system. This part of your nervous system causes you to respond to outside stimuli, such as smell, sight, and sound. Your uncontrollable sweating, caused by the anxiety of the race, is controlled by your autonomic nervous system. This portion of the nervous system is involuntary (separated from your conscious effort).

If you were to touch something hot, your sensory nerves would send a "pain" message to your brain. Instantly, your brain would tell your hand to pull away from the heat source. All of these reactions occur in a fraction of a second.

Health Alert! Problems in the Nervous System
Pinched nerve: When an injury occurs to the spinal cord, a nerve can be pinched or squeezed.

Infections: Polio and rabies are infections that directly affect the nervous system.

Epilepsy: Epilepsy is a brain disorder that results from a sudden burst of nerve action. Some medicines can control the seizures caused by epilepsy.

Cerebral Palsy: CP is a condition in which the cerebrum of the brain is damaged. It can cause muscular spasms, poor balance, or problems with seeing, hearing, and talking. There's no cure for CP to date, but therapy is used to help the individual cope with the condition.

Multiple Sclerosis: MS is a disease in which the outer coating that protects some nerves is destroyed. As a result, the individual loses control over certain body movements. It can also affect a person's speaking and hearing. Some medicine and therapy may help control the symptoms. As yet, however, there's no cure for MS.

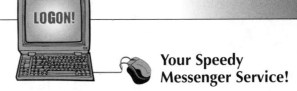

Your Speedy Messenger Service!

Did you know that you have about 45 miles of nerves throughout your body? Many of these neurons can send a message as fast as 248 miles per hour!

The Endocrine System
The endocrine system works closely with your nervous system to maintain a stable, internal balance (homeostasis). Your nervous system sends messages to muscles and glands by way of nerve impulses. Similarly, your **endocrine system** secretes hormones into your bloodstream as messages to your cells. Your nervous

> *If you were to touch something hot, your sensory nerves would send a "pain" message to your brain. Instantly, your brain would tell your hand to pull away from the heat source.*

system can send messages very rapidly throughout your body for a very quick response. In contrast, the effects of the hormones of your endocrine system often require minutes, hours, or days to get started. After the hormonal actions begin, they may continue for a very long time.

The chemicals released by the glands of your endocrine system are called **hormones**. These hormones can be called "chemical messengers." Their release is out of your control. They're working silently within your body. When you hear the word "hormone," you may think of only those hormones relating to your sexual development. There are, however, eight *glands* (a cell, group of cells, or organ that releases a substance) that are very important to many of the daily functions of your body. These eight glands are described below.

The pituitary gland is responsible for releasing your growth hormone (GH) that determines your rate of development.

Your **pituitary gland**, located at the base of your brain, is only about 1 cm in size. This small gland is also called "the master gland" because its function is so important. This gland is responsible for releasing your growth hormone (GH) that determines your rate of development. If your pituitary gland had released too little GH into your system, then you would be much smaller than you are. If it had released too much GH into your system, you would have grown unusually large.

Your **thyroid gland** is located in your throat. It's controlled by the pituitary gland. The release of your thyroid hormone, controls how fast your body metabolizes (uses) food for energy.

Your **adrenal glands** are located near your kidneys. A gland sits on top of each kidney like a cap. Your adrenals release certain hormones in response to various types of stress. When you feel fearful, for instance, these glands help you in your "fight or flight" response. When your adrenals release the hormone called adrena-

line, your body begins its appropriate stress response. Your body begins to defend itself by increasing your heart rate, breathing faster, and preparing your muscles for action.

Your *Islets of Langerhans* are several masses of endocrine cells located in your pancreas. They were named after the man who first described them, Paul Langerhans, a German anatomist who lived in the nineteenth century. Your Islets release the hormones *glucagon* and *insulin*. These two hormones are vitally important in the control of your blood sugar levels.

Your *pineal gland* is a small gland located in your brain. Although the function of this gland is not totally understood, researchers believe that it secretes a hormone called melatonin. Melatonin is thought to stimulate your hypothalamus. Your hypothalamus affects your pituitary gland's function in your sexual development.

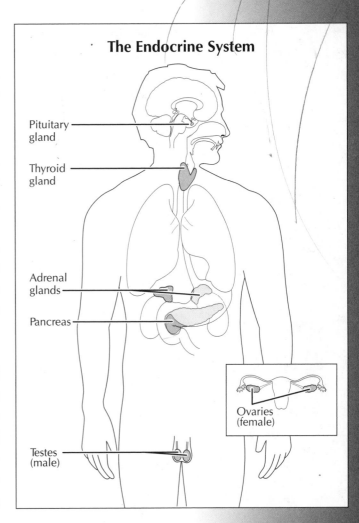

The Endocrine System

Pituitary gland

Thyroid gland

Adrenal glands

Pancreas

Ovaries (female)

Testes (male)

Your *thymus gland* is located behind your sternum and between your lungs. This gland is thought to be involved in the lymphatic system, which deals primarily with your body's immune system.

The **ovaries** are the glands of the female reproductive system. They are located inside a female's lower abdomen, one on each side. The **testes** are the glands of the male reproductive system. Unlike the ovaries which lie inside the female's body, the testes are located outside the male's body. Both of these glands gradually release hormones during puberty. They influence the development of male and female sex characteristics.

Health Alert! Problems in the Endocrine System

The most common problem associated with the endocrine system is **diabetes mellitus**. When people suffer from diabetes, their bodies cannot properly utilize the sugar that they need. Either insulin isn't released or it's not properly used. A careful diet or insulin shots may be needed to control this condition. Did you know that when insulin is commercially made, it comes from the pancreas of a pig or an ox?

The thyroid gland can also cause problems, if it's not functioning properly. *Hyperthyroidism* occurs when the thyroid is overactive (*hyper*=over). *Hypothyroidism* occurs when the thyroid is underactive (*hypo*=under). Both conditions can be treated with medication. A diet that's low in iodine can cause a swelling of the thyroid called a *goiter*.

Chapter 2 Review

Defining the Terms

Healthy	Blood pressure	Alimentary canal
Cells	Stroke	Large intestine
Tissues	Pharynx	Small intestine
Organ	Trachea	Kidneys
Arteries	Esophagus	Hormones
Veins	Epiglottis	Pituitary gland
Capillaries	Lungs	Thyroid gland
Plasma	Diaphragm	Adrenal glands
Red blood cells	Skeletal muscle	Homeostasis
White blood cells	Smooth muscle	Ovaries
Platelets	Cardiac muscle	Testes
Arteriosclerosis	Digestion	

Recalling the Facts

1. Explain the common characteristics of every single cell.

2. List the four primary types of tissues in the body and explain their general function.

3. Explain how the circulatory system is like a "roadway" network in your body. Include in your answer its four main functions.

4. Explain how the act of breathing is both voluntary and involuntary.

5. What are the four main functions of the skeletal system?

6. Explain what is meant by the phrase: "For every action there is an equal and opposite reaction of a muscle". Give one example of this principle.

7. Explain how the excretory system is like the exhaust system of a car.

Applying the Truth

1. What body systems are helped by consistent physical activity? How does exercise help them?

2. Which body systems are hurt by the poor eating habits a person might have? How does a poor diet hurt these systems? Give an example of how you might change your personal diet to help these systems of your body.

3. After reading this chapter, list four facts or observations about your body that show how awesome of a creation it is.

"I have given you every herb...and every tree whose fruit yields seed... for food."

Genesis 1:29

NUTRITION 3
ENTERING THE FOOD ZONE

What's Coming Up...

3•1 The Great Pizza Potential: A Balanced Diet

• •

You enter your local pizza parlor with your friends. You smell the fresh, hot, mouth-watering aromas of garlic and pepperoni. You glance at the menu. Everything looks good: the Canadian bacon & pineapple, the combination supreme with thick crust, the tomato/onion veggie, and the Italian sausage with extra cheese. What do you order? What do you feel like devouring tonight? Did you know that pizza has real potential for being a source of good nutrition? I like to call it The Great Pizza Potential. Before you decide to order your next pizza, however, you might want to read on and see if your particular pizza choice reaches its full nutritional potential.

Food is the fuel that energizes your body. When you feel hungry, your body is telling you that it's time to "refuel." Nutritious food means a diet that gives your body the best fuel (all the proper nutrients that it needs to cleanse, build, and maintain itself for optimal performance). Eating a **balanced diet** means making food choices that include a wide variety from all that God has given us in nature.

THE FOUR SOURCES OF CALORIES

Source	Calories per gram
Carbohydrate	4
Protein	4
Fat	9
Alcohol	7

A **calorie** is the name given to a unit of heat that your body uses for activity. Foods that are high in calories have a higher energy value. Typically, people who are trying to lose weight "count calories." If you eat foods that contain mostly **"empty calories"** (those which don't have any nutritive value), you're actually starving your body. Be aware of the empty calories you may be choosing to feed yourself. It's very important for you as a growing teenager, to eat a healthy, balanced diet. (A healthy diet doesn't have to taste "yucky" if you'll retrain your taste buds a little.) Your body is undergoing so many rapid changes, it needs all of the nutritional help that it can get. These changes require adequate sleep, plenty of pure water, and nutritious food.

If you knew that eating healthy food everyday would give you more energy, improve your looks, help you handle stress, take off extra pounds, and raise your grades, would you eat any better? All of these benefits could be yours, but why do most teens not change their daily eating habits? First, it's because most of what you eat and drink is out of habit. You've always chosen French fries and a chocolate shake from the drive-through menu, for example, so you continue ordering the same items. Second, you consume certain foods because they appeal to your five senses. When something looks good, smells delicious, and tastes great, you eat it—even if it's bad for you.

When was the last time you consciously chose to eat healthy food? Making healthy food choices may mean that you have to choose something different than a friend. It may also include making a choice against what you really want to have at the moment. If you can start the habit of making healthy food choices, however, your body will begin to crave nutritious food instead of "junk food". The more "junk food" you eat, the more "junk food" you want. The more good food you eat, the more good food you want. It's like an addiction. Why feed your body bad fuel? It'll only make your engine (body) break down sooner and more frequently.

Nutritionists have identified many different kinds of **nutrients** (substances in foods that your body needs). The six main nutrients are proteins, carbohydrates, fats, vitamins, minerals, and water.

Proteins build new cells and tissues. They're an essential part of every cell. The main component of every protein is a string of *amino acids*. The body extracts the amino acids from the proteins you eat and rearranges them into new proteins. These new proteins are then used by the body for growth and maintenance of cells. By itself, your body produces 14 of the 22 amino acids. The other eight are called **"essential" amino acids** because they must come from the foods you eat.

It's important to include protein in your daily diet. You probably eat animal protein such as meat, poultry, fish, cheese, and eggs. You don't have to eat animal protein to be healthy, however. A **vegetarian diet** (one that typically excludes animal products) can be carefully planned to ensure that the proper nutritional requirements are met (e.g., using B_{12} supplements). Protein is also found in foods such as nuts, legumes (beans), and grains.

Active people require diets that are high in carbohydrates and low in saturated fats.

Carbohydrates are your body's energy-producers. Sugars and starches are the main source of carbohydrates in foods. Your system turns carbohydrates into a type of sugar called *glucose*. Glucose is fuel for your body. Other foods that contain carbohydrates are vegetables (peas and carrots are high in natural sugar), fruits, cereals, and bread products.

Fats are a concentrated source of energy. Fats can provide more than twice as much energy as carbohydrates. *Essential fatty acids* (those fats that are needed by the body) provide insulation for the body and cushioning for vital organs. Fats keep your skin from becoming too dry. They also aid in the transportation of certain vitamins and the manufacture of certain hormones.

DANGER!

Try this. Fry hamburger meat in a pan. Pour out this grease into a jar or can. Let the grease cool. What do you see? What was once a liquid when it was hot has now become hardened. This grease is saturated fat. Eating it is injecting white, fat globules directly into your bloodstream.

"Non-fat," "Low-fat," "2% milk fat"…what's the big fuss over fats? More people are becoming aware of the health dangers of eating too much of the wrong kind of fat. Most Americans eat far more fat than their bodies actually need. A very important characteristic of fat is the degree of saturation. **Saturated fat** tends to increase blood **cholesterol**, a fatty substance in the blood which increases the risk of heart disease. These fats are hard at room temperature. Your body doesn't need any saturated fat in its diet. High levels of saturated fats are found in red meats, pork products, egg yolks, butter, hard margarines, many cheeses, dairy products, tropical oils (coconut, palm, and palm kernel), and hydrogenated oils (those which have had hydrogen added).

Unsaturated fats don't tend to raise cholesterol levels. They're usually liquid at room temperature. Corn, safflower, cottonseed, and canola oils are examples of unsaturated fats. Any act of frying your food, however, changes any unsaturated fat to a saturated fat. That's why French fries, fried chicken, and donuts are full of the unhealthy kind of fat.

Why Are Hamburgers Called *Ham*burgers?

There are "chickenburgers", "gardenburgers", and "fishburgers", but have you ever wondered why hamburgers are called *ham*burgers and not beefburgers? The popular beef patty in a bun is thought to have originated in Hamburg, Germany and was brought to this country by immigrants, whose descendants now make up a huge portion of the population of this country. The name hamburger never referred to the type of meat used. But, now that the misconception is ingrained, imagine the difficulty of anyone who wanted to make a burger-type sandwich with *ham*. What would they call it?[1]

Vitamins are organic (derived from living things) substances your body needs in small amounts. Vitamins help regulate and co-ordinate the functions of your body. They are essential for maintaining a healthy balance throughout all eleven of your body systems. The best source of vitamins comes from the foods you eat. Do you know what vitamins you may be lacking? Age, sex, heredity, illness, diet, stress, as well as the amount you exercise, all contribute to your body's need for nutrients. The **RDA** (Rec-ommended Daily Allowance) is a daily dosage amount of vitamins and minerals that is recommended by the **FDA** (U.S. Food and Drug Administration) for the average non-pregnant adult to main-tain minimal health. The RDA amounts are not enough for a person to maintain excellent health; only the minimal amount needed to prevent deficiency diseases.

There are two main types of vitamins: water-soluble and fat-soluble. **Water-soluble** vitamins are those that dissolve in water. Vitamins C and B, for example, are water-soluble. That means that they can be excreted from your body. Because of this, you need to replenish your supply of them everyday. **Fat-soluble** vitamins don't dissolve in water. They can be stored in the body. Vitamins A, D, E, and K are fat-soluble vitamins.

Minerals are inorganic (not having the structure of living bod-ies) substances that are essential for your body. Minerals are needed in small amounts to help your body form bones, teeth, and blood cells. They help regulate your body's fluids and aid in the chemical reactions of cells. You must get minerals from the foods you eat. Although everyone needs minerals, there are certain times when people's physical needs change. During your teen years, your body is undergoing huge growth changes. It's essential that you make wise food choices to give your body the adequate nutrition it requires. Calcium, phosphorus, iron, potassium, zinc, chlo-ride and magnesium are some of the minerals your body needs.

It's important to drink plenty of water, especially if you're active in sports or strenuous activity.

DANGER!

If you have a habit of drinking soda (pop), coffee, tea, or other liquids containing caffeine, you may be more likely to become dehydrated. These drinks act as diuretics (removing water from the body). If your body needs water, it'll take it from your body organs. Your skin will become dry (lips are especially affected). Your energy will decrease. You may become constipated (difficulty in having a bowel movement). Listen to your body! It's trying to tell you to drink something it can really use!

Water is the most common nutrient. About 60% of your body is made up of water. How important is water? You could live without food for an extended period of time. But, without water, dehydration (lack of water) would set in and you would die very soon.

Your body uses water for many functions. Some of these include: cleansing waste and toxins, lubricating joints, transporting nutrients, regulating body temperature, losing weight, and digesting food. Usually your body will tell you when it's hungry. But, if your body has to tell you that it's thirsty, you may already be somewhat dehydrated. Your body needs at least seven to ten eight-ounce glasses of purified water a day. Your body may need more if you are losing a lot of body fluids through perspiration from strenuous work or exercise.

A healthy pizza can be a nutritious and delicious meal.

Let's go back to the pizza parlor. What do the ingredients of a great tasting pizza have to do with a balanced diet? Today, many pizza parlors are creating healthier pizzas. They're using "veggies," low-fat cheese, and whole-wheat crust. Let's make a special order and see if we can have a delicious-yet-healthy pizza!

• Whole-wheat crust (*carbohydrates/fat*): A whole-wheat crust gives you more fiber and necessary nutrients than a crust made out of white flour and white sugar.

• Pizza sauce/seasoning (*flavor*): Pizza sauce usually contains very few nutrients if it comes from a can. However, you can

add all sorts of healthy ingredients to it, e.g., garlic. Real to-
mato sauce is high in vitamin C. Pizza sauces from a can are
normally very high in sodium. If you're not making your own
sauce, check the label and buy a low-sodium brand.

- Low-fat or mozzarella cheese (*protein/low-fat*): Skip the ched-
dar cheese. It's very high in fat and calories. Skip the meats.
The low-fat cheese gives you the protein you need.

- Veggies (*vitamins/minerals*): Try peppers, onions, black olives,
artichoke hearts, tomatoes, spinach, zucchini, mushrooms,
low-fat refried beans—whatever!

This delicious-yet-healthy pizza contains a balance of the main
nutrients for a healthy meal. "Where's the cola or root beer?" you're
probably wondering. Stop and think. It would be a healthier
choice—before you ate your pizza—to drink a large glass of purified water to give your body more of a sense of being full. Then,
when your pizza was ready, you'd be less inclined to drink cola or
root beer with it. Drinking any liquid during a meal dilutes the
digestive enzymes that your digestive system needs to digest your
food properly. So, skip the pop, save some money, and enjoy a
healthier meal.

3 • 2   Food Zone 101: Good Health from Good Choices
· ·

*How much of your
diet contains
empty calories?*

"I know that donuts, potato chips, and cookies
aren't the healthiest, but just how bad can they
be?" "I've never felt any big difference in my body
between when I've eaten a candy bar and when
I've eaten an apple." "When I get older and weaker,
then I'll start watching what I eat. My Dad's doctor didn't tell him to eat less salt until after he
had his first heart attack…." Do any of these statements sound familiar? If so, try to remember the
following fact. Just because you don't feel the consequences of your food choices immediately, it

doesn't mean that nothing unhealthy is happening inside of your body. Every food you choose to put into your body does something either negatively or positively (or both) to your cells.

Consider the following. You eat a candy bar. It tastes delicious. Your mouth begins to digest the ingredients. Your bloodstream immediately begins to absorb the simple sugars. Because of the high sugar level of your snack, your pancreas immediately shoots insulin into your bloodstream so that you won't feel sick. The enzymes in your stomach start to break down the contents to find any usable nutrients. The partially digested candy goes into your small intestine. Your digestive system still attempts to identify functional nutrients to absorb into your body, but it can't find any! What does your body do next? It sends the saturated fat to your fat cells for storage. It gradually escorts all but a tiny amount of the original candy bar to your colon where it's eventually evacuated. This is what commonly happens whenever you consume good-tasting—yet "empty"—calories.

Have you ever wondered what is in a typical hot dog?

A piece of candy gives your taste buds five minutes of "palatable pleasure." Nevertheless, it does nothing for your body. "Junk food" damages your body on the cellular level. It leaves behind debris inside your body where you can't see or feel it at first. Consequently, after a period of time, your body begins to show negative symptoms, e.g., excessive gas (flatulence) in the intestines, constipation, diarrhea, excess weight, or possibly an increase in acne. If you choose to continue these "junk food" eating patterns, you'll have started bad eating habits that'll be difficult to break. As an adult, you may develop problems such as hypoglycemia, diabetes, fatigue, colitis, heart disease, or even cancer. When do healthy food choices begin to count? They begin to make a difference right now. What you choose to eat today is already beginning to affect your health tomorrow!

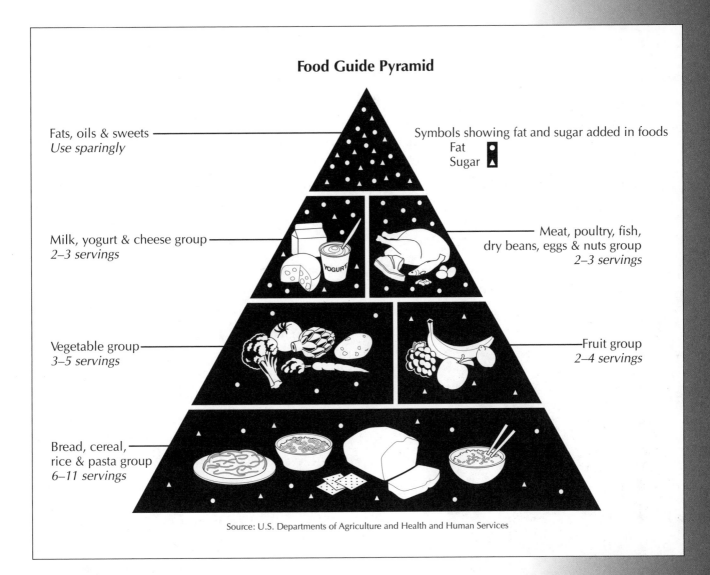

Food Guide Pyramid

Fats, oils & sweets
Use sparingly

Symbols showing fat and sugar added in foods
Fat
Sugar

Milk, yogurt & cheese group
2–3 servings

Meat, poultry, fish,
dry beans, eggs & nuts group
2–3 servings

Vegetable group
3–5 servings

Fruit group
2–4 servings

Bread, cereal,
rice & pasta group
6–11 servings

Source: U.S. Departments of Agriculture and Health and Human Services

The Food Pyramid

In addition to being motivated to eat healthy, making nutritious food choices begins with having accurate information. The USDA (United States Department of Agriculture) first released its food pyramid in 1992. It was presented as a concise, visual guide to healthy eating. Since then, new food pyramids have been emerging every year. Much of these changes occurred due to cultural differences while others resulted from the lack of a clear definition of portion size and cooking techniques. A food pyramid is still a great way to help you to visualize a balanced diet. An even healthier food pyramid would be to have fresh fruits and vegetables at the bottom and whole-wheat bread and grains on the next level.

The Whole Grains Group: Breads, Cereals, Rice, and Pasta

The whole grains group is the largest section at the base of the food pyramid. Grains should be included in your diet every day. Although you may not eat as many as 11 servings a day, the two most important health points to remember are (1) Eat whole grains (white bread and most packaged cereals don't contain whole grains), and (2) Eat high-fiber foods (e.g., bran muffins, apples, bananas, celery, and broccoli). When purchasing a breakfast cereal, try to choose one that has less than three grams of sugar and at least 3–4 grams of protein per serving.

The Fruits and Vegetables Group: Fresh is the Best

The average American teenager doesn't eat enough fruits or vegetables to maintain good health. Take a close look at your present

An even healthier food pyramid would be to have fresh vegetables and fruit at the bottom and whole-wheat bread and grains on the next level.

diet. How often do you eat fresh vegetables, e.g., lettuce, carrots, spinach, or corn? The longer vegetables are cooked, the less nutrients remain in them. It's best to steam, microwave, or eat them raw. Canned vegetables aren't as healthy for you because of the sodium that's added to them to extend their shelf life. The thin slice of iceberg lettuce on your hamburger isn't a full vegetable serving. For optimum health, you should eat at least 3–5 servings of vegetables every day. Dark green and yellow vegetables add folic acid, magnesium, zinc, and fiber to your diet. Starchy vegetables, such as peas and potatoes, give you fiber, carbohydrates, vitamin C, B_6, iron, and magnesium. Why not try a tossed salad, a baked potato, or a cup of steamed broccoli with your next dinner?

How often do you eat fresh fruits, e.g., apples, bananas, pineapple, grapefruit, or oranges? Canned fruit isn't as nutritious as fresh fruit because of the sugar added to extend shelf life. Even if fruit is canned in its own juice, the fruit loses much of its nutritional value. For optimum health, you should eat at least 2–4 servings of fruit every day. Fruits—especially citrus fruits—are good sources of vitamin C. Fruits also provide you with folic acid, potassium, and fiber. Some good daily serving ideas for fruit would be: taking one banana with you to school and eating it on your first break, drinking a glass of fresh orange juice before you go to school, or snacking on a large handful of raisins. Fruit in the morning is a great way to start your day. It's easy on your digestive system, cleanses you from what you ate the day before, and is a good source of energy.

The Dairy Group: Milk, Yogurt, and Cheese

There are various opinions concerning the value of dairy in your diet. Although this group is the primary source of calcium, some people cannot tolerate the lactose that milk and milk products contain. Lactose-intolerant people can obtain milk substitutes or lactose-free products that are still high in calcium. Saturated fat is also a concern with the dairy group. Do you remember our delicious-but-healthy pizza? We chose low-fat cheese, preferably mozzarella. You can also choose low or non-fat milk products to keep the saturated fat content as low as possible. The foods in the dairy group provide you with protein, vitamin A, riboflavin (B_2), B_6, and B_{12}. Good choices in this group would be non-fat yogurt (light on the sugar), an eight-ounce cup of non-fat milk or milk substitute (such as rice, almond, goat's or soy milk), one ounce of non-fat or low-fat cheese, and lowfat ice cream.

Gone fishing lately? Including fish regularly in your diet is an excellent food choice.

The Protein Group: Meat, Poultry, Fish, Beans, Eggs, and Nuts

This group is very important because it provides your body with protein, vitamins, and minerals. In order for you to obtain the valued nutrients without the excess saturated fats from foods in this group, you should:

1. Eat salmon and halibut. They provide omega 3 fatty acids (good fats!). Avoid shellfish because it's high in cholesterol.

2. Eat your chicken and turkey without the skin. Most of the fat is contained in the skin. White meat is leaner than dark meat.

3. Eat only extra lean red meats, e.g., hamburger with less than 9% fat. The extra lean cuts cost a bit more, but they reduce your risk of heart disease.

4. Eat egg yokes sparingly. They are high in cholesterol. Egg whites are okay. Cholesterol-free egg substitutes are becoming more and more popular.

Traditionally, a typical American meal was built around red meat, fish, or poultry. Today, however, legumes and beans are an accepted alternative. The foods contained in this group are good sources of protein, phosphorus, niacin, iron, zinc, B_6, B_{12}, as well as trace minerals. A healthy snack would be a large handful of raw almonds mixed with raisins. This combination would keep your blood sugar in proper balance. The raisins would give you sugar for energy while the almonds would provide you with protein.

The Fats, Oils, and Sweets Group

Did you know that your body actually needs fat? Good fats help give your body energy as well as act as an internal lubricant to your system. To be more precise, your body needs the correct amount of the "right" kind of fat (unsaturated). Some sources of good fats are olive oil and flaxseed oil. You can purchase EFA (essential fatty acids) supplements, too.

The average American consumes 700 pounds of sugar a year!

When you read labels, you'll find that there's lots of white sugar, sucrose, glucose, fructose, and corn syrup added to all kinds of foods you eat. The next time you buy your favorite breakfast cereal, take a moment to read the label to see how much sugar was added. White sugar is one of the main "poisons" included in the typical American diet. Outside of certain specialty breads, did you know that the only kind of breads that have no sugar added are sprouted wheat or sourdough? Snacks and desserts are the most common ways teens consume foods from this group. Chips, crackers, pastries, candy, cookies, cakes, pies, and soft drinks are full of "empty calories." To be the most healthy now and in the future, consider these snack foods as "once-in-a-while" treats—not as a regular part of your diet.

How to Read a Label

A good way to be a wise consumer is to read product labels. The FDA (Food and Drug Administration) is requiring manufacturers to supply more nutritional information on their labels to help consumers make more informed choices. Avoid products that only list ingredients, because you don't know how much of what you're eating. When reading an ingredients list, remember that the list of ingredients is in the order of weight, from the highest to the lowest. If sugar is listed first in the ingredients list, for example, it would be the most-used ingredient in the product.

If sugar is listed first in the ingredients list, for example, it would be the most-used ingredient in the product.

Keeping "In Step" With Product Labels

Step #1: Don't be swayed by the bright or fancy packaging. Don't be fooled by the claims that products are "lite" or "light." Although they may be reduced in fat, the calories may be higher to compensate for flavor-loss. Also avoid products with lots of sodium, sugar, colorings, and preservatives.

Step #2: Check the serving size. This is usually found at the top of the nutritional box. If your cereal box is describing the contents for a serving size of only 1/2 cup, make sure you more than double the label numbers if you serve yourself a full bowl for breakfast. Companies normally keep the serving size low because they know that most people will only read the other numbers in the chart and won't take the time to figure it out.

Step #3: Check the label for saturated fat and cholesterol amounts. Choose foods that are low in both fat and cholesterol. A good rule of thumb is to choose products where there is a big difference between the total number of calories and the total number of *fat* calories. Try to keep your cholesterol consumption below 300 mg a day.

DANGER!

Have you ever read a label that contained hydrogenated or partially hydrogenated oil? Avoid both of them. *Hydrogenation* is a chemical process used to make an unsaturated fat more saturated. This method extends the shelf life of the product, but it also produces *trans fatty acids* which have been shown to raise the bad cholesterol levels in the blood.

What are your eating habits? Do you eat before going to bed? Do you forget to drink water throughout the day?

Step #4: Check the carbohydrate-to-protein ratio. Choose only those products that have three or less grams of sugar per serving. Make sure there is also a good amount of protein. The protein is important when sugar is present because it helps to keep your blood sugar in balance.

Step #5: Check what types of oils are contained in the product. Avoid products that describe their ingredients with the phrase "one or more of the following ingredients" because they're too general. If the list contains both coconut oil (a bad oil) and safflower oil (a better oil), you don't know exactly how much of each was really used. As a result, you can't make an educated choice. It's wisest, however, to avoid tropical oils altogether.

Keeping a Food Journal
"What's a Food Journal?"

A food journal is a diary of all the food and beverages you consume. The result is an honest evaluation of your diet. The journal can be kept for one week or for an indefinite period of time. You may be quite surprised by what you learn from your own personal food journal. By noting patterns in their journals, some teens have improved their diets.

"What Are the Keys to a Great Food Journal?"

- Be totally honest! Write down everything you eat and drink.

- Be as exact as possible. Instead of writing, "I ate a few crackers," count the crackers and record, "I ate ten crackers."

- Make no dietary changes when beginning your journal.

- Write down the time of day you ate or drank something.

- Be accountable to someone. Trust someone to look over your journal or to ask you if you're keeping up with it.

- Fill in the comment section with statements like, "I ate cookies when I was angry at my Mom," or "I got a headache after I ate that soda and chocolate candy."

"What Will My Food Journal Show Me?"

A food journal can serve several different purposes. At first, you may only want to see what times of the day you make poor food choices. For example, do you eat a large snack just before going to bed? If so, what is it? Do you skip breakfast? If so, how often? After you keep your food journal for a week, evaluate it. Do you find some eating habits that you want to change? How easy are these changes to make? When you begin to feel pressure to make some changes, don't stop keeping your journal; just start to make the changes very slowly. As you continue to monitor your changes, set realistic goals for yourself. If you forget to drink water, make a goal that each time you pass a water fountain, you'll take a drink for a count of ten seconds. Another goal might be to avoid eating an unhealthy snack after school before dinner.

A food journal is a diary of all the food and beverages you consume. The result is an honest evaluation of your diet.

Goals to Get You on Track

- Buy one liter of bottled water. After you finish drinking the water, keep the container and refill it with purified water. Carry that container of water wherever you go. Make a goal that you must drink two of these containers before you allow yourself a soda.

- If chips are your weakness, allow yourself to eat only a certain number of chips from a bag. If you buy a small bag, only eat half of the bag. Give the rest to a friend or throw the rest away.

- Don't eat anything after 8:00 PM at night. Digestion is very slow during sleep.

- Carry a bag of almonds and raisins with you wherever you go. Whenever you have a "snack attack," munch on them instead of a candy bar.

- Don't leave the house without breakfast. If you're always in a hurry, try a banana or an apple as you walk out the door.

Your fast-paced lifestyle can lead you to make poor food choices based on convenience.

Have you ever wondered what it would be like to wake up every morning to a quick, healthy meal on the table all prepared for you? The Bible describes a time in history when God provided the people of Israel with everything they needed. Each morning "manna" was waiting for them to eat (Exodus 16:15). Although the people complained about the lack of variety, the manna supplied their daily nutritional needs and kept them healthy.

It's just the opposite in Western culture. You have so much variety from which to choose, it has become increasingly difficult to make certain that your food choices are healthy ones. Another problem is the role of fast food. (You can be sure that the healthy Israelites never rode their camels to a drive-through for a quick burger and fries!) Your fast-paced lifestyle can lead you to make poor food choices based on convenience. Even the prepared frozen dinners that you can pop into the microwave oven leave very little room for good nutrition. They are usually very high in fat and sodium.

One Olympic athlete put it this way regarding eating fruits and vegetables:

Fit means achieving the balance between nutrition and exercise that works best for your body. Someone I consider to be fit is aware of the food she eats and includes fruits and vegetables.
I think most foods are okay in moderation.[2]
Tara Lipinski, 1998 U.S. Olympic Figure Skating Gold Medal Winner

Food Zone 101

Change takes time, but if you have even the slightest desire to make better food choices in your life, it's certainly doable. Keep the following ten statements in mind when making your food choices.

- Eat a variety of foods.
- Maintain your ideal weight.
- Exercise to keep your metabolism high.
- Increase your dietary fiber to 25–35 grams a day.
- Eat less sugar.
- Eat less sodium (2,500 milligrams or less per day).
- Eat less saturated fat.
- Avoid alcohol and tobacco.
- Drink plenty of water (purified or filtered whenever possible).
- Avoid eating while under stress.

3•3 What's the Buzz on Dieting?

· ·

Do you ever think about trying to lose some weight just before summer vacation hits? The top teen magazines today all focus around being thin. All of the young, innocent-faced actors in Hollywood are slender. Each of the female models is thin. Every advertisement focuses around being thin (or how to get thin). Guys, girls, love, romance, sex, make-up—all in the context of being skinny. It's not just tough to "match up" to the body types of these teen actors and models, it's impossible!

Thin is In and Stout is Out!?

The pressure to be thin is incredible. It's not only focused upon teens. Adults also are bombarded with the same images. Society has fed us the line that "Thin is in and Stout is out!" Advertisements and products for weight loss programs have skyrocketed in the past several years. In spite of this heightened interest in weight loss, weight problems remain. Why is obesity still on the rise when thousands of Americans use these weight-reduction products? Why do most of the participants in weight loss programs eventually gain back all the weight they lost—and even more?

Why do most of the participants in weight loss programs eventually gain back all the weight they lost—and even more?

Diets Don't Work

The simple answer to these questions is that *diets don't work.* Research shows that there are two main reasons for this. First, when you begin to cut your calories, your body thinks it's starving and begins to hold onto its fat. Your metabolism slows down while your body stores more and more fat. When you go off your "diet" and you eat a 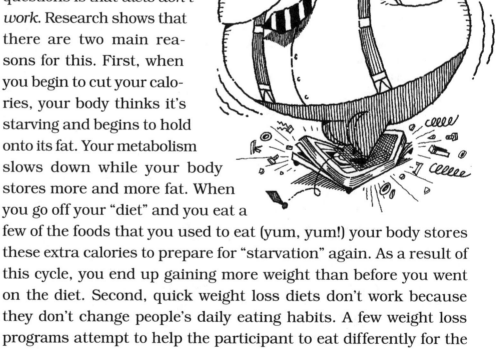 few of the foods that you used to eat (yum, yum!) your body stores these extra calories to prepare for "starvation" again. As a result of this cycle, you end up gaining more weight than before you went on the diet. Second, quick weight loss diets don't work because they don't change people's daily eating habits. A few weight loss programs attempt to help the participant to eat differently for the rest of their lives, but at the end of their training, it's still up to each individual to choose to eat healthy every day. Losing extra pounds in a short amount of time by feeling like you're starving yourself is not only unsafe, it's also no guarantee of permanent results. It's actually worse for your body to be "yo-yo" dieting (losing and gaining weight repeatedly), than it is to stay at a comfortable weight—even if you are a few pounds over the ideal. "Yo-yo" dieting reduces your **metabolic rate** (the speed at which your body burns calories). This puts added stress on your body.

Losing weight doesn't have to be a constant or complicated stressor. The principle of weight loss is straightforward: calories in, calories out. If you take in more calories than you burn in activity or exercise, then the excess will be stored as fat. A diet is not something you turn on and off like a water faucet. Your present **diet** consists of all the foods you choose to eat right now. It includes everything you eat on a regular basis. So, what does your diet look like?

"Am I Obese or Just a Little Overweight?"

What does it mean to be overweight or obese? When teens are considered **overweight**, they weigh more than the desired weight for their age, sex, height, and frame size. Teens who are considered **obese** have too much fat in their bodies. These teens are more than 20% over their ideal weight. Being obese is considered a very serious health hazard. Experts estimate that 10 to 25% of all teenagers fall into the obese category. Research also shows that an obese teenager is more likely to become an obese adult. Don't lose heart, however, a shift in your eating habits can help you take the weight off—and keep it off.

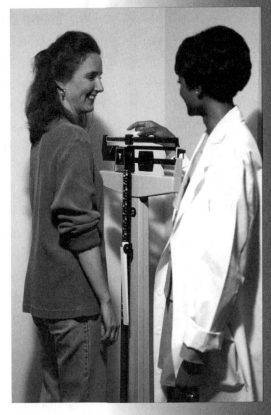

Beware!

"Lose 30 lbs. in 30 Days or Your Money Back!" "Lose Weight While Eating All You Want!" "Chocolate Shake for Breakfast. Vanilla Shake for Lunch. Complete Meal—All in a Can!" Do any of these sales lines sound familiar? There are hundreds of dietary programs that try to get you to buy their products. Be suspicious of the programs that make claims sounding too good to be true. If they sound too good to be true, it's usually because they are! Never limit your calories to lower than 1,000 calories a day unless prescribed by a doctor. Read the labels on those "diet shakes." Notice the amount of sugar in them. You may lose the weight they claim, but as you begin to eat normal food again,

To lose weight and keep it off, you must make a commitment to change your eating habits and your lifestyle. Eat healthy and get off the couch!

your weight will skyrocket and your metabolism will be messed-up. Avoid using appetite suppressants. Some expand like sponges in your stomach and give you a false sense of being full. If you want to lose weight, don't diet! Dieting makes you think only of the short-term. To lose weight and keep it off, you must make a commitment to change your eating habits and your lifestyle. Eat healthy and get off the couch!

Eating Disorders: Going to Extremes

When I was about to enter junior high, I noticed that my older sister, Ann, had some habits that seemed pretty weird to me. Every night before going to bed, Ann would do several minutes of intense exercise in addition to her usual daily jog. At dinner, Ann would pick the fat out of her hamburger meat before cooking it, drink just half a glass of skim milk, and eat only a few bits of rice or potato—with absolutely no butter. Ironically, Ann loved to bake. After she would bake a batch of mouth-watering chocolate chip cookies, she would watch everyone else eat them. She'd make sure that she didn't lick any of the dough off her finger. Even the kids at school began to ask me questions about Ann. They didn't know how to deal with her strange eating habits and weight loss. (Ann's weight was down to 70 lbs. in eighth grade!)

People who suffer from anorexia are totally consumed with the way they look.

Like many families, we thought that ignoring Ann's problem would make it go away. We told ourselves that it was "just a phase." Unfortunately, this wasn't the case. I didn't know how to talk to Ann about it. Whenever I blurted out, "Why do you act like this?" she just ignored me. I felt uncomfortable eating around her. I felt embarrassed about the food I was eating.

Fortunately, by the grace of God, Ann snapped out of it. I later discovered that she had been suffering from an eating disorder called anorexia nervosa. To this day, neither of us know why she acted so extremely. Anorexia was very damaging to Ann's health. During her early teens, a critical time in her physical development, she withheld from her body many important nutrients. As a result, even her female hormones were affected.

Our family will never know for sure, but Ann's bout with anorexia during her early teen years may have been the beginning (on the cellular level, anyway) of the MS (multiple sclerosis) with which she was diagnosed twenty years later.

This true story about my sister, Ann, is very typical. In the privacy of their own homes, many families have experienced the frustration that accompanies any eating disorder. All health problems put an added strain upon families. Good family communication is hard enough without the added stress that comes with strange behaviors and attitudes. Symptoms of an eating disorder may appear during adolescence or even adulthood. Although eating disorders are more common among young girls, some guys suffer from them as well. Hopefully, you don't have an eating disorder. It's very likely, however, that either you know someone who does or will meet someone who suffers from one sometime during your teen years. In either case, the following information will provide you with an overall understanding of the problem.

In the privacy of their own homes, many families have experienced the frustration that accompanies any eating disorder.

Anorexia, Bulimia, and Chronic Overeating

The three eating disorders that can cause you serious mental and physical damage are anorexia nervosa, bulimia, and chronic overeating. **Anorexia** is self-induced starvation. It results in extreme weight loss. It's characterized by an intense fear of gaining weight. People with anorexia, like my sister, Ann, see themselves in need of losing weight even when they are ex-

DANGER!

Anorexia actually means, "without appetite" and nervosa means "of a nervous (possibly emotional) origin." Anorexic teens seem to have a desire for the "perfect body." Their perfectionistic tendencies, probably fueled by the "Barbie™ doll" images of the media, lead them to extreme behaviors and an obsession about their weight.

tremely underweight. This disorder can lead to malnutrition, starvation, and even death.

Bulimia is a pattern of "binging" (eating large portions of food) followed by "purging" (self-induced vomiting in an attempt not to gain weight). Bulimics may also use laxatives to expel the food from their bodies. As a result, teenagers with this disorder don't allow enough time for any of the food's nutrients to nourish their bodies. Bulimic teens may show no outward signs of the disorder. They may be thin or even a little overweight. Although they may appear okay on the outside, they have deep emotional pain on the inside. Bulimia damages your body through malnutrition, dehydration, excessive acidity in the digestive track (from continual vomiting), and stress on the heart.

Feelings of rejection by peers or adults can lead to depression and loneliness, where food becomes a teen's only "friend."

Chronic overeating is the habit of eating more food than your body needs. It's much more common than anorexia or bulimia. For some teens, the habit of overeating began in childhood. For others, it started during their emotional teen years. Whether by overeating or something else, whenever you choose to place undue stress on any of your body systems, it can result in many physical problems.

There are many possible causes for eating disorders among teens. Every teenager has his own personal struggles. If there is a common thread between all of the eating disorders, however, it would seem to be a teen's attempt to meet his or her unmet emotional needs with food in some way. When teens feel unaccepted, inferior, ugly, rejected, out of control, criticized, or worthless, they may look to food (in one way or another) as a way of trying to make them feel better about themselves. Both anorexic and bulimic teens seem to have a need to be in control. Through personally controlling what they eat, when they eat, and if they eat, they may feel like they're more in charge of their lives. Teens who overeat may feel very lonely. They may be using food as a friend and an emotional comfort.

There are different approaches to curing eating disorders. Often it takes a professional to help the individual. Here are a few suggestions in how to approach those who have an eating disorder:

1. Encourage them to talk about their feelings to an adult they trust.

2. Don't nag them about their food.

3. Help them to realize that it's normal to experience times in their lives when they spend extra effort and energy trying to accomplish something.

4. Be there for them, especially if their parents don't understand their highs and lows.

5. Show them love and acceptance as people—just as they are—with no strings attached.

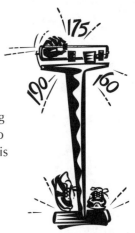

The Ultimate Child Abuse

Today's extreme emphasis on physical attractiveness is harmful to adults—and potentially life-threatening to children. A recent study states that 80% of girls in the fourth grade have attempted to diet because they see themselves as fat. One elementary schoolgirl justified her dieting by saying that she wanted to be skinny so that no one would tease her. How sad it is that children in this culture have been taught to hate their bodies, to measure their worth by comparison to a standard that they can never achieve.[3]

If you find yourself continually obsessed with being thin or needing food to make you feel better about yourself, please don't try to "go it alone." Lean on God to help you. God understands the way you feel. He will be there by your side through every trial. Also, look to your parents to support you. Furthermore, trust a professional for help.

Yea, though I walk through the valley of the shadow of death,
I will fear no evil; For you are with me; Your rod and Your staff,
they comfort me…. Surely goodness and mercy shall
follow me all the days of my life; And I will dwell
in the house of the Lord forever.
Psalm 23:4,6

Chapter 3 Review

Defining the Terms

Balanced diet	Vitamins
Calorie	RDA
Empty calories	Water-soluble
Nutrients	Fat-soluble
Proteins	Minerals
Essential amino acids	Metabolic rate
Vegetarian diet	Diet
Carbohydrates	Overweight
Fats	Obese
Saturated fat	Anorexia
Cholesterol	Bulimia
Unsaturated fats	Chronic overeating

Recalling the Facts

1. What are the guidelines on the Daily Food Pyramid? Include a possible adjustment to the Pyramid recommendations that might be even healthier.

2. Explain the difference between saturated fats and unsaturated fats. Which are more dangerous for your body and why? Give one food example for each.

3. Explain why your body needs an adequate amount of water each day. Include in your answer six ways your body uses water.

4. What is the main purpose of keeping a food journal?

5. What are four better ways of making food choices in your life?

6. What are the dangers of "fad" diets? Why do "diets" make you think only of the short-term?

Applying the Truth

1. Explain how a pizza could be a potentially healthy meal. With this in mind, describe what kind of "healthy" pizza you would order.

2. Choose three "keys to a great food journal". Explain why each might be difficult to do.

3. What in the Food Guide Pyramid surprised you? How might following the Food Guide Pyramid be different than your food choices you are making now?

4. Explain one reason why package labels can be misleading to consumers.

5. Imagine that you have a friend about whose poor eating habits you are very concerned. How might you determine if they have a problem with anorexia or bulimia? What might you say and/or do to help your friend?

"...your body is the temple of the Holy Spirit who is in you..."

I Corinthians 6:19

FITNESS AND EXERCISE 4

What's Coming Up...

4•1   Feeling the Benefits of Exercise

● ●

> *I consider people fit if they not only feel good*
> *on the outside but feel good on the inside.*[1]
> Dominique Dawes, Olympic gymnast

Why take the time and effort to be active? Why make exercise an important part of your routine? Why "sweat it"? It's because exercise and activity will make you look and feel so much better! I always felt better after I actively participated in my P.E. class. After riding my bike, I always had more energy. Following a good workout, I felt more excited about my life. Upon finishing sports practice, I had a

greater sense of self-confidence. It's the same for me today. Even when I do a minimum amount of exercise, I feel healthier. You can feel better, too! If you choose to increase your activity level, you'll feel better about yourself, others, and even God.

LOGON!

Feeling Depressed?

If you're like most teens, you experience times of depression. Sometimes, you know why you're depressed, but other times, you may just have an overall "blah" feeling. Did you know that exercise is a natural cure for depression? During vigorous exercise (30 minutes or more), your body releases natural hormones called endorphins. These hormones give your body a feeling of well-being which often results in a more positive outlook on life. So, the next time you're feeling depressed, don't reach for the cookie jar or the remote control. Instead, take a walk or jump on your bike and experience the benefits of exercise.

Playing a sport helps me to keep my life in balance. It takes my mind off of schoolwork, guys, and relationships. It's also great when I'm in a bad mood because it always cheers me up.

Andrea

Benefits of Exercise

1. Increases strength and stamina
2. Reduces stress and tension
3. Improves mental alertness and concentration
4. Relieves depression
5. Melts away excess fat and weight
6. Increases Basal Metabolic Rate (lets you burn more calories)
7. Gives more restful sleep
8. Increases body flexibility
9. Delays signs of aging
10. Improves digestive and excretory systems
11. Betters cardiovascular and circulatory systems
12. Encourages social outlook
13. Inspires spiritual outlook and perspective on life
14. Brightens the countenance
15. Promotes general health (less illness, more time for work and play)
16. Helps friendships

Exercise makes your whole life more fun and efficient—body, mind, and spirit!

4•2 Knowing Your Fitness Condition

• •

What do you think it means to be "fit"? Does it mean that girls need to look like Barbie™ dolls and guys like Mr. Universe? Teens have a variety of definitions for the term. Here's how one Olympic gymnast describes a condition of good fitness:

> *Teens that are physically fit must have good muscle tone, flexibility, and stamina.*[2]
> Dominique Dawes, Olympic gymnast

Generally, **fitness** is the ability of your mind and body to work together to their highest possible level. Your overall physical health includes four areas of fitness: *cardiovascular fitness*, *muscular fitness*, *flexibility*, and your body's *fat-vs-lean body weight*.

Cardiovascular Fitness

> *A person needs to be in good cardiovascular shape in order to be fit. Cardiovascular fitness doesn't automatically come from being thin. It comes from being physically active.*[3]
> Holly McPeak, professional beach volleyball player

Even with a slight increase in your activity level, you will feel the benefits.

The most important measurement of your physical fitness is the condition of your heart. Your heart, lungs, and blood vessels work together to supply oxygenated blood to your whole body. Like any of your muscles, your heart needs exercise. When you exercise, your muscles actually change in their physical composition. When a long period of time lapses between your workouts, your muscles will **atrophy** (decrease in size and strength). "Use It or Lose It" applies to your muscles. Your heart is no exception. Regular exercise is needed to increase your heart's efficiency.

Cardiovascular disease is the number one killer in America. It claims more than one million lives in this country every year. A healthy heart is better able to resist it. By controlling your blood pressure and cholesterol levels through aerobic exercise, you can increase your chances of living a longer and more productive life.

DANGER!

What does exercise do for your heart? Consistent aerobic exercise can lower your heart rate by as much as 10 to 15 beats per minute. That is 15,000 to 20,000 beats less each day and in one year over 7 million beats! So, give your heart a rest and begin a regular exercise program!

Some people think that their heart will automatically stay in excellent condition no matter what they eat, just as long as they are fairly active. I knew one teacher who said, "The only purpose of eating the main course of a meal is to get to the dessert!" He also thought that it wasn't necessary for him to participate in any form of cardiovascular exercise since he walked from building to building (on a very small campus) to teach his classes. The truth is, however, that even those people who play some sports may find that the condition of their heart is much worse than they think. Covert Bailey, a leading nutritionist and exercise authority, had such an eye-opening experience:

When I was in college, I played a lot of hard squash and thought that I was in great shape. Occasionally, I played squash with a dentist friend who did a lot of running. He usually lost, but he seemed to have a lot of endurance on the squash court. One day, he talked me into taking a long, slow run with him. After about half a mile, I had to stop and vomit.[4]

To gain the benefits of exercise, it's important to know how to give your heart the workout it needs. Have you ever attended or observed an aerobics class? Do you know what the word "aerobic" means? The word "aerobic" means "requiring oxygen for life or movement". Every moment, your body needs oxygen to produce energy. When your muscles demand more oxygen than normal, the activity is called **aerobic**. Besides diet, the amount of aerobic exercise in your life is the key ingredient to your overall fitness level. It's vital to have some aerobic activity included in your personal fitness program. Some of the benefits of aerobic exercise include cardiovascular improvement, weight loss, improved mental outlook, and a longer life expectancy. Aerobics is not just a class to attend at a health club or an exercise video to play in your living room. Aerobics is a fundamental principle of fitness, and a very healthy way of life.

Besides diet, the amount of aerobic exercise in your life is the key ingredient to your overall fitness level. It's vital to have some aerobic activity included in your personal fitness program.

Anaerobic exercise is short bursts of physical energy without the use of much oxygen (e.g., sprinting, golf, or weight training). The benefits of anaerobic activity are not as great as those of aerobic activity. The main benefit of anaerobic exercise is improved muscular strength. Enhanced muscular strength can be a very important part of your overall fitness program.

Muscular Fitness

Muscle strength and muscle endurance are two components that make up your **muscular fitness**. Your *muscle strength* is measured by the most work one of your muscles can do at any one given time. An example of this would be how much weight you could bench press. *Muscle endurance* is measured by how well one of your muscle groups can perform over a given period of time without becoming overly weak. An example of muscle endurance would be how many repetitions you could bench press. Your muscles will grow in their strength and endurance with increased exercise.

The muscles in your body are made up of fixed groups of fibers. These groups of fibers are of two types: slow

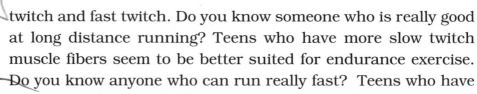

twitch and fast twitch. Do you know someone who is really good at long distance running? Teens who have more slow twitch muscle fibers seem to be better suited for endurance exercise. Do you know anyone who can run really fast? Teens who have more fast twitch fibers are better suited for fast bursts of movement such as sprinting. Each muscle works by contracting (shortening or pulling) its individual fibers in order to cause a desired movement. Muscles are made to pull rather than to push.

Flexibility

Being flexible also protects you against injury.

Have you ever tried to do the splits? If so, could you go all the way down to the ground? If not, do you really wish you could? Throughout my years of physical exercise and competitive sports, the least enjoyable activity for me was stretching. Because my body was very inflexible, I didn't enjoy stretching exercises. The importance of **flexibility** (the ability to move your joints and muscles through a full range of motion), however, is often overlooked. Some people seem naturally flexible. They can effortlessly bend over and touch their palms to the floor while keeping their legs straight. Whether you're naturally flexible or not, being able to extend your muscles and joints is very important in fitness. Flexibility gives you agility that you can use in other sports. It also provides you with a greater ability to practice new skills.

Without a natural outlet of daily exercise, your body stores up tension. You may feel it as a headache or backache or even a stiff neck in the morning. Without releasing this tension, your muscles will become weak and stiff. Stretching, if done correctly,

DANGER!

Have you ever heard the phrase, "No pain, No gain"? The belief that the more you hurt during exercise the more you benefit, is false. Anytime you stretch your muscle fibers too far (either by bouncing or overstretching), a nerve reflex protects your muscle by sending a signal to the muscles to contract; the pain is a warning to stop. This response keeps the muscle from getting injured. When you stretch too far, you're actually tightening the very muscles you're trying to loosen!

will feel good. It's not stressful but relaxing. The key is to stretch regularly and not to try to compete with your friends who seem more flexible than you. Work slowly and enjoy the benefits of stretching.

You don't have to be an athlete to benefit from stretching. Regular stretching, done correctly, will do the following:[5]

- reduce muscle tension and make your body feel more relaxed,

- help coordination by allowing for easier movement,

- increase your range of motion,

- prevent injuries,

- make strenuous activities like running and skiing easier,

- help clear the mind,

- improve circulation, and

- make you feel good.

Fat-vs-Lean Body Weight

Have you ever heard of the term "body composition"? Your **body composition** is the relationship between your fat and lean (muscle) body weight. It's not how much you weigh. It's what the relationship in your body is between "muscle weight" and "fat weight". There are some definite benefits to you of increasing your lean muscle mass. First, you may decrease your "fat weight." Since muscle weighs more than fat, an overweight individual with 35% body fat, may actually weigh less than an individual with 25% body fat. You may actually gain weight as you exercise because you are losing fat but gaining muscular fitness. Another benefit of increasing your lean muscle mass is that muscles burn more calories than fat. You will burn more calories sleeping if you increase your muscular strength. If weighing yourself on a scale has been your only measurement of fitness—throw the scale out!

If weighing yourself on a scale has been your only measurement of fitness—throw the scale out!

How "Fit" Are You?

- **Flexibility.** Can you touch your toes? If not, sit with your legs out in front of you and reach for your toes. It's fine to spread your legs apart and slightly bend your knees. How close can you come to touching them?

- **Cardiovascular test.** This fitness check measures your heart rate and your recovery time. Ask an experienced physical educator or qualified aerobics instructor to administer this test to you. It's sometimes referred to as the bench step-up test.

- **Muscular fitness.** How much weight can you lift at one time? This test should only be done under the supervision of a qualified physical education instructor or trainer. Trying to lift too much weight by using your back can cause serious injury. You may also take the sit-up test. How many sit-ups can you properly do in one minute?

- **Resting heart rate.** Take your pulse first thing in the morning before you get out of bed. Place your fingers on your carotid artery on your neck or on your wrist just below the line of the thumb. When taking your pulse, don't use your thumb. Your thumb has its own pulse and would confuse your measurement. Count the beats-per-minute by counting the beats for 10 seconds and multiplying that number by six. Take your pulse for three consecutive days and figure the average reading. If your average morning pulse rate decreases over time your cardiovascular fitness is improving.

- **Doctor's physical examination.** If you're severely overweight or have other health conditions, for example, asthma or diabetes, you should consult with a doctor before beginning any exercise program. No matter how healthy you are, it's always a good idea to receive a complete physical examination from your family doctor before participating in any competitive sports.

4•3 Increasing Your Activity Level

I know I should exercise regularly, but I really don't have time with school activities, my homework, and my family. Besides, I'm not good at anything, and working out isn't fun to me.

Kristine

Accidental Workouts

Do you want to feel better? Just because you may not have been the first person picked for the basketball team in gym class, it doesn't mean that you can't live a very active and healthy life.

You may not own a cool bike or have the opportunity to ride horses, but that doesn't mean that you have to miss out on the benefits of being fit and feeling great. Working out doesn't have to be a high-intensity exercise routine that you must do every day. Getting fit and feeling better may simply mean adding more physical activity and movement to your life.

Getting fit and feeling better may simply mean adding more physical activity and movement to your life.

Until I was in junior high, I had P.E. (Physical Education) class every day. I always looked forward to the class. Sometimes, our P.E. teacher was our home room instructor. For other classes, we had a specialist teach us something unique like gymnastics or trampoline. I loved getting out of the classroom and getting some exercise. In junior high, however, our school cut back the P.E. class to only three days a week. Because of this decrease in my planned workout times, I was glad that I had many other activities in my life that gave me an "accidental workout".

After school, I quickly changed my clothes and got ready to go to the ranch to ride my horse. I started riding when I was in second grade. Even though riding wasn't very cardiovascular (heart-pumping), it made me feel great. When I rode trails in the fresh air, I felt a great sense of adventure. It was fun and motivating. Without thinking, "I'm going to ride today for my daily exercise," riding became an excellent "accidental workout" for me. Besides providing me with a lot of fun, I found that riding also strengthened my back and stomach muscles. It worked muscles I never

Accidental Workouts

- Make your bed and clean your room in a short amount of time. Concentrate on body movement and a thorough and quick job. Time yourself. Try to beat your old record.

- Mow the yard, pick berries, or work in the garden. Mowing, gardening, weeding, planting, harvesting, and picking can be strenuous exercise. You might use muscles you never thought you had. By the way, gardening isn't "women's work". I knew a man who was a multi-millionaire who relaxed from his fast-paced lifestyle by working in his garden and orchard every weekend.

- Wash cars. You could earn extra money as well as burn extra calories.

- Ride your bike to school or to other activities. Depending on where you live, taking your bike could be a great lifestyle habit. Just make sure that you leave in plenty of time!

thought I had! By having to sit on my horse in a certain way, riding also helped my posture.

When I didn't ride my horse, I rode my bike with my friends. Bike riding was also an "accidental workout" for me because I received several physical benefits from it while I was really enjoying myself. Bike riding worked my heart and my lungs. It also increased my sense of balance and coordination.

Some of my other enjoyable "accidental workouts"—along with their physical benefits—included: skateboarding (balance, coordination, leg strength, flexibility, back and stomach muscle development), in-line skating (great general conditioner, balance, coordination, heart and leg muscle strengthening), and tennis (development of a specialized skill, upper and lower body strength). Can you think of one of your favorite activities and its physical benefits?

Living an active life helps you to enjoy physical activity.

Even though our family had a TV, we didn't have a VCR. I couldn't watch videos. Since video game systems did not yet exist, I couldn't play video games. We didn't have a computer either. My lifestyle was very active. Every day was full of movement and fun. I was frequently getting an "accidental workout"! Little did I know that I was not only laying the groundwork for a healthy lifestyle, but also a college degree and a career.

What keeps you from doing some kind of activity or exercise? Do you feel that you have to be "good" at a sport before you participate in it? This is one of the main hindrances to involvement in physical exercise. If you were to go out for a competitive sport that required you to learn a specific set of skills, then you would need to develop some talent in order to try it. Having fun, however, or just exercising for health reasons, requires nothing but desire and determination.

Many people choose **lifetime sports**, activities that they can participate in throughout their lives. Being skilled at something usually makes an activity more fun. In many cases, however, just practicing a sport can increase your ability enough to keep you interested. Can you think of any examples of lifetime sports that would interest you?

One of the most important aspects of good health is having an active lifestyle and getting regular exercise. What's your lifestyle like? Is it active or *sedentary* (non-active)? Your lifestyle has a great influence on your health and general sense of well-being. Your level of activity can also affect your personality, social involvements, family life, and attitude toward living. Have you ever thought about the patterns you're now setting for the rest of your life? The habits that you're presently forming in the areas of eating, being active, and even working around your house, will determine your lifestyle as an adult.

Can you think of any examples of lifetime sports that would interest you?

4•4   Avoiding the Comparison Trap
· ·

When I exercise, the feeling of power in my muscles and in my whole body is much more important that my looks. But, looks is a nice benefit. Sometimes, my looks are even the reason behind my exercising.

Cindy

Some teens don't really care how physically "fit" they are as long as they are "fitting" into the clothes they bought or aren't getting sick all the time. No matter how you've been measuring your personal fitness up to this point, it's a good idea honestly to evaluate your fitness level by some objective measurements.

In measuring your overall physical condition, please remember that you aren't comparing yourself with anyone else. You're only

How "Fit" Are You Looking?

- **Mirror test.** Look in the mirror. Are you pleased with what you see? Are you at a desirable weight? Are your muscles toned? Do you have good posture? Do you look "fit"?

- **Fat-skin fold measurements.** Can you pinch an inch or more of skin from around your waist, back of arm, or your back? If so, then you may have a few pounds to lose.

- **Body frame size.** Are you large-, medium-, or small-boned? There's a correlation between your weight and your frame (bone) size. There's a "proper range" for your height and weight only when you consider your frame size. Take a weight chart seriously only if it considers frame size.

God never intended for you to compare yourself with others. He only expects you to do your best and become the finest person you can become with the resources that He's given to you

measuring yourself against yourself in order to see how fit you could be if you really worked at it. Comparison is one of the greatest enemies to your mind. It'll either make you feel superior to others who aren't as good as you, or it'll make you feel inferior to others who are better than you. For this reason, God never intended for you to compare yourself with others. The apostle Paul criticized some of the people in his day who were going around comparing themselves with each other (2 Corinthians 10:12). Paul made it clear that each person stands or falls before God as an individual (Romans 14:4). God only expects you to do your best and become the finest person you can become with the resources that He's given to you (See the Parable of the Talents, Matthew 25:14-30).

4•5 Staying Strong and Motivated

Proper Preparation

When you see a professional athlete finish a race, win a game, make a goal, or sink a basket, it looks so easy, doesn't it? But, as you know, many years of training and practice have gone into his/her great "one minute" performance. As it is in professional sports, so it is in all successful physical activity. Before any great performance or accomplishment, there has to be adequate preparation.

The Warm-Up

The warm-up prepares your muscles for activity. First, a good warm-up includes you doing some activity to raise your body temperature, for example, jogging or fast walking. Second, a warm-up contains very light stretching of your major muscle groups. Only after your body is warm should you stretch slowly and thoroughly. The warm-up should last anywhere between eight to fifteen minutes. Breaking a sweat is one sign that the body is ready for increased exercise. The warm-up is essential to prepare the body for the workout that follows.

The Warm-Down

A proper warm-down is often overlooked. During exercise, your muscles demand more oxygenated blood to help them move efficiently. When your workout is strenuous, your muscles can experience a *lactic acid* build-up. Without a proper warm-down, you may experience unnecessary muscle soreness, light- headedness, nausea, and/or muscle cramping. A proper warm-down includes light movement like a slow jog or a walk. Stretching large muscle groups such as the back, legs, and arms will also help to prevent stiffness and injury.

Injury Prevention
Reducing Your Risk

I'm continually amazed at the risks young people take. They seem to have the amount of energy and courage needed to push past pain and dangerous circumstances in order to have fun or to reach a goal. When I look back, I can't believe all the chances I took when I was in junior high. I must have kept my Mom on the edge of her seat many times.

Long hours of practice are behind the performance of trained athletes.

Even though taking a certain number of risks is a healthy part of living, your body *is* destructible. Your body can and does suffer injury, and quite easily at times. Have you ever broken an arm, sprained an ankle, or stubbed a toe? If so, did you ever ask yourself whether any of your injuries were preventable? Would you like to know how you can prevent yourself from being injured? If so, the answer is being fit. Being physically healthy actually lowers your risk of injury. Being fit makes you more physically and mentally able to handle a dangerous or stressful situation.

Tips for the Prevention of Injuries

1. Choose a realistic and appropriate program for yourself.
2. Begin the program slowly.
3. Use quality equipment including shoes, helmets, guards, etc.
4. Make sure you know the proper form for the activity.
5. Always have a warm-up no matter how little time you have.
6. Always have a warm-down no matter how rushed you are.
7. STOP when you feel faint, dizzy, or pain.
8. Vary your activity by cross-training to avoid stress injuries.

Attending to Injuries

When you're injured, it's very important to treat your injury immediately so that no further damage is done. When I tried out for our high school basketball team, I felt a sharp pain in my thigh as we ran. When the coach noticed that I was hurting, he had me sit down for a few minutes. I wanted to make the team so badly, however, that I ignored my pain and rejoined the workout as soon as I could. The pain in my thigh kept bothering me throughout the season, but I didn't want to stop playing. My leg injury became worse. Four months later, track season came, and I ran the mile relay. My leg injury prevented me from making my fastest times in my events. Because I ignored the pain in my leg by trying to be "tough" and "cool", I still have a knot in my leg. To this day, I haven't been able to "fix" it. The knot in my leg hinders me from strenuous workouts. It's a continual reminder to me of how I should have attended to my injury as soon as I felt the pain.

Wearing protective gear such as a bike helmet has proven to save many lives.

If you or one of your friends is injured, stop the activity and get help. If the injury seems serious, contact a doctor who specializes in sports medicine. If the injury is mild, it's still a good idea to check with a doctor if the condition doesn't improve after a few days.

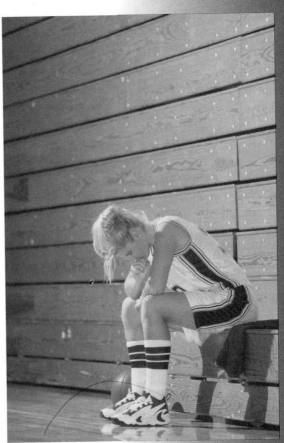

For the immediate treatment of injuries, follow the acronym RICE:

- **R**est the injured area.

- **I**ce the injured area (to prevent swelling).

- **C**ompress the injured area with a towel or bandage (to prevent swelling).

- **E**levate the injured area above the level of the heart (to help drain fluid that might collect at the injury).

Motivation: "How Can I Stay Motivated?"

It's fairly easy to stay active when you're young because you have more free time to enjoy exercise just for the fun of it. As a younger teen, try to be active after you get home from school. Actively participate in your Physical Education classes. Walk or ride your bike whenever it's possible instead of riding in the car. If you really need help staying motivated with a particular exercise program, here are a few ideas that might help:

When you're injured, it's very important to treat your injury immediately so that no further damage is done.

1. Keep an exercise journal. Evaluate your progress. Record inspirational quotes. Report how you felt during the activity along with any comments about what you want to improve.

2. Set realistic goals. Continually evaluate them.

3. Remind yourself often of the benefits of exercise. Have a list of the benefits in your journal, on your mirror, or inside your binder.

4. Read sports, fitness, walking, or running magazines.

Working out with a friend can help keep you motivated.

5. Add music or talking tapes to your routine.

6. Exercise with a friend, sister, brother, Mom, or Dad.

7. Enter a competition like a fun walk/run race.

8. Take lessons for a particular sport (swimming, tennis, golf, gymnastics, etc).

9. Join a sports team. If not at school, join a YMCA/YWCA team or city league.

10. Reward yourself when you reach a goal.

Chapter 4 Review

Defining the Terms

Fitness

Cardiovascular fitness

Atrophy

Aerobic

Anaerobic

Muscular fitness

Flexibility

Body composition

Lifetime sport(s)

Recalling the Facts

1. List ten benefits of exercise.

2. Explain why the most important measurement of your fitness is cardiovascular fitness.

3. Explain the difference between aerobic and anaerobic exercise and give one example of each kind of activity. Why are they both important?

4. Why is the phrase, "No pain, No gain" incorrect when it comes to stretching and exercise?

5. Explain the importance of a good warm-up and warm-down when exercising.

Applying the Truth

1. What is the important role that exercise has in controlling one's weight? How might you include more activity in your lifestyle?

2. What is meant by the phrase, "accidental workout"? Include in your answer any accidental workouts that your personal lifestyle already includes.

3. Many teenagers compare themselves with others. How can comparison be dangerous, and what does God think about it?

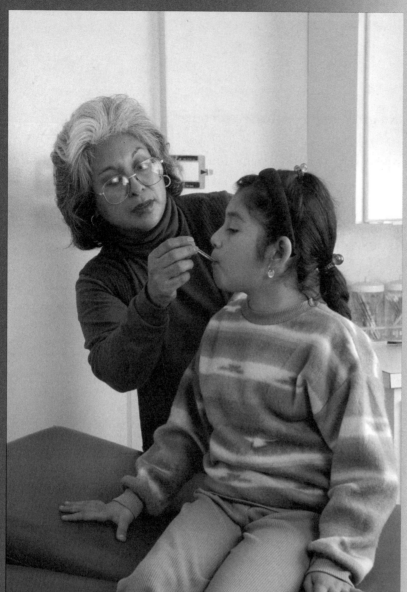

"If you diligently give ear to His commandments...I will put none of the diseases on you which I have brought on the Egyptians..."

Exodus 15:26

DISEASES 5
THE BODY UNDER ATTACK

What's Coming Up...

5 • 1   The Body Under Attack

. . . .

> *Two years ago, I would sometimes come home from school*
> *and cry because my friends were ignoring me or I got a low grade.*
> *That seems so silly to me now. These days when I cry, it's because*
> *I know I'm going to die; probably sometime soon. I have*
> *terminal bone cancer, and there's nothing I can do to stop it.*
> *All I can do is live each day as it comes.*[1]
> Kristen, diagnosed with cancer at age 13, died at age 15

Imagine for a moment where you might be five years from now. What school would you be attending? Who might be your friends? Where would you be living? You'll probably have your driver's license. You could even be enjoying the steady income of a part-time job. All of this sounds good, doesn't it?

On the other hand, what have you possibly forgotten to consider in this scenario? You've thought about your future school, friends, location, driver's license, and income, but what about your health? How do you think Kristen felt when her whole life changed overnight? One moment she was a happy, healthy teenager who was anticipating the joys of young adulthood. The next moment, she was diagnosed with a terminal illness.

Do you take your health for granted? I think that all teens have a tendency to get so excited about the future that they don't consider their good health as a gift from God. The apostle James wrote, "Every good gift and every perfect gift is from above and comes down from the Father of lights..." (James 1:17). Sometimes, you're reminded of your body's weaknesses when you experience a slight cold or a more serious flu bug. Diseases, both infectious and noninfectious, can attack your body without much warning. As you learn about diseases in this chapter, consider what your role might be in trying to prevent them.

Your body fights to stay in balance all the time. Every system of your body, including your body temperature and your need for rest, is constantly struggling to maintain normal functioning and good health. Whenever your good health is threatened, your body immediately begins to try to regain its balance. God gave you an amazing creation when He gave you your body. He made your body to serve you well all the days of your life. When you think about it, it becomes clear why the psalmist exclaimed:

God gave you an amazing creation when He gave you your body.

I will praise You, Lord, for I am fearfully and wonderfully made. Marvelous are Your works, and that I know very well.
Psalm 139:14

Many diseases, like Kristen's, are beyond human control. Kristen was a healthy, athletic, young lady. She ate well, exercised regularly, and had no known cancer in her family history. Yet, she developed terminal bone cancer. You won't be able to explain or prevent some tragic events in life. This is the bad news. However, this is not the whole story. There is hope. The good news is the fact that you can prevent most sickness and disease by making wise lifestyle choices. As the old adage goes, "An ounce of prevention is worth a pound of cure". Prevention really is the best medicine. Making wise decisions according to the principles that God has given to you in His word is a way of preventing sickness and disease in your life. "You're not just a body attacked by germs and waiting for medicines," Dr. Paul Brand writes, "you're a body with a mind and a spirit. You can't be truly healthy or happy unless you follow the laws of the God who made you".[2]

Can you remember the last time you were sick? Did you enjoy it? If you had not had a TV to watch while you were laying in bed recuperating, it would have been even more miserable, wouldn't it? No matter what sickness you may have, being ill is no fun. The word **disease** can be used to describe any condition that negatively affects the healthy and normal functioning of your mind or body. There are two categories of diseases. The first category is infectious (or, communicable) diseases. **Infectious diseases** are caused by germs that spread from one person to another. The second category is noninfectious (or, noncommunicable) diseases. **Noninfectious diseases** are caused by heredity, the environment, and/or a person's lifestyle.

Although there have been great medical advances in the last century, many diseases still puzzle scientists.

5 • 2   Infectious Diseases

• •

There are thousands of different diseases that afflict mankind today. Although there have been great medical advances in the last century, many diseases still puzzle scientists. Infectious diseases are caused by the spread of **germs** or **pathogens**. These tiny particles may be plant or animal in origin. They're so small that they may only be seen under a microscope. These

germs attack your body. They use your body's cells to live and grow. One day you may be feeling fine, then suddenly you begin to feel sick. The fact that you develop symptoms such as a stuffy nose or a sore throat shows that you have an *infection*. Some of the infections that are caused by *fungus* are athlete's foot, ringworm, and candidiasis. Others are caused by *parasites* like tapeworms or roundworms. Parasites can produce intestinal problems, some forms of anemia, and trichinosis. Most infections are caused by either viruses or bacteria.

DANGER!

When sick people go to see their doctors, they receive written prescriptions for certain medications. Many times, after they've finished their prescriptions, it's as if "poof" their infection disappears. Recently, however, there's a growing concern with the widespread use of prescription drugs. Some strains of bacteria and viruses are changing to resist the medicines that once destroyed them. As a result, it's even more important to keep your immune system strong so that your body can resist germs. Be careful not to rely upon antibiotics and medications but on your own body's ability to defend itself.

Viruses

When you're suffering from the common cold, you're suffering from a virus. **Viruses** are much smaller in size than bacteria. While bacteria produce toxins (poisons) in your body, viruses attack individual cells. The virus chooses the tissue it wants to damage and then invades the cells of that tissue. Viruses that cause cold sores, for example, invade your skin cells. Viruses that cause the flu attack your respiratory system. Viruses are also responsible for diseases such as the mumps, measles, chicken pox, smallpox, rabies, polio, most cases of hepatitis, and AIDS.

When you're suffering from the common cold, you're suffering from a virus, not a bacteria.

After a virus invades one of your cells, it begins to multiply. After damaging one cell, it moves on to injure other cells. When your impaired cells cannot function properly, your body begins to tell you that something is wrong. To do this, your body develops **symptoms** to let you know that it's trying to fight an "intruder". In order to win the battle, your body has to redirect much of the energy that you would normally use for daily activities. As a result, you feel tired. Instead of trying to push yourself past your own body's clear signals, it's best to *listen to your body*. Help your body win the battle by giving it nutritious food, purified water, and sufficient rest.

Bacteria

Bacteria are tiny single-celled organisms. They come in many shapes: rodlike (bacillus), round (coccus), and spiral (spirochete). Not all bacteria are harmful. Your body produces "friendly" bacteria that grow in your intestines and are vital for proper digestion. The good bacteria are called **resident bacteria**.

Good Bacteria Are Your Friends.

Did you know that when you take an antibiotic to fight "bad" bacteria, it also kills the "good" or "friendly" bacteria in your body? It's very important that you replace the "friendly" bacteria that was destroyed by the antibiotic so that your immune system can regain its strength. You can do this by including lots of yogurt in your diet and/or taking a supplement of "friendly flora" (a combination of good bacteria). If you take an antibiotic like tetracycline for your acne, you should also include "good" bacteria in your daily diet.

Bacteria need food for energy, like all other living creatures. Bacteria also produce waste products. These disease-bearing organisms produce poisonous wastes (toxins) that are harmful to your body. Your body works hard to stop the growth of these bad bacteria and to neutralize any toxins they produce. Sometimes, a doctor may prescribe an antibiotic to help fight the bacteria. When the growth of the bacteria is under control, your body eliminates the poisons, and you recover. Some diseases that are caused by bacteria are: strep throat, staph infections, cholera, pneumonia, tuberculosis, some food poisoning, and certain venereal diseases (STDs) such as gonorrhea and syphilis. If left untreated, some bacteria can even cause death.

Learning the Hard Way

Susan Boe

Have you ever had a sinus infection? If so, then you've felt the throbbing headache behind your nose and eyes. It's horrible, isn't it? My Mom always told me that I must have inherited my grandmother's sinus problems. At least once a year as I was growing up, I experienced a very painful sinus infection. I learned that the main difference between a sinus infection (a bacteria) or a cold (a virus) is that green stuff that you blow out of your nose. When the color changes to green mucus, you can bet you have a bacterial infection and not just a cold virus. I don't know from where all the green mucus comes, but it's manufactured in great quantities! Anyway, I always took an antibiotic and the infection would clear up. One summer while I was in college, I worked as a lifeguard at our university's indoor pool. But, when the chlorine in the air began to irritate my sinuses, I knew that I was in big trouble. One morning, I called in sick because I thought my head was going to explode. I went to a doctor, and he prescribed for me the same medication I had taken when I was in high school. It seemed to help me, so I went back to work. About one week after I had finished the medication, I awoke with another one of "those" headaches. I called in to work sick—again. The doctor prescribed for me even a stronger antibiotic. It was "sure to work", but it didn't. My boss was getting so upset with my sinus infections that he wanted me to come in and "swim it off"! When I went back to the same doctor, he told me, "You're going to have to ride this one out on your own. I can't write anymore prescriptions for you. Once your body has built up its own immune system enough to fight this infection by itself, you should be better". So, I suffered through it, and my body did fight back. Lifeguarding that summer was very painful for me, but I haven't had a sinus infection since.

The Infectious Disease Process

To protect yourself against infectious diseases, it's important to know how germs are spread. Germs are "caught" in four ways.

Contact with an airborne germ. Infections, such as colds, are spread when a person sneezes or coughs. Germs travel through the air by way of tiny droplets and enter another person's nasal passages or lungs.

Contact with a person. Some germs spread through direct physical contact with an infected person, for example, STDs and AIDS. Touching athlete's foot or ringworm may also cause the germ to spread.

Contact with animals. Bites from various animals may cause disease. Certain flies, mosquitoes, and fleas can carry diseases such as malaria, dysentery, typhoid, and typhus.

Contact with an object. Touching objects that an infected person has handled, for example, towels, door handles, drinking glasses, soda pop cans, toothbrushes, or the telephone, can cause the spread of germs.

From the time you become infected to the time you develop symptoms is called the **incubation period**. The incubation period is the most infectious time of the disease and is often called the **contagious period**. Why is it that you and a friend may share the same can of pop, but you're the only one who ends up getting sick? People respond differently to the same germ. A person who is carrying the germ but doesn't seem to be suffering from the illness is called a **carrier**. Your **resistance**, or ability to fight the invading germ, has much to do with the severity of symptoms you will experience. Building a strong immune system through proper nutrition, exercise, lots of purified water, and adequate sleep, will help you to resist the invasion of a virus or a bacterium. If you're infected, you become the new home (host) for the germ, and the cycle continues.

Exercise helps strengthen your resistance to germs.

Your Defenses: Physical and Spiritual

Sometimes, no matter how careful you are, germs will infect your body. In the battle against any disease, infectious or noninfectious, there are always two lines of defense. One is not more important than the other. Both methods of defense play a vital role in your

fight against disease as well as in your process of recovery. Your two defenses are the physical and the spiritual.

The human body is a remarkable creation. Researchers who invest their lives studying it are continually amazed at its intricate designs and functions. God designed your body with its own physical defense system to fight off sickness. It's called your immune system.

LOGON!

Wash, Wash, Wash!

Did you know that most germs are carried by way of contact with hands? The last time that you used the public restroom at the mall, did you wash your hands before leaving? Even if you did wash your hands when you were leaving, if you touched the doorknob, you may have contracted more germs. After using the restroom, you go to the food court and order something to eat. You eat the food with your hands, and may infect yourself with the germs you picked up in the restroom! One way to avoid this germ cycle is for you always to wash your hands after using the restroom, then use a tissue or paper towel to open the door as you leave, making sure you don't pick up any germs on your way out! Also, whenever you're around a sick person, at home or in school, wash your hands regularly with antibacterial soap. Also, try to keep your hands away from your face (nose, mouth, and eyes).

Your *skin* is part of your first line of defense against an infectious disease. It's your outer barrier that prevents germs from entering your body. Most substances (with the exception of poisonous plants) cannot penetrate your unbroken skin. It's important to wash your hands often throughout the day. The *mucous membranes* in your mouth, nose, and throat protect you from invading germs. The mucus secreted in your nose and throat gives you a way to blow out or cough up germs. The small hairs inside your nose keep small particles out.

When harmful germs penetrate your first line of defense, your body sets up for a counterattack. Your body's white blood cells (lymphocytes) begin to produce special proteins called **antibodies**. If your body's resistance is strong enough, the antibodies destroy the pathogen(s). After destroying the invader, your lymphocytes make a "mental note" of the germ and can destroy it quickly if it ever reappears in your body again. Antibodies instinctively know to attack viruses and bacteria but not to attack your body's healthy cells. If a germ, however, has found a way inside one of your body's cells, antibodies will not attack it. As a result, your cells need to have their own line of defense. If invaded, a cell produces interferon. **Interferon** is like a communication system between your cells. The release of this chemical informs the other cells to prepare to fight the virus. If the virus cannot enter these other cells, the infection is stopped.

Did you know that a fever can be good for your body?

Have you ever had a fever? If so, you probably tried to get rid of it as soon as you could, didn't you? Did you know that a fever can be *good* for your body? A fever is another way your body defends itself against invasion. A certain body temperature will destroy some germs. If you have a low fever (102° and under), it may be good to let the fever run its course so that your body can drive out whatever it's trying to get rid of. If your temperature is really high and accompanied by severe body aches and pains, a non-aspirin medication can be taken to make you more comfortable until the fever breaks.

Your lymphatic system plays a part in your immune system. White blood cells not only travel in your bloodstream, they also travel in a secondary circulatory system called your *lymphatic system*. Your lymphatic network includes vessels that circulate a special body fluid called *lymph*. Lymphatic vessels lead to specialized organs called *lymph nodes*. One function of your lymph nodes is to manufacture white blood cells called **lymphocytes**. Lymphocytes travel through your lymphatic system fighting germs.

Scientists have discovered that an injection of weakened or destroyed cells of a particular germ (mumps, measles, chicken pox, or polio) will cause your body to produce enough antibodies against

that particular germ to destroy it. Such an injection is called a **vaccine**. As a result of the vaccine, your body is prepared to fight the germ or disease if it's ever exposed to it again.

Your Spiritual Defenses

Any illness or physical condition can be addressed purely on a physical level. The Bible, however, gives you insights into the physical as well as the spiritual defenses that you have available to defend your body against attack.

Faith in God's Power

How does your faith in God affect your perspective on health and healing? This is a very personal and sometimes controversial

question. As you're getting to know God for yourself and using the Word of God more and more in your daily life, the role of faith and healing may become an issue for you. Some families who experience personal tragedy in relation to sickness and possibly even death may still hold to a very strong conviction in the area of healing. Other Christians wouldn't. Your walk with Christ becomes "personal" as you search the Scriptures for yourself and pray over areas that concern you.

The life of Christ shows us the great power God has over disease and even death. Jesus, moved with compassion, healed many who were sick. Sometimes, He healed everyone who came to Him for healing (Matthew 8:16). Jesus didn't always have to touch the sick for them to be healed. Sick people could receive healing by exercising their own faith in Jesus (Mark 5:34) or even by having one of their friends or relatives exercise it for them (Matthew 8:8).

Faith in God's Control

No matter what the circumstances, God wants your *faith* (deep trust) in Him to grow. He is *sovereign* in His ways. God is sovereign in that He is the king, the highest ruler, and the lawmaker of the

God is sovereign in that He is the king, the highest ruler, and the lawmaker of the entire universe.

entire universe. He rules the galaxies according to His character of holiness, justice, goodness, love, and mercy. He rules over all things in ways that you can't always understand. Although you may not always understand "why" things happen, for example, the death of a loved one, sickness, accidents, etc., God understands the anguish you feel in every painful situation. You may even blame God for a tragedy in your life. However you're feeling, God wants to draw you close to Himself and comfort you. The life of Job is an excellent example of a man who had "bad things" happen to him (Job 1:13-19). Through all of his suffering and complaining (3:1-26), his trust and faith in God were finally restored after he received a deeper understanding of God's sovereignty (chapters 38-41). After he humbled himself before God, saw himself as totally ignorant before the Sovereign One (40:3-5; 42:1-6), and prayed for the friends who had condemned him (42:8-10), God restored his life to more than he had at the first (42:10-17).

5 • 3   Sexually Transmitted Diseases

· ·

Sexually transmitted diseases (STDs) are a widespread problem. STDs are not limited to age, race, gender (male or female), or economic class (rich or poor). The only common thread that determines whether an STD (with the exception of AIDS) may affect you or someone you know is the decision to be sexually active. **STDs or venereal diseases** are diseases that pass from one person to another through sexual contact.

STDs are diseases that pass from one person to another through sexual contact.

There are many different kinds of STDs. The most serious ones are chlamydia, gonorrhea, syphilis, herpes simplex II, and HIV that causes AIDS. Serious complications can result from many of these diseases. Chlamydia and gonorrhea can both cause **sterility** (inability to produce

offspring). Syphilis can cause blindness, heart and other organ damage, and even death.

Although STDs can be treated with some medications, the only way to prevent getting an STD is through sexual abstinence. As you are shaping your own **convictions** (strong beliefs), it's important to consider making a firm decision about being sexually pure *before* you find yourself facing a temptation. Talk with your parent(s) or a mature Christian adult about your questions concerning sexual activity. Ask God to give you the strength to be pure. Make a commitment to stay away from any sexually compromising situations. If you don't make a decision ahead of time, you may find yourself doing something you really don't want to do. The consequences can be deadly.

AIDS

AIDS stands for acquired immunodeficiency syndrome. AIDS itself is not a disease but a result of **HIV** (human immunodeficiency virus). Although scientists are learning more about this disease each year, there remain three undisputed facts about AIDS: (1) It's always fatal. (2) There's no known cure at this time. (3) It's preventable. Abstaining from sexual activity until marriage is not only pleasing to God, but a wise health decision, too.

5 • 4 Noninfectious Diseases

*The disease I fear the most is cancer—
what if someone in my family got it?*

Lisa

Do you have any health-related fear like Lisa? Sometimes, if you know someone who has a bad disease or hear about it on the news, it can cause you to worry. But 'borrowing trouble' will only

As you are shaping your own convictions (strong beliefs), it's important to consider making a firm decision about being sexually pure before you find yourself facing a temptation.

put fear in your heart. If you find yourself worrying about potential illness, try to learn all you can about preventing disease, live a healthy lifestyle, and then leave the rest up to God!

Noninfectious diseases are not contagious. These diseases are said to be **degenerative** because the body's tissues break down, don't grow, or malfunction. The primary causes of noninfectious diseases are *heredity*, *environment*, and *lifestyle*.

Although the symptoms of a noninfectious disease may show up suddenly, the disease itself may have been developing over a long period of time. Jim's doctors, for example, just informed him that he has colon cancer (cancer of the large intestine). Jim was shocked. No one had ever told him about the direct connection between lifestyle and degenerative disease. For many years, Jim's diet lacked sufficient fiber and nutrients. He frequently suffered from symptoms such as constipation, diarrhea, and an irritable bowel, but he just ignored them. Now Jim is suffering a degenerative disease due, in most part, to his poor eating habits. Can you think of another example where a person's lifestyle might contribute to the cause of a particular noninfectious disease?

Cancer

If I could find a cure to any disease today,
I would want to cure cancer because so many people
have died from it, and so many people suffer from it.

Katy

The Big 'C' Word
Susan Boe

When I was in seventh grade, I had a classmate named Teresa. During the school year, Teresa's mother was diagnosed with cancer—the big 'C' word. None of the students in our class ever talked about it. All of us felt too uncomfortable to ask Teresa how her mother was doing. We didn't want her to get upset. We didn't realize the seriousness of cancer. Before we graduated from eighth grade, Teresa's mother died. As I look back, I wish I had been more of a support to her.

When going through a difficult time such as a serious illness in the family, it's important to talk about your feelings with someone you trust.

More than any other disease, cancer is accompanied with feelings of intense fear. Not very often do you hear about the triumphs or victories over this disease. Although cancer is a complicated disease, its definition is simple. **Cancer** occurs when abnormal cells grow out of control. Your body is composed of trillions of cells. Many cells die each minute and are replaced with new ones. It's hard to imagine the constant activity that is taking place every minute on the cellular level within your body. God made every cell in your body to serve a certain purpose. At times, however, cells change, become abnormal, and rebel. They may form masses of cells called **tumors**. Tumors can either be *benign* (not cancerous) or *malignant* (cancerous).

A tumor is called benign if its effect is fairly localized and it stays within membrane boundaries. Malignant tumors, however, don't stay in one location. They multiply without any checks on growth, spreading rapidly throughout the body, choking out normal cells. White cells, armed against foreign invaders, will not attack the body's own mutinous cells. Physicians fear no other malfunction more deeply. For still mysterious reasons, these cells—and they may be cells from the brain, liver, kidney, bone, blood, skin, or other tissues—grow wild, out of control. These abnormal cells use vital nutrients from the body. As a result, the tumor lives while the body starves.[3]

The Cause of Cancer

The specific cause of cancer is unknown. However, there are certain factors that researchers believe increase your chances of developing the disease. Some of these factors are out of your control, others are not. The following is a list of the major factors which contribute to the development of cancer. Which of the following factors do you believe you can directly control?

- Genetic make-up (heredity)

- Lifestyle habits (diet, exercise, tobacco, alcohol, stress)

- Environmental factors (air and water pollution)

- Occupational hazards (dust, chemicals, toxins)

- Your body's reaction to a virus (weakened immune system)

Any substance that tends to produce cancer is called a **carcinogen**. There are both natural and man-made carcinogens. The sun is a natural carcinogen. Many people, in an effort to get a "great tan", contract skin cancer every year by exposing themselves too much to the sun's rays. Tobacco smoke, saccharine (a sugar substitute), as well as pollutants from factories, are all man-made carcinogens.

How can teenagers include more fresh fruits and vegetables in their diets?

The Prevention of Cancer

Although you can't change your heredity or some of the factors in your environment, you can adjust your lifestyle. Scientists believe that the way you choose to live has much to do with your individual risk of cancer.

According to the American Cancer Society, vitamin A (in dark green and deep yellow fruits and vegetables) may reduce the risk of some cancers. Vitamin C (in citrus fruits) is also a strong anticarcinogen. Although your favorite foods may be "fast food" (hotdogs, hamburgers, French fries, pop), a diet high in these foods actually increases your risk of cancer because they are high-fat, low-nutrient, and chemically-laden foods. Research on diet-related cancer has shown that a person whose diet is high in plant-rich foods (fruits, vegetables, nuts, seeds, whole grains) has less of a chance of contracting cancer than does one who eats red meats (high fat).

Noticing Changes

Every unusual change that your body experiences is not an automatic sign of cancer. However, there's truth in learning how to

"listen" to your body. Your body speaks to you through different signs and symptoms.

DANGER!

The American Cancer Society's Seven Warning Signs of Cancer spell out the word **CAUTION**. Knowing these signs is important for early detection and treatment.

- **C**hange in bowel or bladder habits
- **A** sore that does not heal
- **U**nusual bleeding or discharge
- **T**hickening or lump in the breast or elsewhere
- **I**ndigestion or difficulty in swallowing
- **O**bvious change in a wart or mole
- **N**agging cough or hoarseness

Treatment of Cancer

The presence of cancer is confirmed by a microscopic examination of tissue cells. Cancer cells look different from normal cells under a microscope. Doctors obtain these tissues by performing a biopsy on a person. A biopsy is the removal of living tissue from a person's body for the purpose of closer examination.

You can learn to "listen" to your body. Your body speaks to you through different symptoms.

Although scientists are researching new treatments for cancer, there are presently four main types of treatment:

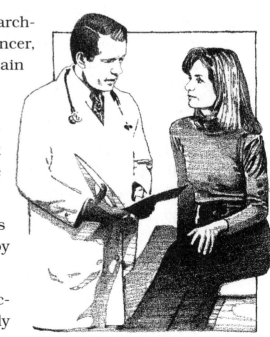

1. *Surgery* removes the cancer cells that have not spread throughout the body.

2. *Chemotherapy* uses drugs and chemicals to destroy cancer cells.

3. *Radiation* applies radioactive energy (x-rays) directly

to cancerous cells while attempting to avoid healthy cells.

4. *Immunotherapy* takes measures to strengthen the immune system so that it can better fight and control the cancerous cells.

Today, the word "cancer" is not synonymous with death. Both the cure and survival rates of cancer victims continue to improve. Through avoiding the high-risk causes of cancer, you can lower your chances of developing this disease. Knowing whether cancer is a part of your family's health history (heredity) is also an important part of being responsible for your personal health.

LOGON!

Your Humor, Your Health

A person's attitude and outlook on life can have a profound effect on one's health. The Book of Proverbs says that laughter is like a good medicine (Proverbs 17:22). A movie was actually produced based on the story that a man supposedly healed himself of cancer through laughter. Can you see a connection between laughter and health? Do you think that laughter actually releases a certain positive chemical into the bloodstream? Include laughter in your lifestyle—it can't hurt!

Heart Disease

"Star Athlete Dies on Basketball Court of a Major Heart Attack," newspaper headlines sometimes read. What could cause a young or healthy athlete to have a heart attack? We usually think that the young and athletic will have the least problem with their hearts because they're so active. When a young person suffers from cardiovascular disease, however, it's usually attributed to a **congenital** (at birth) heart condition. Congenital heart defects may or may not be serious. Obviously, heart attacks are more common among older people than they are among younger people. Nevertheless, the number one killer in the United States is heart disease. Every 33 seconds, someone dies from a heart attack or stroke. Whether old or young,

The bicycle test is one way doctors measure how healthy the heart is.

inactive or athletic, most cardiovascular disease is caused by a person's lifestyle. If a person's cholesterol level is over 200, for example, he has twice the risk of a heart attack; if over 240, he has three times the risk.

Arteriosclerosis and Atherosclerosis

The phrase, "hardening of the arteries" refers to *arteriosclerosis*. Fat deposits on the artery walls called atherosclerosis cause the most common type of hardening of the arteries. These fat deposits make it difficult for the blood to pass through. Unfortunately, a person who has atherosclerosis may experience no warning symptoms until the blockage is so severe that the blood flow is seriously restricted. At this stage, the person may experience *angina* (a pain or tightening in the chest) or a *myocardial infarction* (a heart attack caused by the blood flow being so reduced that the heart is starved for oxygen and stops functioning).

Stroke

A *stroke* occurs when a person's brain is damaged by a lack of blood supply. The four main causes of a stroke are: (1) blockage by a clot that has built up on the wall of the brain artery (2) blockage by a clot that drifts into an artery in the brain (3) the rupture of a blood vessel in the brain, and (4) bleeding within the brain area. Arteries of the brain that are damaged or weakened may rupture and cause a *cerebral hemorrhage*. When a brain artery expands like a balloon and bursts, it's called a *cerebral aneurysm*.

Prevention of Heart Disease

Although doctors have isolated several risk factors for heart disease, prevention is still the best medicine. You can start right now to have a healthy heart. You can begin at a young age to prevent heart disease by discovering whether there's heart disease in your family. It's very important to know your family health history so that you can make choices that can decrease your risk of developing the disease. Just because you may have heart disease in your family doesn't mean you have to suffer from it, too. Of the risk factors that contribute to heart disease, only your age (the older are

Including fresh fruits and vegetables in your diet is a great way to help prevent heart disease.

114

more likely to get it that the younger), your gender (males are more likely to have heart attacks than females), and your family history are out of your control. Most, if not all, of the other risk factors, are up to you.

Risk Factors Contributing to Heart Disease

- *High blood pressure (hypertension).* The force of your blood on the inside walls of your main arteries is called your blood pressure. It's important for you to keep your blood pressure in a healthy range. If it gets too high and remains at a dangerous level, it can cause a heart attack. Hypertension is often called the "silent killer" because many people don't know they have it until after they suffer a heart attack.

- *High cholesterol.* Cholesterol is the waxy substance that's carried around in your bloodstream. There is good and bad cholesterol. High levels of LDL (bad cholesterol) in your blood can increase your risk of developing heart disease.

- *Smoking.* Smoking increases your chances of heart disease because it damages and constricts (makes smaller) your blood vessels.

- *Diabetes.* Those who suffer from diabetes have a greater risk of developing heart disease.

- *Alcohol.* Those who drink alcohol excessively are more likely to develop complications from heart disease than those who don't drink heavily.

- *Obesity.* People who are overweight are more likely to have heart disease than people who maintain their ideal weight because their weight makes their heart work overtime.

- *Lack of exercise.* Regular exercise not only helps you maintain your ideal weight, it also keeps your heart muscle strong. Exercise can also help you manage your blood pressure and reduce stress.

- *Stress.* Managing your stress level is an important part of decreasing your risk of heart disease.

DANGER!

Sure, we all get angry sometimes. But, are you always on the verge of blowing your top? Do you find yourself constantly annoyed—about everyone and everything? Evaluate your anger level to see if you are starting a dangerous habit that could increase your risk of heart attack and other health problems. If you feel you have a problem with rage, find ways to get the harmful emotions of rage, unforgiveness, and resentment under control. Talk to someone you can trust about your strong feelings. Whether you let it out or hold it in—persistent anger may still damage your heart.

Diabetes Mellitus

It's important for me just to blend in—like being able to hang out with my friends and get a diet soda after track practice. Sometimes I feel different from other kids, like I can't sleep in. I have to eat breakfast at a regular time and then prepare my equipment and my snacks for the day. I have to have a lot of discipline.

Mark, a 14-year-old diabetic

Having to cope with diabetes during the school routine can be hard.

It's not easy for anyone to have a disease. Mark knows what it's like to have to face each day with diabetes. Diabetes mellitus is the most common form of diabetes. It's a noninfectious disease that affects approximately 5.5 million Americans (as of 1998). Studies show that there are 5 million adults with undetected type II diabetes. Another 20 million adults have impaired blood sugar tolerance that may eventually give them the full disease. Complications of diabetes are the third leading cause of death in the United States.[4]

Having to cope with diabetes during the school routine can be hard, but moving from elementary school to middle school or high school can be even more difficult. It's important for those around a young person with diabetes to know and understand the symptoms of the disease. For example, when Mark started ninth grade, not many of his teachers, counselors, or coaches knew that he had **diabetes mellitus**. Mark kept it to himself and handled his disease on his own. This is how many young people feel about having diabetes—different from their peers.

Mark's pancreas wasn't able to produce adequate amounts of insulin. **Insulin** is the hormone produced by your pancreas to control how your body uses sugar to give you the energy you need. The more sugar Mark has in his blood, the more insulin is released to regulate it.

Hypoglycemia is a condition in which the pancreas releases too much insulin. If you were hypoglycemic, your blood sugar levels would be very low and your symptoms would include shakiness, lightheadedness, nausea, and even fainting. Have you ever gone without eating for longer than usual? If so, did you experience weakness or strong hunger pangs? If you did, it wasn't necessarily a sign that you have a blood sugar problem. Although you may not have symptoms at your age, it's good to keep the amount of white sugar in your diet to a minimum. Did you know that in one twelve-ounce can of regular soda pop there are 39 grams of sugar (high fructose corn syrup)? That is equivalent to 9 teaspoons of sugar for every twelve-ounce can and 25 teaspoons for each liter of regular pop you drink!

The cause of diabetes is not totally understood. Its significant risk factors include a family history of diabetes, obesity, age, and, probably most important, diet.

A diet high in refined, processed foods and low in fiber and complex carbohydrates is believed to be behind most cases of diabetes.

Perhaps more than most diseases, diabetes mellitus is associated with diet. It is a chronic disorder of carbohydrate metabolism... Although genetics may make a person susceptible to diabetes, a diet high in refined, processed foods and low in fiber and complex carbohydrates is believed to be behind most cases of the disease. Those who are overweight face the greatest risk of developing diabetes.[5]

You may know someone who has diabetes but does not have to take insulin. Diabetes mellitus is generally divided into two categories: type I, called insulin-dependent or juvenile diabetes, and type II in which the onset of the disease occurs during adulthood. If you suffered from **diabetes type I** (insulin-dependent), your pancreas would be producing little or no insulin. Mark suffers from type I diabetes. This is a more severe form of the disease. Insulin-dependent sufferers are usually young (between the ages of 10 and 16). Type I, however, may also develop in people up to the age of 35. Without the treatment of regular injections of insulin, the individual who has diabetes type I could die.

Symptoms of Type I Diabetes (insulin-dependent)

- Frequent urination
- Extreme thirst
- Increased appetite
- Unexplained weight loss
- Vomiting and nausea
- Weakness and fatigue

Diabetes type II (noninsulin-dependent) usually appears gradually in people over the age of 40. In this type of diabetes, either the pancreas doesn't produce enough insulin to meet the body's needs, or the body can't use it correctly. Diet, weight control, exercise, and oral medications can help to keep diabetes type II under control.

Symptoms of Type II Diabetes (noninsulin-dependent)

- Tingling and numbness in hands and feet
- Blurred vision
- Lack of energy
- Skin abrasions that heal slowly
- Itching

Diabetics must learn to monitor their blood sugar levels by using a daily blood test. Although there's no agreed-upon cure for diabetes as yet, diabetics can live fairly normal lives by learning to control their symptoms.

Chapter 5 Review

· ·

Defining the Terms

Disease	Convictions
Infectious disease	AIDS
Noninfectious disease	HIV
Germ(s) or pathogen(s)	Cancer
Symptom(s)	Tumors
Viruses	Carcinogen
Bacteria	Congenital
Resident bacteria	Insulin
Antibodies	Hypoglycemia
Lymphocytes	Diabetes type I
Vaccine	Diabetes type II
STDs	

Recalling the Facts

1. Why is homeostasis so important for your body?

2. Explain the infectious disease process.

3. How might you explain to a friend that the human body has both good and bad bacteria? Why are good bacteria considered as "friendly" bacteria?

4. How are most germs carried and passed on to another human being? What can a person do to help decrease the spread of germs?

5. Explain how God has designed your body with its own physical defenses to fight off sickness.

6. What is the only way to prevent getting a sexually transmitted disease?

7. What factors increase your chance of developing cancer? Which of these factors do you believe you can directly control?

8. How can you begin at a young age to prevent heart disease?

Applying the Truth

1. What can you learn from Kristen's attitude about life (story section 5.1)? How might her story relate to James 1:17, "Every good gift and every perfect gift is from above and comes down from the Father of lights..."?

2. What is meant by the phrase "Listen to your body"?

3. What other defenses do you have as a Christian to fight off disease and sickness?

4. As you evaluate your present lifestyle, what aspects could you change to help you prevent disease as you get older?

5. Why is it important to develop strong convictions about your personal sexual boundaries before you find yourself in a relationship with the opposite sex?

Unit 2 • Mental Health

"Who am I, O Lord?"

II Samuel 7:18

"WHO AM I?" 6

6 • 1 Change Is Normal

. . . .

*I used to think that I was the only one having so many problems.
But, when I talk to my friends, I find that they have the same problems
as I do! I'm really glad that I'm not alone in this world.*

Ashley

God plans for you to make a successful transition (change) from being a teenager to being an adult. Someone has said that teenagers are really "in-between-agers" because they're in the years just before they find a full-time career and start their own lives and/or families. Such a time of transition includes many changes that must take place for you to be prepared to establish your own direction in life.

Changes are occurring in every area of your life, aren't they? You're experiencing physical, emotional, intellectual, social, as well as spiritual adjustments. The most obvious changes are physical ones, for example, acne, increase in height and weight, and the need to shower more often. Some of the mental or emotional transitions that you may be feeling include increased stress, feelings of independence, an inability to "relate" to adults, and that general feeling of "No one understands". Socially, some of the changes involve tension at home, attraction to the opposite sex, increased peer pressure, and the desire for more freedom.

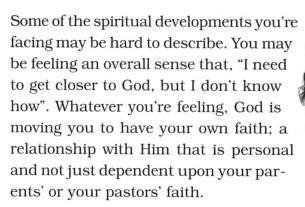

Some of the spiritual developments you're facing may be hard to describe. You may be feeling an overall sense that, "I need to get closer to God, but I don't know how". Whatever you're feeling, God is moving you to have your own faith; a relationship with Him that is personal and not just dependent upon your parents' or your pastors' faith.

Whatever you're feeling, God is moving you to have your own faith; a relationship with Him that is personal and not just dependent upon your parents' or your pastors' faith.

"Who Am I, Anyway?"
Susan Boe

When I entered junior high, our class had the privilege of moving to the upper floor in our school building. We were upstairs while the "little kids" were still downstairs. The change in location made me feel more mature. I wanted more freedom and responsibility. The change also gave me higher expectations of myself. I would spend hours on my hair and struggle over what I would wear. I wanted to act more mature. I desired to hangout with those who were older than me, but I didn't fit in. My feelings were like a roller-coaster. One day I would feel "up", and the next day I would feel "down". I really wanted to talk to someone. My teachers never talked to me about the changes I was experiencing. My parents never warned me that it would be this hard. My four older brothers and sisters were into their own friends. I had no one to talk to. I felt alone, insecure, and confused. Although I was now more grown-up, I still didn't feel confident or secure. I acted one way around some friends and another way around others. I struggled with the questions, "Why can't I just be myself?...Who am I, anyway?"

Can you relate to the way Susan felt in junior high? She had a deep feeling of confusion and frustration because of all of the changes that were happening in her life. Little did she know that these changes were all a part of God's plan. Although she felt alone, God had never left her. On the contrary, He was closer to her than she realized.

He's the Potter, You're the Clay

When an artist creates a masterpiece, perfection seldom occurs in one sweeping moment. Each small change to the clay brings it one step closer to what the artist wants it to become. Have you ever thought of God as an artist? He created the world without copying any famous work. He formed the universe, the animal kingdom, and mankind, all from His own imagination. Human artists make mistakes and even give up on their works. God, however, never makes a mistake; but when *you* do, He just keeps working on you.

> *Each small change to the clay brings it one step closer to what the artist wants it to become.*

> *Then I went down to the potter's house*
> *and there he was, making something at the wheel.*
> *And the vessel that he made of clay was marred (ruined)*
> *in the hand of the potter; so he made it again into another*
> *vessel, as it seemed good to the potter to make.*
> Jeremiah 18:3-4

Apply Jeremiah's words to your life. God's the potter, and you're the clay. For an artist, the natural process for 'throwing a pot' is quite extensive. The clay must be clean (free of any dirt or debris), soft (wet, moldable), flawless (to stand the next baking), and kilne-fired (to harden it for practical use).

LOGON!

Hot, Hotter, Hottest!

An artist keeps changing the clay throughout the formation process. Some changes are drastic, and others are very small. In the eyes of the artist, however, each change is necessary to produce the perfect vessel. Once the artist believes the vessel will not break under the heat, he places it in the kilne (fire). Depending upon the purpose for the piece, the pottery may have to be placed in the fire over and over again to strengthen it. For example, a delicate piece of china must endure tremendous heat. Once complete, the vessel is placed in a dark room to set. When the time comes, the piece is brought out into the light and begins to fulfill its purpose. The purpose for the vessel is even determined before the potter begins to work with the clay.

In the same way, God has a wonderful purpose for your life. He wants to help you to **mature** (grow) spiritually, physically, mentally, and socially. If you remain moldable in His hands, and allow God to form your life as He sees fit, you'll be able to develop the friendships and gifts that God has given to you. You'll also find the strength to endure the trials that you'll face in order to reach your destiny.

How Do You Feel About These Changes?

Have you ever felt...

- uncertain about who you're supposed to become?
- unable to keep a close friend?
- inadequate to make decisions?
- doubtful about yourself?
- fearful about your future?
- uninterested in "God, everyone, and everything"?
- tired of getting up in the morning day after day?
- worried and depressed?
- isolated and all alone?
- misunderstood by many people?
- stressed-out from the pressure of so many *changes, changes, changes*?

One day you may be in a great mood and get along with everyone, the next day you may feel totally the opposite.

If so, there are many other teens who feel the same way as you. Which feelings in the above list have you felt the most over the last year? Which feelings do you feel now? Teens usually experience certain feelings more intensely than adults because of the many changes that are taking place in their lives.

What do you think about all of these changes in your life? Do you think that they're good, bad, or in-between? Do you consider them normal and natural or do you look at them as interruptions that make you feel guilty, criticized, or depressed—moments to be avoided? Changes can make you feel very confused. One day you may be in a great mood and get along with everyone, the next day you may feel totally the opposite. It may be very difficult to understand what's happening, but the fact is that all of the changes that you're experiencing are very normal and natural.

How to Replace Worry with Faith

With so many changes going on, you might find yourself worrying. You might wonder about what your future holds or how you'll get through this school year. In any situation, you can either choose to worry or choose not to worry. If you choose to worry, you'll probably feel uneasy and anxious. In order to replace worry with faith, it's helpful to identify your worries, starting with the greatest one. From the following list, decide what's the greatest worry in your life right now.

Many teens worry about what other people think of them. Do you think this is healthy?

- What other people think of you

- Your parents splitting up

- If you'll ever get married

- Being overweight

- Being underweight

- If you're going to heaven when you die

- If you'll give in to peer pressure

- If your Mom or Dad will die before they get old

- If you'll get cancer

- If you'll ever have a boyfriend or girlfriend

After you decide what the greatest source of worry is in your life right now, begin to share with God why you feel worried about it. As you share with Him, He'll give you His full attention and begin to share with you some words of encouragement. As you're talking with God, helpful thoughts will pop into your mind that will

Through talking honestly with God and others about your concerns, you'll begin to replace worry with faith and peace.

surprise you. God will also begin to give you inward peace about your concern.

Next, talk to someone you trust. If you choose to talk only to your friends, you'll only get their limited opinion. But, if you decide to talk to a trusted adult, you'll probably find (from their greater experience and perspective) words that will really help you. Through talking honestly with God and others about your concerns, you'll begin to replace worry with faith and peace. You'll grow in your awareness that God is in full control of your life and has many good experiences planned for you.

Change in any form is usually very difficult, especially when God is trying to mold your character into His likeness. The good news is that God's grace (power) is always available to you, if you'll just ask for it. If you ask Him, God will give you new desires and new abilities to handle your difficulties. When you allow the changes to mold your character, you may even find yourself "enjoying the ride" because your heart will be the happiest the more it becomes like Jesus. God is very gentle and will only move you along at the pace that He knows that you can move. God is not expecting you to adjust overnight to all of these changes. Being made into the image that pleases Him is a lifelong process.

As you change (mature), you can look forward to more responsibility, privileges, and freedoms. Right now, God is slowly but surely forming you into the person that He wants you to be. He is causing the fruit of His Spirit to grow inside of you: His love, joy, peace, patience, kindness, goodness, faithfulness, gentleness, and self-control (Galatians 5:22-23). It's exciting to see your life as a picture still being painted, a book still being written, or a sculpture still being formed. That gives you hope!

Why Do "Bad" Things Happen to "Good" Teenagers?

Every teenager who's having a tough life isn't alone. Every teen has their problems in some way or another. Their problems might be small or big. But, for the big ones, I've had to stay close to God every step of the way in order to keep myself from going insane. I go to God when I feel down, and I don't blame Him. He has reasons for everything.

John

John went through a very tough time in his life when he was about thirteen: his parents got a divorce. What has really helped John through this hardship is his faith in God: "I go to God when I feel down, and I don't blame Him. He has reasons for everything." Eventually, John began to see a divine purpose behind some of the painful events in his life.

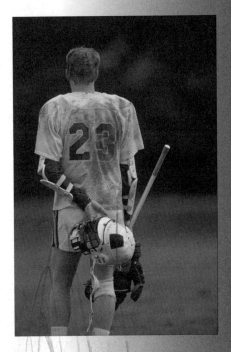

During his parents' divorce, John became very angry. This was totally normal and natural. It was healthy for him not to hide his anger. Instead, he faced up to it and asked for prayer for it. As with John's explosive anger, Jesus understands your weaknesses, too. He doesn't try to expose you to embarrass or punish you. He wants you to see your increasing need for His strength and help. Through turning to God, you'll change and grow in many positive ways.

Even though it may be painful, your ability to accept change can help you grow spiritually. You'll grow in your ability to see Romans 8:28 come to pass in your life: "And we know that all things work together for good to those who love God, to those who are the called according to His purpose." Such an outlook can also help you with your attitude toward the people that God is allowing to "bring" the changes into your life. Instead of resenting them, you can grow to appreciate how God is using them.

"I go to God when I feel down, and I don't blame Him. He has reasons for everything."

Sometimes, bad things happen to teens—even a good teen like yourself. Many times, you won't understand why something is happening. "Why doesn't God answer all of my prayers when I want Him to?" "Why did He let my parents split up?" "If God is so loving, why did He allow my best friend to die?" There are no easy answers for these tough questions. However, the Scriptures as well as many Christians' lives have shown through the centuries that God has a unique way of making something good come out of something bad. Satan hates when God brings good out of bad because his plan is to use the bad things to cause you to become so discouraged that you stop serving God. This is what the devil tried to do in Job's life when God allowed him to take everything away from Job (Job 1:9-12). Many teens are going through some very tough experiences, but God is helping those who ask Him.

God has made you with a unique identity. There's no one else in this whole universe like you!

6 • 2 "Why All These Changes?"

To Be More Like Jesus

One of the main purposes behind the changes in your life is that God is beginning to make you more like Jesus. Paul put it this way,

> *For whom He foreknew, He also predestined*
> *to be conformed to the image of His Son…*
> **Romans 8:29**

Part of the image of Jesus that God is working into your life right now is learning who God has created you to be as a Christian human being. It's one thing to know what your calling is (doctor, plumber, missionary, teacher, etc.) but it's even more important to know yourself as the person God has made with a unique identity. There's no one else in this whole universe like you. Because of your uniqueness, do you ever find yourself worrying about fitting in? Read what John learned from his experiences.

I wish I would not have worried so much about 'fitting in' because I wasted a lot of valuable time. I think I would have enjoyed school and the friends I had a lot more. When I just was myself, not trying to be someone I wasn't, I found good friends. I also wish I wouldn't have worried about having friends because eventually I found my niche.

John

John found good friends when he started being himself. With so many changes happening in your life, however, it's hard to know who you are at times. That's okay, because going through a "neutral zone" is all a part of growing up. Even when you know that God wants to change some aspects of who you really are, the only way that He can do that is if you are yourself first. If you keep lying to yourself about who you really are, then how can you bring yourself to God for real change? You'll constantly be pushed by the people around you not to be who you really are. In order to feel accepted, you'll be tempted to be who you're not, just like John was. In the end, however, you'll find that "fitting in" will not make you happy when you're really someone different on the inside.

Learning to know who or what the Lord is making you to be is like finding your "niche". Your niche is the place, position, or function that no one can fill except you. God has a niche waiting for you. Believe it or not, one of the ways that God uses for you to find your niche is by allowing you to see what is *not* your niche! You learn, for example, what subjects in school you like by taking subjects that you don't like. Being the person that God has created you to be is what will really make you happy.

To Develop Identity, Confidence, and Openness

God is forming identity, confidence, and openness in you right now. Because Jesus knew who He was (had **personal identity**), He was very **confident** (no feelings of inferiority) in His obeying what the Father told Him to do. His inner confidence toward God allowed Him to be very open (not defensive) with God as well as other people.

These are the same character qualities that God is working into you right now. He is showing you who you are as a Christian teenager. From this identity, He's go-

Being the person that God has created you to be is what will really make you happy.

ing to remove any sense of feeling inferior that you may have as you stop comparing yourself with others. Then, out of the inner confidence that will form when you do this, He's going to remove any defensiveness that you might have toward others. In the place of defensiveness, He'll show you the great time you can have in life from being an open and honest person.

When you know who you are, then you will have the confidence and willingness to be able to do what God asks you to do—no matter what it is. Because Jesus knew where He had come from (the Father) and where He was going (back to the Father), He was able to humble Himself as a servant and wash His disciples' feet (John 13:1-5).

Even those closest to Jesus struggled with who they were and where they were going. As a result, they suffered from feelings of inferiority that caused them to compare themselves with each other. They were close friends. They had found their niche as Jesus' disciples. However, that didn't mean that they were exempt from making unhealthy comparisons. Comparing themselves did not help them, it just made them be more defensive and proud.

After eating the Passover, Jesus told His disciples that one of them sitting at the table was going to betray Him. Immediately, the disciples began to ask each other which one of them it was. As they were asking each other who the betrayer could be ("Are you the one?"), they began strongly to defend themselves ("No, I'm not the one!"). They also argued as to which one of them was the greatest (Luke 22:24). Each of the disciples probably began to

Even those closest to Jesus struggled with who they were and where they were going. As a result, they suffered from feelings of inferiority that caused them to compare themselves with each other.

recount all of his personal spiritual successes in order to impress all of the others and erase any doubt in their minds that he might be the betrayer. Apparently, Peter, the one who had walked on the water, kept defending himself the most. Because of this, Jesus had to interrupt him, "Simon! Simon!" (Luke 22:31). Jesus told Peter that Satan had asked for his soul. Even though Peter was trying to convince everyone else that he was willing to be martyred for the Master (Luke 22:33), he was indeed going to deny Him! Peter's pride and over-confidence set him up for a fall![1]

Why was Peter so defensive about the weak condition of his own heart? It was because he wasn't being honest with his own inward condition. His lack of honesty required the Lord first to expose his heart's true condition, then forgive him, and then begin to change it. As one author writes, "We should realize that the greatest defense we can have against the devil is to maintain an honest heart before God. When the Holy Spirit shows us an area that needs repentance, we must overcome the instinct to defend ourselves. We must silence the little lawyer who steps out from a dark closet in our minds, pleading, "My client is not so bad". Your "defense attorney" will defend you until the day you die—and, if you listen to him, you will never see what is wrong in you nor face what needs to change."[2]

Have you ever fallen into the trap of comparison? If so, you probably know what **jealousy** is like; that feeling of resentment against another teen for having a success or talent that you want to have. What are some of the things that you might compare with others? Appearance, grades, friends, parents, money, and talents are just a few areas. If you didn't compare, then you wouldn't be jealous. Why does God warn us against comparison and jealousy (Proverbs 27:4)? First of all, they ruin relationships. They put a big wedge between you and others. They also affect your thoughts about yourself. The more you compare, the more likely you'll find fault with yourself. Further, and maybe

Have you ever fallen into the trap of comparison? If so, you probably know what jealousy is like.

worst of all, they lead you into **pride** because as you compare yourself with others, you might find yourself a little "better" than someone else. Finally, they cause you not to accept yourself as God has made you (or others as God has made them).

Why does God warn us against comparison and jealousy (Proverbs 27:4)?

Being willing to listen to God speak to you—whenever and however He chooses—is the first step in you becoming the young adult that He's planned for you to become. God works with you 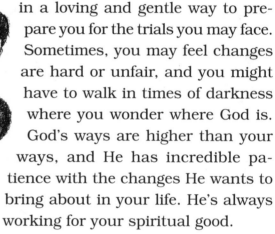 in a loving and gentle way to prepare you for the trials you may face. Sometimes, you may feel changes are hard or unfair, and you might have to walk in times of darkness where you wonder where God is. God's ways are higher than your ways, and He has incredible patience with the changes He wants to bring about in your life. He's always working for your spiritual good.

6 • 3 Your Character Counts

When someone mentions the word character, what comes to your mind? Is it being honest and sincere? **Character** is what you truly are on the inside. It's what you do when no one else is watching. Just as God uses word pictures to help you understand important truths, God also teaches you valuable lessons from the lives of people in Scripture. Each of the following biblical examples shows how important good character is.

The Faithful Servant: Increase Your Personal Responsibilities

I feel that I'm mature enough to handle more responsibility. My parents, however, aren't letting me have very many responsibilities or privileges.

Bob

Do you ever think that your parents should give you more freedom? Do you feel like you're only one small step away from being a young adult, and, therefore, should be treated with more respect? If so, life can be very frustrating in middle school. You may feel caught in the middle of grade school and high school.

It's normal and natural for you to feel that you want to have more independence. Most every teen wants to have more freedom. Do you want to know how to get it? Here's the secret: you have to earn it. The more you sensibly use the privileges that you've already been given, the more privileges will be given to you. With each measure of freedom you gain, comes a new level of responsibility. As you are faithful with each new level of freedom—and don't abuse it—you'll be

building a strong foundation of trust with your parents and other adults. Trust is the key. Be honest: how much do your parents feel that they can trust you? Upon what can they base this trust? In Bob's case, maybe he hasn't really *earned* the greater privileges that he wants from his parents. When you show you're able to be trusted to make wise choices with your time, talents, money, freedom, and friends, the more will be given to you. The Scripture says, "He who is faithful in little, will also be faithful in much" (Luke 16:10).

There's a clear biblical relationship between the fulfillment of responsibility (the proper use of freedom) and increase in privileges. The Parable of the Talents is a good illustration. Each servant was given a certain number of talents (dollars) to invest while their master was gone. Two of the servants showed responsibility with their talents by doubling their worth. But, the third servant buried his talent and didn't increase it. When the master returned, he blessed the servants who showed responsibility but took everything away from the third, saying, "You wicked and lazy servant…[You will be] cast…into the outer darkness…[where there will be] weeping and gnashing of teeth" (Matthew 25:28-30).

When you show you're able to be trusted to make wise choices with your time, talents, money, freedom, and friends, the more will be given to you.

You'll develop the habit of making good choices— not because they're easy or immediately rewarding— but because they're right.

Developing a good sense of personal responsibility is actually an extension of your personal identity. When you were a child, you may have done your chores to get a star on a chart or made your bed to please your Mom. As you grow into adulthood, what you do (or don't do) reflects who you really are inside your own heart. No more stars on charts or pats on the back for cleaning your room. You'll have to live with the choices you make. You'll have to face the personal consequences for each of those choices. The reason you fulfill your responsibilities will be more mature. You'll learn to use your privileges wisely because it pleases God. You'll develop the habit of making good choices—not because they're always easy or immediately rewarding—but because they're right.

Samuel: Focus on What Really Matters

I'm insecure about the way I look... Since I can't afford to buy brand name clothes, I feel uncomfortable around my classmates.

Liz

My biggest insecurity comes from people teasing me because I'm so short.

Joe

Can you relate to Liz or Joe? Is there something about yourself that you don't like? Do you feel insecure about your looks? Do you get mad if you don't get an "A+" on a math test? Do you feel like a bad person if you don't score on the basketball court? If you feel insecure or angry like this very often, you may have chosen to focus on your appearance, performance, or accomplishments in order to feel good about yourself. All of your experiences up to now help to determine your **self-esteem**, the way you feel about yourself. How others have treated you, including all the words that they've spoken to you, can also affect the way you feel about yourself.

I guess guys think that they have to like the most popular and pretty girl in the class to be cool. This isn't fair to the rest of us girls. I really want a guy to like me, but I'm not that pretty or popular. I really wish that guys would like girls for who they were instead of for how they looked.

Kathy

Physical appearance, talent, wealth, popularity, and intelligence are the ways of being accepted and seen as successful in the American culture. But, God has a different opinion about the importance of all these externals. When God sent the prophet Samuel, for example, to search for the next king of Israel, He led him to the home of Jesse who lived in the city of Bethlehem. Jesse was a shepherd and the father of eight sons. When Samuel came to Jesse, he told him that he was going to anoint one of his sons as the next king of Israel. Jesse presented all of his sons (except one) to the prophet, starting with the eldest. The man of God rejected all of them. God chose and anointed the youngest and most unlikely son, David. Although our culture rewards outward appearance and talent, God sees beyond the natural and the external to the heart, to that which is deep on the inside of a person.

> **But the Lord said to Samuel, "Do not look at his appearance or at the height of his stature because I have refused him. For the Lord does not see as man sees; for man looks at the outward appearance, but the Lord looks at the heart."**
> **I Samuel 16:7**

After David became king, his life was not free from major failures. From adultery to murder, David made more than his share of mistakes. His spirit, however, was always tender before God. David was used mightily by God, not because of his outward skills alone, but because he was a man "after God's own heart" (Acts 13:22). As we look at a man who made serious mistakes yet was close to

Physical appearance, talent, wealth, popularity, and intelligence are the ways of being accepted and seen as successful in the American culture.

God because of his honest and humble heart, we begin to catch a glimpse of what really matters the most to God.

David: Grow in Openness to God

When something bad is happening in my life, I talk to God. Even though I may not hear His voice out loud, I listen in my heart. When bad things come, something good has always come out of it. It has happened to me so I can trust God more. I read the Bible, and if any scripture just jumps out at me, I write it down. I also pray to God in my journal writing.

Christina

With all of the emotional challenges that face Christina in her life, she's formed several spiritual habits that are very healthy for her to do. Each of these habits involves acknowledging the way she feels. First, she "listens to her heart". She tries to hear God's voice or feel Him in her spirit. Second, Christina reads the Bible and writes down any scripture that "jumps out" at her. How can she tell when a verse "jumps out at her" if she's not in touch with her inner feelings and questions? Third, she prays to God in her "journal writing". To write her thoughts and feelings down in a journal means that Christina is able to "feel" what's deep down inside of her heart. Writing helps her to put her feelings into words.

To write her thoughts and feelings down in a journal means that Christina is able to "feel" what's deep down inside of her heart. She learns to put her feelings into words.

Christina has learned to do what David did as he wrote the Book of Psalms (songs) in the Bible. David freely expressed his feelings in words and music. David was a very intense and sensitive man of God. He experienced many emotional heights of joy: "[My] soul has escaped as a bird from the snare of the fowlers!" (Psalm 124:7). He also felt moments of deep anxiety and discouragement: "My God, My God, why have you forsaken me?" (Psalm 22:1). The Book of Psalms is full of David's true feelings. There are songs in which he even questioned God's ways and complained about being pursued by his enemies. But, in the end—even without an answer from God—David ended his songs with worship, praise, and trust in his Maker.

David's life was like clay that was moldable in God's hands. Although he faced trials and made some major mistakes, God was still able to make him into a powerful king. David's closeness with God is an incredible example to follow. Do you express your true feelings to God? Do you tell Him when you're feeling good and when you're feeling down? If not, try to develop more of an open friendship with God. See how much closer your relationship will become, and how it will benefit all of the other areas of your life.

Judas: Avoid Secrecy and Isolation

I don't have anyone to talk to because nobody understands me.
I like to handle things on my own.

Allen

With all of the changes that you're experiencing, it's natural for you to desire to spend some time alone. Spending time alone can give you time to collect your thoughts and "process" what you're feeling. All teens need some time alone. Some teens need it more than others. However, when a teenager, like Allen, says, "I like to handle things on my own," there may be some cause for concern. Just as Satan caused Eve to isolate herself from her husband, Adam, and not share with him the struggle that she was facing, so the enemy can do the same to you. Satan still uses the same trick of secrecy and isolation on teens today.

In addition to Eve, Satan used secrecy and isolation on another Bible character. His name was Judas Iscariot, who was one of the original twelve apostles of Jesus. Judas was the treasurer of the disciples. He carried the moneybag and had a greedy heart. He went to the chief priests to see how much money they would pay him if he would show them where Jesus was so that they could have Him arrested.

All teens need some time alone. Some teens need it more than others. However, when a teenager, like Allen, says, "I like to handle things on my own," there may be some cause for concern.

The chief priests told him that they'd pay him thirty pieces of silver for his help (Matthew 26:14-16).

Before he betrayed Jesus, Judas was a faithful follower of Christ. Something went wrong with his thinking. It wasn't as if he had no one to talk to. He could have talked to any of the other apostles—even Jesus, the most understanding of them all. The battle for Judas began in his thoughts. He allowed Satan to put distance between him and the others. What if Judas had responded to these thoughts by talking to someone?! Let's imagine that Judas chose to talk to John because he thought that he would be more understanding than Peter and the others.

The battle for Judas began in his thoughts. He allowed Satan to put distance between him and the others.

The Difference One Conversation Can Make

Judas: John, could I talk with you for a minute?

John: Sure, Judas, what's on your mind?

Judas: Well, I've really been struggling with some thoughts that I don't understand. I've felt a big temptation to do something wrong, and I don't know how to handle it.

John: Can you tell me what it is?

Judas: I have these thoughts about turning the Master over to the chief priests. All of us know how much they hate Him. They've even offered me money. I feel so bad for letting this thought into my mind even for one second; but I don't know what to do!

John: Judas, I can understand why you might feel this way. It's been hard for all of us to be rejected by all of our friends in the temple—and even some of our own family members! Where do you think these thoughts are coming from? Don't you think that they're coming from Satan? Let me pray with you that God will give you the strength to overcome this temptation. If you want me to, I'll stay extra close to you until this temptation passes. I also suggest that both of us go and talk to Jesus about this right away...

For awhile, Judas was having doubts—serious doubts—about his relationship with Jesus. I can just imagine some of the thoughts that may have been going through his head; thoughts like: "Nobody likes me", "I just don't fit into this group", "Jesus likes the others more than He likes me", "Jesus never really talks to me",

"I don't think that I could tell Him my true feelings", "I'm tired of being poor", or "When am I going to get to do what I want?"

> ## DANGER!
>
> If you allow yourself to become isolated from the positive influence of other strong Christians, it will give Satan greater freedom to deceive you. Eventually, the result will be manifested in your actions—sin. Think about writing the following progression in your Bible, or where you often can read it:
>
> Total isolation → secrecy.
> Secrecy → deception.
> Deception → sin.
> Sin → self-destruction.
>
> While Satan wants to make you believe that you can and should handle all of your problems and temptations on your own, that's not the way God made you. God made you to need other Christians for strength, encouragement, counsel, and prayer.

When a flaw in a piece of clay goes unnoticed, it'll eventually cause the vessel to break in the heat of the fire. Judas didn't allow anyone to see his flaw of greediness or to help him handle the incredible pressure he was feeling. Although it may seem hard, you can learn to open up to others and listen to their input. The next time you're tempted to try to handle all of your burdens on your own, remember these verses:

As iron sharpens iron,
so a man sharpens the countenance of his friend.
Proverbs 27:17

He who covers his sins will not prosper, but whoever
confesses and forsakes them will have mercy.
Proverbs 28:13

Confess your trespasses to one another, and
pray for one another, that you may be healed. The
effective, fervent prayer of a righteous man avails much.
James 5:16

Joseph: Learn How to Forgive Those Who Hurt You

*Sometimes I get angry about the things my older brother does,
but I always end up forgiving him.*

Tom

Have you ever felt really angry toward someone for a long time? Have you ever felt rejected? You may have been overlooked when you weren't included in an activity with your friends. You might have blamed yourself when your parents were divorced. You may

have frequently been ignored when you walked into a room. It's true that people can be very cruel and unkind. It's also true that teens can blame themselves for happenings that are not their responsibility.

Each experience of rejection can plant thoughts of worthlessness and depression inside of your mind. You can be tempted to believe that no one likes you—including God. The more you allow yourself to feel unloved and worthless, the lower self-esteem you'll

If you allow yourself to think only negative thoughts about yourself, you might begin to live your life accordingly.

have. If you allow yourself to think only negative thoughts about yourself, you might begin to live your life accordingly.

Consider the life of Joseph. When Joseph was a teenager, his older brothers became jealous of him, tossed him into a deep pit, and abandoned him (Genesis 37:4). Later, Pharaoh, the king of Egypt, falsely accused him and slammed him into jail (Genesis 39:20). Just when he thought that he would get an early release from prison, his plans failed, and Joseph had to stay in prison for another two years (Genesis 40:23). What did Joseph get for serving God and being kind to others? God gave Joseph the ability to forgive everyone who had rejected, forgotten, or abused him. Instead of crying out, "It's just not fair!", he chose to believe that his life was under God's control. Even when he felt hopeless and discouraged, he chose to trust the Lord with his future. God didn't fail him. Joseph learned that what really made him happy—

what really mattered the most—was forgiving everyone who had hurt him while trusting the Lord during the dark times.

Peter: Learn to Have Stand-Alone Courage

I really want to be Lisa's friend. She's so popular and seems to be part of the 'in' crowd. Sometimes, she's really nice to me and includes me in the group. Other times, she makes fun of my clothes, criticizes my looks, and puts me down in front of others. This really embarrasses me. I never know what to expect…I find that I act differently around her…
Sometimes I don't know how to act or what to say…
Why do I want to be her friend when she's so mean to me?

Sue

How might you answer Sue's question? How would you help her with her friendship with Lisa? Before you answer, you might want to ask yourself a few questions. Have you ever felt like Sue? Have you ever wanted to be so popular that you were even willing to put up with a lot of hurtful teasing? Do you only feel good about yourself when a certain "clique" of your peers accepts you? Have you ever acted one way around a group of your friends but then felt unsure about how to act around others?

If your answer to any of these questions was "Yes", then you're certainly not alone. You may be like a lot of teens who wear masks, hiding who they really are (for different reasons). Sometimes, your insecurity comes from not knowing who you really are, what you really think, or how you really feel about something. That's normal because your identity is still "under development". At other times, you may fear you will be teased or rejected. Deep down inside, you want to be liked, accepted, and respected.

Have you ever acted one way around a group of your friends but then felt unsure about how to act around others?

If your friends' opinions of you mean a lot to you, it's okay. God wants you to have close friends. But, do you know that God doesn't want you to be controlled by your friends' opinions? He wants you to be controlled by the Holy Spirit living in your heart. Even though people don't love or accept you just the way you are, God does. As you get closer to Jesus and are filled with more of His love and acceptance, He'll help you outgrow your dependence on what your friends think about you.

Teens aren't the only ones who act weirdly or strangely in order to be accepted. Satan can even use your feelings of insecurity to tempt you to behave in ways you never thought you would. This happened to some of the guys who followed Jesus. Peter, for example, stood up for Jesus in the Garden by cutting off the ear of an arresting officer. Later, however, he denied Jesus three times so that he would not be criticized or rejected (Mark 14:66-72). In order to "fit" into the "in" crowd, Peter even cursed and swore that he had never known Him (Mark 14:71). Peter was horrified after he realized what he had done. God allowed this incident to show Peter that he wasn't able to stand alone without God's strength.

Even though people don't love or accept you just the way you are, God does.

Awhile after Peter's experience of failure, he showed that he had learned to depend totally on God. When he was on his way to prayer, God used him to heal a lame man. After the healing, a humble and courageous Peter spoke to the gathering crowd. "Why do you look so intently at us, as though by our own power or godliness we had made this man walk? The God of Abraham...glorified His servant Jesus...and...through faith in His name has made this man strong... Repent, therefore, and be converted [totally changed]..." (Acts 3:11-26).

After God showed Peter what a coward he was, He changed him into a man of great courage. God can work the same change in you, too.

Chapter 6 Review

Defining the Terms

Mature

Confident

Personal identity

Jealousy

Pride

Character

Self-esteem

Recalling the Facts

1. List some of the physical, mental (emotional), social, and spiritual changes that take place in a teen's life.

2. Why do teens usually experience certain feelings, like frustration and disappointment, more intensely than adults?

3. Explain how you can begin to replace feelings of worry with feelings of faith and trust in God.

4. What is one of the main purposes behind the changes in your life?

Applying the Truth

1. Read Jeremiah 18:3-4 about the potter and the clay. Describe the process required to create a beautiful vessel. Apply this truth to the changes taking place in your own life.

2. If a very angry friend asked you, "If God really loves me, why did He let my parents split up?", what would you say to your friend?

3. Why does God warn us against comparison and jealousy?

4. Choose one of the following biblical illustrations and write an essay explaining what principle(s) of life can be learned from their example: The Faithful Servant (Luke 16:10), Samuel (I Samuel 16:7), King David (Psalms 22:1, 124:7), Judas (Matthew 26:14-16), Joseph (Genesis 37:4, 39:20, 40:23), and Peter (Mark 14:66-72; Acts 3:11-26).

"**…observe to do all according to all the law… For then you…will have good success.**"

Joshua 1:7-8

LET'S TALK ABOUT "SUCCESS" 7

What's Coming Up...

7 • 1 Success: What Does It Mean to You?

> *Success is being able to accomplish something. Success is not*
> *necessarily being perfect or first. It means different things to*
> *different people. In order for me to be fulfilled, I believe*
> *my desires have to be equal to what I'm doing.*
> *I need to be doing what I really want to be doing.*
>
> John

What kind of message do you get from society about success? Does success mean having a lot of money and/or enjoying fame? Or, does it mean being the most popular person in your class? No matter how you define success, experiencing it is like climbing a big rock or mountain. In this section, you'll see how being a success is much like learning how to rock climb. Have you ever seen people scaling up the side of a huge rock wall? How did you feel when you saw them slowly going up to the summit? Did you want to buy some climbing equipment and go up with them, or did you cringe with fear or worry?

Chad, age 18, is a great rock climber. Chad used to be very afraid of climbing rocks. When he was twelve, he thought to himself, "There's no way that I could ever become a rock climber. There're just too many steps that I'd have to take to get there. Besides, the people that do it are crazy. It's just too dangerous!" Chad was not only afraid of rock climbing, he was also very shy and withdrawn socially. But, Chad changed. He now is an excellent rock climber and climbs every weekend. Why? Because he learned how to face his fears, set goals, and achieve them patiently. Chad found a healthy activity in which he eventually became interested. He learned how to become a success at it. In the same way, so can you.

7 • 2 The Seven Steps to Success

Like rock climbing, the road to success is slow and gradual.

1. Make Wise Choices.

I wish that more kids got to know God. Their decisions would be better and their problems would be less.

Lindsey

God has given you safe and proven paths in His Word to enable you to climb your mountains to success. As you read the Bible, you become aware that it tells you to "refuse the evil and choose the good" (Isaiah 7:15). But, the big question is still *how* are you to make wise decisions that please God and bring success? Here are a few ideas.

Learn from Others' Experiences.

Chad tells those who are interested in learning how to rock climb,

Don't try to blaze your own trail. Go where others have gone. You'll see chalk marks on the hand holds in front of you because they're stable and trustworthy. Because this is what I've done, I've never had a big fall.

Have you ever noticed how younger family members don't always get into trouble? They learn to watch their older brothers and sisters and avoid the same mistakes. One of the positive reasons to be an avid reader of history is to discover great lessons from others' experiences. More importantly, get to know the men and women in the Bible and learn from their victories as well as from their defeats.

Get Input from Mature Adults You Trust.

> *When I have a problem or a question, I don't feel*
> *I have anyone to talk to so I talk to my friends.*
>
> Matt

Can you relate to Matt? Since he feels that no one will understand him, he talks to his friends about his questions and problems. If you feel similarly, it may feel 'right' only to share with your friends. Asking your peers' advice on a particular decision, however, may not be your best move. Making wise choices often means asking the advice of spiritually mature adults whom you respect. King Solomon wrote, "Where there is no counsel, the people fall; but in the multitude of counselors there is safety" (Proverbs 11:14).

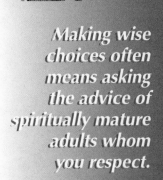

You love your dog or cat so much. Sometimes, he/ she even seems like one of your best friends. Suddenly, your pet gets really sick. You take him/her to your usual veterinarian. Your vet tells you that you should put your pet to sleep since he/she has an incurable disease. What do you do? Do you act purely on your vet's advice? Or, do you seek a second or third opinion from other vets before you say good-bye to your pet forever?

Making wise choices often means asking the advice of spiritually mature adults whom you respect.

Sometimes, very important decisions are made on the basis of a single opinion instead of getting input from several different sources. Many teens make decisions with only a few ideas or alternatives in their minds. Because this takes much less thought and energy, they simply go for the first alternative that is presented.

Take Time to Think About Your Decisions.

Have you ever accepted an invitation at school to go over to a friend's house for a party without first thinking about all of the kids who would be there; and then when you got there, wished you could leave? If so, one of the ways to avoid making hasty decisions is to tell yourself beforehand, "Every time I'm invited to go somewhere, I'm going first to think about it at home before I make a commitment. Each time, I'll tell those who invite me, 'Thanks for the invite! I'll think about it and tell you tomorrow.'" By taking some time to think about your decisions, you can get yourself out of some uncomfortable situations. King Solomon also said, "It is not good for a soul to be without knowledge, and he sins who hastens with his feet" (Proverbs 19:2).

Every time you're invited to a party, take time to think about it first.

Pray for Wisdom.

My relationship with God is kinda like a roller-coaster. I admit that some days I really want to talk to Jesus, but some days I forget.

Megan

Even if you don't or can't ask Jesus for wisdom each day, one way that you can make successful decisions is to ask yourself, "What would Jesus do"? Do you recognize "W.W.J.D.™"? Although this abbreviation may now be overused or commercialized, it's still a valid way to help you make good choices. Do you think that you personally know Jesus well enough to tell what He would do if He was in your particular situation? As you get closer to Jesus, you'll make wiser decisions. The more wise choices you make, the more you'll enjoy personal fulfillment and spiritual success. When you do ask Jesus what to do, He will certainly tell you. James, the Lord's brother, put it this way:

If any man lacks wisdom, let him ask of God, Who gives to all liberally and without reproach, and it will be given to him. But, let him ask in faith, with no doubting.

James 1:5-6

2. Stay Mentally Focused.

*When you're climbing a rock, don't look ahead
too much. If you do, you'll miss your steps. This is really true
if you're on a new or unfamiliar route. Keep your eyes on
what you're doing right now.*

Chad

Chad knows that in order to reach the top of a rock successfully, he's going to have to be mentally focused on his climb. He realizes that he's not going to make it if he's distracted by the terrain he's already climbed or the steep rock up ahead. Have you ever been so focused on what you were doing that nothing else could distract you? Maybe you were glued to your favorite TV show or movie. When your Mom asked you to turn off the show and come to the dinner table, you didn't even hear her. Maybe you were on the free throw line in the last five minutes of your team's championship basketball game. Not even the shouts of the opposing team could get your attention. Whatever it was, you've probably experienced total concentration in some way in your life.

Staying focused on what you need to accomplish takes discipline and concentration.

It's not too difficult to stay focused on those activities which you really enjoy, for example, sports, bikes, friends, and pizza parties. The hard part is staying focused on what you don't really enjoy but know you would be more successful if you did, like homework. The word "**distract**" means to divide the mind. James also wrote, "A double-minded man [is] unstable in all his ways" (1:8). What distracts you from totally focusing on your task at hand? Do TV, movies, friends, music, computer/video games, sports, food, or reading teen magazines get in your way? What else comes to mind?

Here are some practical ideas to help you stay focused:

1. Wear earplugs when studying.

2. Reward yourself for completing your homework.

3. Don't do homework in front of the TV/VCR.

4. Study in a library instead of at home.

5. Begin using a student calendar with a place for assignments.

6. Set up a general daily schedule with a friend and stick to it for at least a week.

7. Don't talk on the phone until after you've done all your chores.

3. Gain Self-Control.

Having self-control is essential when I climb. I have to control my desire to take unnecessary risks. If I try to take a shortcut, I'll leave my route and get stuck. Beginners especially have to learn self-control. Many will try to climb just as fast as they can in order to escape their inner fears. But a fast, uncontrolled ascent won't get them to the top safely.

Chad

Have you ever seen someone out of control? Have you ever felt out of control? Your Dad sees that your room isn't clean. He grounds you for a week. You get mad, throw your books on the floor, and run outside—slamming the door behind you. You're out of control! To have **self-control** means that you're able to restrain your words and behaviors that might hurt you or someone else. One of the signs that the Holy Spirit is in charge is self-control (Galatians 5:23).

Don't forget to ask God for help in hitting your "target areas".

God wants to help you to develop the inner quality of self-control so that you might be a success. Many times, the teens that don't exercise self-restraint don't succeed at work because their bosses can't trust them. What areas of your life do you feel are out of control right now? Is it your busy schedule, anger, choice of words, lack of sleep, attitude toward your parents, gossiping, procrastinating, or just not really caring? God wants to help you regain self-control in every area of your life.

It's clear that the Bible asks you to control your tongue (James 1:26; 3:5,6,8), attitudes (Philippians 2:5-8), and lack

of discipline (I Corinthians 9:24-27). Each area that needs self-restraint can be called a "target area". One of the best verses on self-control is Proverbs 16:32, which says: "He who is slow to anger is better than the mighty, and he who rules his spirit than he who takes a city." What does this verse mean to you?

Have you ever wondered what Jesus meant when He said, "If your right hand causes you to sin, cut it off!?" (Matthew 5: 29-30) What He meant was that perfect self-control is impossible without God's help. Ask the Spirit to help you, and He will (Galatians 5:24-25).

4. Develop Appropriate Boundaries.

If you don't feel safe going up any higher on a rock, don't be afraid to come down. Whether or not to take the risk is totally up to your present comfort level, your personal boundary line. Once I tried to climb a rock that was completely beyond my ability. I got really scared and climbed down.

Chad

A personal boundary is like a fence with a gate that you control.

Have you ever felt really afraid like Chad? If so, were you able quickly to get out of that situation? Or, did you stay where you were because you weren't able to say "No"? If you aren't able to get out of uncomfortable situations, or if you have a tendency to fill up your schedule with too many commitments, you might have a lack of "boundaries" in your life. A boundary is like a fence with a gate between you and the outside world. It's an invisible line that separates you from everyone and everything else. It's your responsibility to open or close the gate according to your values and priorities. Your personal boundaries have three purposes:

1. to prevent people from hurting you physically or emotionally,

2. to stop you from hurting others' feelings, and

3. to give you a way of protecting yourself by being able to say "No".

A boundary is not a wall that's impossible to get through. You let others in, but you share who you are with others only when you choose. Have you ever known a person who seems very hard to get to know? Sometimes without realizing it, a person can put up invisible "walls" to keep people away from getting to know who they really are. One of the reasons that you could develop high walls instead of proper (flexible) boundaries around your life is to protect you where you feel insecure or afraid.

In junior high, you're really beginning the process of becoming your own person in the Lord. Discovering who you really are and who you really are not—what you truly believe and what you don't truly believe—is all a part of maturing and building your own healthy Christian boundaries.

The next time you feel afraid or think that what someone is doing or saying to you is inappropriate, ask God for the strength to say to them, "No. I don't feel good about this. If you don't stop, I'm going to leave."

"After I reach the top of a rock," Chad says, "I feel ecstatic because I've accomplished my goal."

5. Set Realistic Goals.

After I reach the top of a rock, I feel ecstatic because I've accomplished my goal. I get so excited that I immediately want to help the person who belayed the rope to me so that he can make it up the rock next. When I finish a climb, I'm ready to face a more difficult challenge because my confidence is much greater.

Chad

It's the night before an important test. You feel frustrated. You've not studied enough. On top of that, you also have two unfinished assignments due tomorrow. (You forgot to set any goals for getting your assignments done.) What are you going to do now?... You talked to the coach today. He told you that tryouts for the team were last week and you missed them. He said that there's no more room on the team. (You didn't set a goal on your calendar for team tryouts.) What are you going to do?

Learning to set goals is extremely important to your success. A **goal** is a specific achievement toward which you work. It's your

personal aim, purpose, or end in doing or not doing something. A goal is the "finish line" of some chosen accomplishment. There are two types of goals: short-term and long-term. A **short-term goal** is something that you make specific plans to do within a relatively brief period of time, for example, getting your homework done on time, calling your friend within two days, making every team practice this season, or doing your daily chores. What are some of *your* personal short-term goals? A **long-term goal** is something you make specific plans to get done over a relatively long period of time, for example, planning on graduating from high school, looking forward to marriage after you get out of college, or saving money to buy your first car. What are some of *your* own personal long-term goals? It's important to remember that your goals are very personal and shouldn't be compared with the goals of your peers.

A long-term goal is something you make specific plans to get done over a relatively long period of time.

Above all other goals, you need to keep your spiritual goals as Number One. Paul's ultimate goal in life was to know, love, preach, and become like Jesus Christ. When he described his efforts to reach his goal in the following verses, the successful apostle used the picture of a runner in a race leaning forward with every nerve and muscle in his body toward the finish line. He wrote, "...reaching forward to those things which are ahead, I press toward the goal of the prize of the upward call of God in Christ Jesus" (Philippians 3:13-14).

Whether short-term or long-term, spiritual or practical, reaching a goal makes you feel really good inside.

To me, success is setting a goal and achieving it.
Success makes me feel proud of myself when I've done
the best that I could do at what I've really wanted to do.

Christina

6. Become a Lifelong Learner.

*One time I climbed so high on a rock that I began to feel really scared.
I felt like I was going to fall down if I kept going.
I climbed down right away and continued to train. I realized from
the very start of climbing that I would never know it all.
I would always be learning more. I could always improve.
After training some more, I was able to climb it later.*

Chad

Your interest(s) can be a key to your future success.

Imagine, if you *didn't* have to go to school for the rest of your life! Just think about it—no homework, no grades—but what would you do with all your free time? Sure, you'd probably play sports, enjoy video games, watch movies, go shopping, worship God, and talk to your friends. But is that all that you would do? With so much free time, would you want to spend any of it learning more about something? Would you want to learn more about outer space, making money, Christian missions, decorating a house, the latest fashions, building race cars, or your favorite sport? Whatever your interest is, grab onto it. Continue learning all you can about it. Your present interest or hobby could be a key to your future success.

Lance always liked computers. He was continually learning more about them. When Lance was old enough to pursue a career, he started training to become an electrician. This was a career choice that was in a totally different field from computers. When he began as an apprentice electrician, he noticed that his boss knew nothing about computers. Lance offered his services to his boss for free. When his boss saw how this young man was able to help him build a computer system that kept him more organized, he asked him to build a large database for the entire company! Lance didn't have any idea that his electronics interest would ever pay off directly, but it did. And, it can be the same for you.

The main goal that we want the students to reach in high school is a love for learning. If they can begin to love to learn, then they can do

well at whatever they attempt. They'll be self-motivated to learn
whatever they need to learn in order to be a success.
This will be true whether they're inside or outside of a classroom.

Larry Fletch, Christian high school principal

The Bible encourages lifelong learning, even for the wise. King Solomon wrote:

> ***The heart of the wise teaches his mouth,***
> ***and adds learning to his lips.***
> **Proverbs 16:23**

Paul wanted all Christians to realize that no matter how much they knew about Jesus Christ, they couldn't ever stop learning or

---

A Successful, Lifelong Learner

Successful, lifelong learners:

1. ...develop critical thinking skills. The Bible calls this discernment. Watching TV and movies all the time will dull your ability to analyze, discern, and create. Question what you watch. Make sure you spend less time in front of the TV and more time learning new facts.

2. ...grow in their awareness about the future. What exciting plans does God have for you in the future? The goal of our commercialized American culture is to make you only think about buying something for the present moment. In contrast, the Old Testament says, "O, that they were wise, that they...would consider their latter end!" (Deuteronomy 32:29).

3. ...increase their research skills. There are audio books to listen to while jogging. In cyberspace, you can visit libraries in Europe. Lifelong learners are successful because they know that in the twenty-first century, information is one of the ladders to success.

The more you learn about worthwhile subjects, the more conscious you'll become of the need for more study.

growing in Him. Paul wrote, "And if anyone thinks the he knows anything, he knows nothing yet as he ought to know" (I Corinthians 8:2). The more you learn about worthwhile subjects, the more conscious you'll become of the need for more study.

7. Stay Motivated.

When I first started climbing four years ago, I never dreamed I'd be where I am today. If I had never pushed myself, I wouldn't be at my present level. I never thought I could do what I've done. It gives me a great feeling inside.

Chad

A great feeling of self-confidence and a deep sense of personal accomplishment motivate Chad to continue to climb. Motivation is an inner urge that prompts you to do what others would be afraid to do. Motivation is an inward drive that, many times, comes directly from God. It's really different than an outward "incentive" which promises you more friends, popularity, coolness, or money in order to get you to do something. No one paid Chad money to learn how to rock climb. When he reaches the tops of rocks, he doesn't find any friends that are waiting to tell him how "cool" he is. There is an inner motor that pushes him forward.

It's wonderful for Chad to be inwardly motivated, but how about you? Have you ever lost your motivation for finishing a school project?

It's wonderful for Chad to be inwardly motivated, but how about you? Have you ever lost your motivation for finishing a school project? Did you ever wonder why your drive to serve Jesus may, at times, seem to disappear? Have you ever told your parents that you have no desire to do your chores around the house? If you have, it'll help you to know that it's okay to feel that way at times. Everybody does. It's okay to feel like giving up. It's normal and natural; both David and Elijah did, too (Psalm 22:1; I Kings 19: 3,13,14).

The following is a helpful checklist you can use whenever you feel unmotivated.

☑ Check your motives.

Are you motivated to do this activity because of some outside reward that's driving you, for example, popularity, money, or acceptance? Did you freely choose this activity because you like it and feel that it has value in itself?

☑ Check your interest level.

Do you have a desire to continue pursuing this activity? If you're disinterested, and need to continue for various reasons, try to find a reason for doing it (Ecclesiastes 3:1).

☑ Check your goal's difficulty.

Have you written down a goal that is both clear and realistic (practical and doable)? Reassuring yourself that you're able to do something may restore your inner energy to accomplish it.

☑ Check your friendships.

Are any of your friends draining you of good, spiritual motivation to do what you know is right (I Corinthians 15:33)?

☑ Check your faith level.

Do you really expect to reach your goal doing what you're doing? If you have a deep doubt about that, your motivation may be draining away (Romans 14:23).

☑ Check your values.

Are you going after goals that are truly consistent with your own inward values? Are they goals that God would be pleased for you to pursue? If not, you won't last long doing your activity when you lack sincerity or joy (Romans 14:17).

Children who start training at a young age will someday need to ask themselves, "Is this what God wants me to continue pursuing?"

7 • 3   Rebounding from Mistakes

Even when I make a mistake on a climb, I try to learn from it for my next try. If I don't allow frustration and fear to keep me from climbing again, each error can make me become a better rock climber.

Chad

While Satan wants you to feel depressed, fearful, and unmotivated to change, God can use even your worst mistakes to get your attention.

Chad has learned a valuable lesson: "Learn from your mistakes". No matter your age, errors are an inevitable part of life. How you respond or "rebound" from your mistakes makes all the difference to your success. Sometimes, when you make a serious blunder, it can really set you back. Even after you have properly resolved the issue, it can come back to your mind and haunt you with thoughts such as, "What if I make the same mistake again?" or, "I don't think I can ever get over that terrible wrong I did". Maybe you have heard thoughts like, "I'm sure others remember my mistake and they'll never let me forget it!" Whatever you think about the mistakes you've made (and will make), it's important to know what God thinks about you in the midst of your difficulty.

When you sin, how do you think God feels about you? When asked this question, many of your peers said,

I know God feels sad about what I did, but I also know that He forgives me if I ask.

John

Sometimes, when I make a mistake, I think that God feels so bad and sorry. He doesn't want me to sin because He knows it hurts me.

Jenny

Can you relate to John or Jenny? Do you find it hard to come to God when you know you've made a mistake? Contrary to how you might feel, God waits with open, loving arms for you to come to Him after you've erred. He wants to forgive you and help you learn from your mistakes.

Bible History and the Principles of God

Jeremiah, an Old Testament prophet, confronted the idolatry of God's people for many years. The more he prophesied, the more the people refused to turn back to God. As a result of their continual disobedience, God judged the people by allowing the nation of Babylon to take them into captivity (Jeremiah 18:11-17). Even though the Babylonian Captivity lasted for at least seventy years and was very hard on God's people, God taught the people many good lessons. The best lesson that came from the Captivity was that God's people, as a nation, never again backslid into idolatry. After disciplining His people, God sovereignly brought them back to Palestine in order to witness the birth of the Messiah, Jesus of Nazareth.

While Satan wants you to feel depressed, fearful, and unmotivated to change, God can use even your worst mistakes to get your attention. He has such a creative way of arranging the circumstances of your life—if you let Him. What the enemy would want to use against you, God can use for your good! But your ability to learn from your mistakes results from a heart that wants to respond to God and is willing to change. Are you willing?

What are some of the mistakes that you've experienced? It's important to learn how to resolve them biblically so that Satan cannot use them against you. Here are a few tips to help you to rebound from your mistakes:

- Ask yourself, "Was this a sin or a mistake?" Even though all sins are mistakes, all mistakes are not sins. If you sinned, repent and He will forgive you (I John 1:9). If you made a mistake that wasn't a sin, become aware of your blindspots and become accountable to someone to support you.

- Forgive yourself. Sometimes, teens can be their own worst enemies by listening to constant accusations and reminders of past mistakes. Once you have resolved the issue with God and the other(s) involved, ask God to help you forgive yourself. When teens have a problem forgiving themselves, it's often because they still see some good in their hearts rather than recognizing that in their "flesh" there dwells nothing good (Romans 7:14,18).

Apologize to whomever you may have hurt or offended.

161

- Apologize to whomever you may have hurt or offended. When you hear them say, "I forgive you", you'll feel released.

- Ask a strong Christian to help you find Bible verses on the area of your mistake that will remind and strengthen you about it in an encouraging way.

- Ask safe, strong, Christian adults what they would do if they were you.

God created you to enjoy life. Having good, clean fun is a part of God's plan for you. When you learn how to handle your mistakes with a healthy response, you'll enjoy life to the max!

Chapter 7 Review

Defining the Terms

Distract	Goal(s)
Self-control	Short-term goal
Boundary	Long-term goal

Recalling the Facts

1. What kind of message(s) do you get from society about success? How does this message differ from what God thinks about success?

2. List the seven steps to success.

3. How are you to make wise decisions that please God and bring success?

Applying the Truth

1. It's not very difficult to become mentally focused on activities that you enjoy, but it's often difficult to focus on those that you don't really enjoy. Name three areas in your life where you believe you could become more focused. Explain what personal changes you could make in each area to help you stay focused.

2. What are boundaries? Why are they important in your life?

3. How would you describe the difference between a sin and a mistake?

4. When you sin, how do you think Satan wants you to feel? How does this differ from the way God wants you to feel?

Unit 3 • Social Health

"...there is a friend that sticks closer than a brother."

Proverbs 18:24

BUILDING STRONG FRIENDSHIPS 8

What's Coming Up...

8 • 1   The Value of Friendships

＊＊＊＊＊＊＊＊＊＊＊＊＊＊＊＊＊＊＊＊＊＊＊＊＊＊＊

*I've had good friends who I've taken for granted. I would be
mean to them for no real reason. Their feelings would get hurt,
and I would lose their friendship. I've learned that I have to value the
good friends I have and remember the fun times we've had together.
I'm working at keeping my quality friends.*

Christina

Your ability to get along with different kinds of people is a measurement of your **social health**. Teens who can only relate to their small clique of friends but don't know how to talk with their parents or teachers aren't socially healthy. Neither are the teens who can relate to adults but don't know how to get to know their own peers.

The different kinds of people to which you relate can be divided into two general categories: friendships and relationships. A **friendship** is a social connection in which people willingly share common interests or activities. Even though there are different levels of friendships, friends enjoy each other's company, freely choose to hang around together, and want to get to know each other through some sort of sharing.

How do you feel about your present friendships? Would you rate them as 'great' or would you describe them as only 'average'?

How do you feel about your present friendships? Would you rate them as 'great' or would you describe them as only 'average'? Of those friendships that are 'great', what amount of time, energy, and sharing have you had to put into them to make them so good? Of those that are 'average', what more do you think you might have to invest into them if you want them to be any better than they are right now? Sometimes, the value or importance that you place on a friendship directly affects how fun and fulfilling that friendship is to you. Developing good friendships takes time and effort; it's not always easy. Do you have any friendships that you would like to hang onto forever? Like Christina, you may not realize how valuable a friendship is until you don't have it anymore. Christina is working harder at her friendships because she learned that they were very important to her. How much do you value your friends?

A **relationship** is a tie with people by blood, marriage, work, or social role. Your school teachers and your youth pastor(s), for example, are in your life to perform certain functions, but you might not be developing a close 'friendship' with all of them. The word "relationship" covers many categories. It can describe your connection with your family as well as your connection to the sales clerk where you buy your jeans. Right now, whether you like them or not, you have some sort of a relationship with your peers (both guys and girls), parents (both step- and biological), teachers, fellow students, brothers/sisters (both step- and bio-

logical), grandparents, community leaders, and neighbors. It may be hard right now to get along with some of these people in your life, but God has a unique purpose in every relationship and friendship that He gives to you.

Artificial Relationships: A Substitute for the Real Thing

In sports, coaches choose to make substitutions so that they can increase their team's chances of winning. When on a diet, some people substitute low fat foods for the 'real thing' to avoid the extra calories. Life is full of **substitutions**, replacing one person or thing with another.

With sports or diets, making substitutions is totally acceptable. But, what about making substitutions in the area of your relationships with people? Have you ever substituted a 'thing' for a real person—maybe even a friend? What 'things' in your life might you be inclined to use as a person or relationship replacement? A teen can have a 'relationship' or a 'friendship' with a computer program or game. Some of your friends may have some sort of an emotional connection with a Hollywood actor/actress or a favorite TV character. What about some

A teen can have a 'relationship' or a 'friendship' with a computer program or game.

teens' total fascination with a professional musician or star athlete? What do you think about getting so attached to the characters in a sitcom or soap opera that a teen doesn't only want to catch the next episode but also attentively watches the same program for years and years? For some, such attachments would be considered unreal or **artificial**

DANGER!

Why is it, that so many teens have difficulty finding the words to share how they really feel with others? One reason is the fact that the electronic entertainment they watch all the time doesn't require them to put their own thoughts and feelings into real words. Consider the following:

"There is no doubt that children read fewer books when television is available to them. A child is more likely to turn on the television set when there is 'nothing to do' than to pick up a book to read. This is partly, if not entirely, because reading requires greater mental activity, and it is human nature to opt for an entertainment that requires less effort rather than more." [1]

"As they take in [electronic] words and images hour after hour, day after day, with little of the mental effort that forming their own thoughts and feelings and molding them into words would require, as they relax year after year, a pattern emphasizing nonverbal [thinking] becomes established." [2]

relationships because they involve bonding with someone or something that doesn't really exist.

Unfortunately, many young people are replacing their relationships with people with relationships to things. Sometimes, teens develop artificial relationships when they feel lonely or isolated. Do you know anyone whom you would consider a 'loner'? In His love, the Lord warns you not to become totally isolated from face-to-face relationships. Solomon wrote:

do you frequently feel insecure about opening up to other people— even your own family?

> *A man who isolates himself seeks his own desire;*
> *He rages against all wise judgment.*
> **Proverbs 18:1**

Why do you think that it's so easy to become isolated? Why do you think God warns you against it?

Surface Relationships: A Defense for Your Feelings

Maybe you're not a 'loner', but do you frequently feel insecure about opening up to other people—even your own family? Sharing your thoughts and feelings at home with your family can sometimes be the most difficult. Fortunately, your family knows you[1] the best and also loves you the most.

Do you know how to develop close friendships? If not, you may always want to guard your feelings so that you won't get hurt. If you don't know how to develop close friendships with those you can trust, you may get into the pattern of only developing surface relationships. Does anyone know the real you? Do you have anyone with whom you can share your heart and true feelings without feeling criticized or rejected? Of course, it would not be in your best interest to share all of your feelings with just anyone. Nevertheless, it's important for you to learn how to develop friendships now in which you can be real and not just surface. Developing deep and meaningful friendships is important because how you handle friendships now will carry over into your adult life when it'll become even more meaningful to have these kinds of friends.

A 'Best Friend' Relationship: God's Gift to You

Have you ever met someone with whom everything just "clicked"; someone you knew eventually would become your best friend? A best friend is God's gift to you. God brings people into your life who you need and who need you. He made each person with a need inside for others. You may hear people say, "I don't need anyone", but these people are really denying themselves the love that God wants to show them through best friend relationships.

What makes a best friend truly the 'best'? Have you ever thought why you were best friends with someone? Best friends usually share common interests, have fun together, encourage each other,

What makes a best friend truly the 'best'?

don't try to change each other, and are able to work through conflicts. A good friend is a person who you love and trust. You can count on a good friend to be a 'safe' relationship; one who always keeps your best interest in mind, and one who will not criticize or reject you for who you really are on the inside. Besides a good friend being your close companion, he/she would also be interested in your personal, spiritual growth.

How many close friends do you have? Most people don't have more than a few. If you were to evaluate all of your close friends, would you say that they were truly 'best friends' to you? Best friends help each other to grow and to become better Christians when their common interest is spiritually focused. They challenge you to share, to resolve conflicts, to work hard for something, to learn to forgive, and to love unconditionally, as Jesus loves.

Perhaps the most famous 'best friends' relationship in the Bible was that of David and Jonathan (1 Samuel 18:1-4). What made their friendship so unique was their ability to share deeply with each other and to sacrifice for the good of the other. In your own words, what do you think are some of the characteristics of a 'best friend' relationship from the following verses?

You may not believe it— but your own brother or sister can become one of your best friends!

- *As iron sharpens iron, so a man sharpens the countenance of his friend* (Proverbs 27:17).

- *A friend loves at all times, and a brother is born for adversity* (Proverbs 17:17).

- *Faithful are the wounds of a friend, but the kisses of an enemy are deceitful* (Proverbs 27:6).

- *Ointment and perfume delight the heart, and the sweetness of a man's friend does so by hearty counsel* (Proverbs 27:9).

An Eternal Friend: Jesus

From the beginning of man's existence, God has clearly demonstrated the value of good friends. He did this by comparing His own relationship with His people to a friendship. God called Abraham His friend (2 Chronicles 20:7). God also spoke to Moses "face to face, as a man speaks to his friend" (Exodus 33:11).

The importance of developing good, God-centered friendships is also reflected in the life of Jesus. After Jesus began His public ministry, He spent most of His time developing close relationships with twelve other men, called His apostles ("sent ones"). On the basis of a close and loving relationship that He had developed with each one, He also encouraged them to demonstrate their intimate friendship with Him by doing what He asked them to do (John 15:14). Such obedience was based on a loving relationship.

As you grow in your relationship with Jesus, you will find yourself moving from a lord-to-servant relationship through a teacher-to-disciple relationship to an intimate-friend-to-friend relationship (John 15:15). In this close friendship, Jesus will still be your Lord and Teacher. But, as you experience Him more deeply, you will hear Him speak to you more. You'll be able personally to enjoy all the various aspects of a close friendship. This may take a little time to develop, but it's available to everyone of any age who is willing to surrender all to Him. Of all the friendships in your entire life, your relationship with God has the potential of being the deepest and most fulfilling of all!

Of all the friendships in your entire life, your relationship with God has the potential of being the deepest and most fulfilling of all!

8 • 2 Communication Skills

· ·

I'm very confused about one of my friends. We used to be very close, but now we're really distant. I don't understand what happened, and I really miss our friendship.

Ann

I have a couple of friends who fight almost all the time. When they fight, I tell them who I agree with and why. When I do this, the one I don't agree with totally ignores me.

Casey

I have a friend who never leaves me alone.
Debbie

My sister and I share a room, and we can't get along at all! People tell us that the older we get, the better we'll get along. Our relationship, however, only seems to be getting worse.
Liz

If you were Ann, what would you do to discover what went wrong between you and your friend? How would you feel if you were Casey and one of your good friends ignored you every time you disagreed with him or her? If one of your friends never left you alone—like Debbie—how would you tell your friend that you needed some space? If you were Liz's school counselor, how would you advise her to talk with her sister?

Most people can talk, but not everyone can genuinely communicate.

Just any kind of "talk" won't be enough to resolve these tense situations. Each of the solutions depends on the *kind of talk* that happens. They require true communication. Talking is not the same as communicating. Most people can talk, but not everyone can genuinely communicate. Webster's Dictionary defines **communication** as the act of expressing thoughts, feelings, information, or beliefs easily or effectively through speech, writing, or signs. "Expressing" is only one side of communicating. Expressing yourself "easily and effectively" is the other side. To experience communication that's "effective" means really being able to hear and understand what the other person is saying. Listening is crucial because most of the time, people are coming from opposite perspectives.

Because everyone is different, conflict is inevitable in every relationship. One of the keys to being a success in life is learning how to handle conflicts in the right way. Fighting and calling the other person names doesn't work. Running away and avoiding the person isn't going to help the relationship either. Relation-

ship conflicts can successfully be resolved only if you (1) learn how to express your feelings truthfully and lovingly to the other person, and (2) increase your ability to understand the other person's feelings.

Communication uses both **verbal** (mouth) and nonverbal (body) methods. **Nonverbal** communication is sharing a message without talking. Sign language (the use of hands for communication), for example, is a universally recognized nonverbal language. Can teenagers communicate something just by the way they sit, stand, or walk? Look around the room right now and notice how your classmates are sitting. If their arms are crossed, do they look bored? Are some students' heads resting on their arms? Do they look tired? You have the ability to project powerful messages by your facial expressions and nonverbal cues. Can you think of other examples of nonverbal communication? Do you think that nonverbal communication affects your relationships? If so, how?

Is the Generation Gap Real?

Do you ever feel misunderstood by your parents? Why is it that when you try to talk to your parents, you think they just don't understand you? Have your parents ever told you that they can't understand you either? It sometimes seems that you're on a different planet than your parents, doesn't it? Each of you has a separate perspective because of your different ages, past experiences, hurts, beliefs, home life, successes, failures, prejudices, preferences, and cultures. Because of these factors, it's hard for you to understand each other. As a result, you both may feel like there's a major 'gap' or space between you. If you feel miles away from your parents, and can't seem to connect, you need to work on bridging the gap. Your teen years will be much more enjoyable for everyone, if both you and your parents can work together on improving your communication skills.

One of the keys to being a success in life is learning how to handle conflicts in the right way.

Good Communication Skills

"Duh!" "Yuk!" "Don't know..." "Yeah..." "Never heard that..." "Uhmm..." "Maybe..." "Don't care..." Guess so..." "Nope..." "Don't get it..." "Nothin..." "Stuff like that..." "Whatever..."

How many of the above phrases do you hear every day? How many do you use on a regular basis? It's normal to be experiencing an ever-increasing vocabulary, but when the majority of the way that a teen communicates with others is through words that are "guttural" and require no thinking or formal verbal skills, then something is missing. Words or phrases like "whatever" are lazy words that say nothing.

In order to develop quality relationships, overcome conflicts, and avoid being misunderstood, it is important to work on improving your choice of words. If you'll improve the way you communicate, you'll find yourself better understood and your opinions better accepted.

The following are twelve skills of good communication that you can practice. They will help you build strong relationships.

1. Realize That First Impressions Can Be Misleading.

As soon as you meet someone, you begin to "check them out". You notice what style of clothes they're wearing, how they wear their hair, and what words they use when they talk. Did you know

Reading will improve your vocabulary and enhance your communication skills.

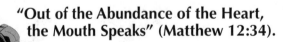

LOGON!

"Out of the Abundance of the Heart, the Mouth Speaks" (Matthew 12:34).

The words that you use to talk with others come from your heart and mind. They include the words you hear most of the time. They also come from what kind of books you're reading— which influence the kinds of thoughts you're thinking, which influence the kind of words you use. When Jesus said that our words came out of our hearts, He meant that if we fill our hearts/minds with nonsense words, nonsense words will be what we speak. But, if we fill our hearts/minds with intelligent, godly, and meaningful words, then we'll use these more productive symbols of communication to share our thoughts and feelings with others. With better speaking skills, you'll be more able to share your faith with others, enjoy better friendships, and persuade others to your way of thinking.

that most of the time first impressions are misleading? They can be misleading because people have "bad days". People feel sick or tired which affects the way they come across to others. Some people are shy and take time to get to know.

When you're talking to someone, try not to jump to conclusions. Many communication problems occur when people make assumptions about what others are saying without giving them time to give an explanation. Suppose your teacher didn't call on you all class period when you raised your hand with an answer, and then—when you *didn't* know the answer—she finally called on you. How embarrassing and upsetting! At that moment, you have a choice. You can choose to make assumptions like, "My teacher always picks on me" or, "My teacher just wanted to embarrass me". These conclusions would most likely be false. Your other choice is not to assume anything but to tell yourself something like, "My teacher had no bad motive behind this" or, "I don't believe that my teacher would purposely embarrass any of his students".

2. Choose the Right Time and Place.

Have you ever seen your younger brother or sister try to talk to one of your parents while they were talking on the phone? Did they get your parents' undivided attention? Probably not. They chose a bad time. Choosing the right time and place to talk is important so that both people feel comfortable sharing. Without both people sharing their true thoughts and feelings, there's not quality communication.

3. Know What Your True Feelings Are—and Stick to Them.

It's important to recognize the real issue in a situation before you just blurt out something. Think before you speak. Get in touch with your true feelings about the subject. Imagine that your sis-

Choosing the right time and place to talk is important.

ter wanted to borrow your new sweater. Deep down inside, you don't want her to. Instead of sticking with your true feelings and kindly telling her "No", you give in and let her wear it. When she returns the sweater the next day, it has a stain on it. She says she's really sorry and will pay for it, but you're still mad. What do you think you could have done to have prevented the stain on your sweater as well as the strain on your relationship with your sister? The answer is if you had not changed your mind about loaning out your sweater. By going against your true feelings, you created an atmosphere in your heart where anger and resentment could grow.

4. Avoid Yelling, Screaming, and Name-Calling.

Have you ever felt so out of control that you yelled or screamed at someone? When people yell, scream, or call each other names, bad feelings only get worse. At such times, not much can be com-

municated except hurtful words and accusations. When hot emotions begin to build up inside of you, you're being mature if you take a "time out". You could say something like, "I'm not comfortable talking about this right now, I need to talk about it later." By agreeing with the other person that you will talk about the issue later, you avoid making statements that you might later regret. The next time you feel like exploding, try to remember the following verses (You can also see Proverbs 19:11; 20:3).

A soft answer turns away wrath, but a harsh word stirs up anger. The tongue of the wise uses knowledge rightly, but the mouth of fools pours forth foolishness.
Proverbs 15:1,2

5. Be an Active and Sensitive Listener.

Do you want to have more friends? Then, become a good listener. Have you ever talked with someone who kept interrupting

you, always finished your sentences for you, or wanted to talk more than listen? Did you want to become his/her best friend? Probably not. If you want to have lots of friends, become an active and sensitive listener. Rather than being passive in the conversation and just 'sitting there', an active listener attempts to understand what the other person is trying to say before sharing his/her opinion. An excellent listener always seeks to understand before seeking to be understood.

Imagine that one of your good friends says to you, "I want to be your best friend". In being an active listener you might respond with, "That sounds really good. But, before I say 'Yes', can I ask you what you mean by 'best friends'?" In first seeking to understand what your friend really means, you'll discover some of your friend's expectations of being best friends and not make a decision that you might later regret.

6. Be Quick to Apologize.

Have you ever sincerely apologized to your parents or to a friend? Have your parents or a friend ever genuinely apologized to you? If so, it made your relationship better, didn't it? Sincere apologizing brings people closer together. It may seem very hard for you to say, "I was wrong" or, "I made a mistake", but it's one of the best ways of building strong relationships. Jesus said, "Why do you look at the speck in your brother's eye, but don't consider the plank in your own eye?" (Matthew 7:3). A good communication skill is to emphasize where you have gone wrong rather than what the other person has done wrong.

7. Accept the Person Even if You Reject the Idea.

Have you ever found yourself really angry at a person just because they disagreed with you? Let's pretend that you want to wear a certain outfit to an activity. Your Mom asks you not to wear it. You're mad because you really find nothing wrong with it and you try to convince your Mom that it looks great. She doesn't

An excellent listener always seeks to understand before seeking to be understood.

177

A wall is anything that comes between people and hinders their honest communication with one another.

see it your way, and she says, "You're not wearing that tonight, and that's final." You put something else on and you head out the door. You couldn't even enjoy the activity because you were so mad at your Mom. You conclude, "My Mom ruined my whole night!" You wake up the next morning still angry. How might this affect your relationship with your Mom? How could you resolve this situation?

8. Recognize Walls in Yourself and Others.

God created you to have close relationships with other people through healthy forms of communication. One of the ways that healthy communication is hindered is through the building of walls (personal defenses). A **wall** is anything that comes between people and hinders their honest communication with one another. Whenever a person feels threatened with criticism, rejection, or attack, they put up walls to protect themselves. A *wall of anger* can be seen in someone who is a natural 'hot head'. A *wall of distance* is shown whenever you ignore the person who is trying to talk with you. A *wall of words* is clear when someone talks non-stop and never listens to what others are saying. Even a *wall of laughter, joking, or sarcasm* can sometimes hinder open and honest communication.

Room for Improvement?

A son wants to talk to his Dad about something that's really important to him. As you read the following brief conversation between son and Dad, do you think that there's any room for improvement?

Son: Dad, do you have ten minutes to talk? I have something kinda serious to ask you.

Dad: Sure son, what's on your mind?

Son: Well, I like this girl at school, and well, uh, I'm not so sure whether she likes me…

Dad: Ha! Ha! Girls, already? No, you don't have to worry about girls yet. You've got plenty of time. Just forget about girls for now.

Son: But, Dad, I was just wondering whether you've ever felt…

Dad: Ha! Ha! Me? Oh, we can talk about that stuff after you get a bit older. Don't you have something better to do with your time than chase girls? Ha! Ha! Ha!…

(End of conversation)

Do you feel that this Dad listened to his son's concern? If you were this son, do you think that you would have come away from this conversation with any encouragement or advice? Do you think that the Dad's laughter helped or hindered genuine communication?

9. Use "I" Statements Instead of "You" Statements.

Imagine that your Dad is upset at you because you watched a TV program or movie that he asked you not to watch. Your Dad comes into the room to talk to you about "the movie". Which of the following statements from your Dad would make you feel that your Dad was correcting your misbehavior and not rejecting you as a person?

(a) "I felt very hurt when I heard that you watched the movie."

(b) "You never do what I ask!" or,

(c) "You've been making me very angry lately with all of your poor choices."

If you chose (a), you were correct. The most effective way of communicating hurt or offended feelings to others is by using an "I" statement instead of a "You" statement. Using the expressions: "I feel angry…." or, "I feel hurt…" or, I feel offended…" is much more effective for communication than using expressions like: "You made me…" or, "You make me feel…".

10. Avoid Statements with the Words "Never" and "Always" in Them.

Has one of your friends ever said to you, "You *never* call me. I *always* have to call you!?" When you think about it, are such statements even true? When you first hear these words, how do you feel? Most of the time, "You always…" or, "You never…" statements are untrue exaggerations which immediately put others on the defensive. Try using statements like: "I sometimes don't hear from you when I call you," or, "Occasionally, I feel frustrated when I don't hear back from you."

Using expressions like "I feel…" is much more effective communication than expressions like "You made me…"

11. Accept the Fact That Some Conflicts Will Take Time to Be Resolved.

Many issues are too deep and complex to be solved by one conversation. Realize that it may take several talks to arrive at a healthy mutual understanding. Making some progress is better than making no progress. If possible, resolve all the issues that are bothering you. If you do, you will be happier and healthier. If you bury your negative feelings, they can easily turn into feelings of resentment and bitterness.

12. Put Yourself in the Other Person's Place.

Another important part of communicating is putting yourself in the other person's shoes. Every teenager deeply desires to be understood. Sometimes, it may seem difficult to talk to your parents, but try to imagine how they might be feeling. Try using phrases like: "I understand how you feel..." or, "I can see your point". Instead of immediately defending yourself when others share some intense feelings with you, try to put yourself in their position. Ask yourself, "How would I feel if that happened to me?"

8 •3 Guy/Girl Friendships

God wants you to develop positive guy/girl friendships in which you're relaxed and can be yourself.

How Do You See It?

*I'm starting to feel like I need a boyfriend,
but I don't want all the mushy stuff.*

Beth

I think guys are great and fun to be with, but I do have some crushes.

Kay

*Girls are God's creation along with us guys. They're not objects
as depicted by the world today. They're good friends.*

Chris

Sometimes, your perspective of the opposite sex affects the way you relate to them. Ask yourself the question, "How do I view the opposite sex?" Remember that God values guys and girls a lot differently than the American culture does.

What really matters is what the person is like on the inside; his or her inner character. Sometimes, teens act shy around the opposite sex because they feel insecure, embarrassed, or ignorant of what to say or do. At other times, teens act loud, rowdy, and obnoxious around them. They may even try to show off for attention or recognition. God wants you to develop positive guy/girl friendships in which you're relaxed and can be yourself. You can successfully do this by starting to see the opposite sex as a casual brother or sister in the Lord. Trying not to show off, put down, or tease others in a hurtful way is a good start in establishing good friendships. Begin by just being good friends who mutually respect one another. Such a wholesome attitude will help you to form healthy guy/girl friendships.

Four Ways to Protect Yourself from Being Emotionally Hurt

I like this one girl. She's one of my best friends, but she likes someone else. All of the other fine girls in my class like other guys, too. I know guys aren't supposed to cry, but almost every night I cry myself to sleep. Pretty dumb, huh?

Randy

I want a boyfriend with whom I won't break up. I hate breaking up.

Rhonda

I don't want to like a guy because he might not like me back.

Kara

The subject of guy/girl friendships brings up different emotions for every teen. You may have been hurt by a guy or rejected by a girl. These emotions are deep and very real. You may choose to avoid these kinds of heartaches. You may decide that they aren't worth it at your age and choose to postpone such friendships until later in your life. The only way to avoid the pain completely is not to get emotionally involved with one person and to remember to have many positive brother/sister friendships. Whatever you choose, there're at least four ways to help you avoid being hurt unnecessarily in guy/girl friendships.

You may have been hurt by a guy or rejected by a girl. These emotions are deep and very real.

1. Keep all guy/girl relationships as friends only.

Do You Want to Go with Me?
Susan Boe

When I was in eighth grade, I had a crush on a guy named Dave. He was from another school and one of my friends told him I liked him. One day, I saw Dave at a school activity. When we were alone, he asked me, "Do you want to go with me?" I must have looked puzzled because my response was, "Go where?" We were both so embarrassed, but luckily we were able to laugh at it. We decided that we didn't have to say that we were going "steady" to like each other. Over the next several months, we talked on the phone and did things in groups with other friends. He's still a good friend today.

Like Susan, many young teens face the decision of whether to "go together". When you allow yourself to get too deeply or emotionally attached to someone of the opposite sex, it will eventually lead to heartbreak. To develop healthy friendships, do activities in groups rather than 'singling-out' any one person.

> *I like guys, but I really don't need a relationship
> in junior high anyway.*
> Carol

> *I think that parents and youth pastors should understand that when
> a guy is 14 years old, he's going to like girls. I think it's very
> natural. I feel that they should accept that fact.
> Just because I like a girl, doesn't mean I'm going
> to do anything bad with her.*
> Joe

Can you relate to Carol or Joe? Sometimes, the whole topic of guy/girl friendships can be so confusing. It's normal and natural to be attracted to someone of the opposite sex. However, some people feel that junior high is too young of an age for emotional guy/girl relationships. What do you think? Before you decide to get emotionally involved with someone, there are a few very important keys to consider:

True Love Is Worth Waiting For...

Pastor Joe was speaking to his youth group one night. As he was speaking, he noticed two young teens, Andy and Julie, in the back row. Throughout the meeting, Joe noticed Andy kiss Julie on several occasions. Knowing that this 'couple' had been 'going together' for a few months, the pastor decided to have a little chat with them. After the meeting, Joe greeted Andy and Julie, "How are you two doing?" "Great!" they responded. Joe continued, "Well, Andy, I can see that you and Julie really like each other." The couple looked at each other and smiled. Looking at Andy, Joe asked, "Do you plan on marrying Julie?" With a surprised look on his face, Andy quickly responded, "Well, of course not!" Pastor Joe commented, "Then why are you kissing another man's wife?"

Think about it...

- **Your definition of the purpose for 'single dating'.** If the purpose for single dating is only to get to know a person, with no expectations of physical contact, then why do two people have to be alone? As you get older, the purpose for single dating may become a lot clearer to you—*to find a marriage partner.* Some people say that dating only prepares you for divorce because all you learn how to do is breakup!

- **Your level of maturity.** What do you think maturity is? Some ideas to consider would be the ability to: make wise choices; be a good judge of people's character; be able to have healthy boundaries and convictions; say "No" without feeling guilty; say "Yes" when appropriate; follow one's conscience; use logic—not just emotion—in one's decisions; have a strong identity in Christ; and be open to adult input. In light of these characteristics of maturity, how mature do you feel that you are? What would others say about you if they were asked how mature you were?

- **Your parents' dating standard for you.** You might agree or disagree with what your parents feel is right for you concerning guy/girl friendships. However, God has given you your parents for your own protection and covering. If you can have ongoing, open, and honest discussions with your parents about dating, appropriate physical and emotional boundaries, and other concerns about relationships, you will be sure to have a healthy view about the opposite sex. If you ever feel pressured

to do something you don't feel right about, you can always use your parents as an excuse to say "No!"

2. Fill your 'love tank' with fuel from your family and same-sex friends.

It's normal to feel a need for attention. Every teen needs to feel recognized for something by somebody. It's normal to feel self-conscious about your looks and about being accepted by other teens because you're still developing your own individual identity. Being genuinely noticed by the opposite sex is a legitimate need in the heart of most young people. Some teens, however, look to guy/girl relationships to meet all of their needs. When you don't feel totally loved and accepted by your family, it's natural to feel a little insecure and to want others to notice you. Andrew expressed his feelings this way, "How do I get a girl to notice me without making a complete fool out of myself?" To avoid this awkwardness, work on deepening your relationships with your family and same-sex friends. When your home life is secure, and you know in your heart that you're loved unconditionally by your family, you may not feel the need to have a boyfriend or girlfriend right now.

Fill your 'love tank' with fuel from your family.

3. Get involved with other activities besides guy/girl relationships.

Friendships require time out of your schedule. Try putting your time into earning good grades and setting personal goals. Focus on pursuing athletics, hobbies, music, talents, genuine same-sex friendships, your relationship with God, youth group meetings, church involvements, and community activities. In these ways, you'll meet many interesting people, and you'll be developing the gifts and abilities that God has given to you.

4. Read a book on courting and discuss it with your parents.

Courting is a way of getting to know someone of the opposite sex. It emphasizes finding someone with godly character, doing group activities together, and actively involving both families. Even if you don't agree with the entire concept of courting, jot down any good ideas that you might be able to apply to your guy/girl friendships. See if there's anything about the values behind courting which could benefit you.

What About Love?

Today a guy gave me a poem in which he told me that he loved me.
This has been going on since the beginning of school.
I'm not sure what to do.

Karen

Have you ever had such strong feelings for someone of the opposite sex that you thought that you were "in love"? It's common for young people to make decisions based on the equation: strong feelings = true love. Think for a moment about the two phrases "I love my Dad" and "I love pizza". Is there a difference in the love you have for your Dad and the love you have for a piece of pizza? Can you explain the difference in words? Throughout your life, you will experience different types of "love". Although each type of love is important, they're all expressed in different ways. When you find someone to marry, you'll love him/her in a different way than you love your Mom or Dad and much differently than the way you love pizza! True love is worth waiting for. God will help you to guard your heart so that you'll be able to save that love for the special someone whom He has waiting for you.

When you feel a strong attraction to a person of the opposite sex, you may be experiencing infatuation. **Infatuation** sometimes feels good and can be totally innocent. Its dark side, however, can include possessive, all-absorbing, irrational, and many times foolish, emotions. It's like being on the largest emotional roller coaster

ride of your life—which can be very damaging. Even though some teens have based relationships on feelings of infatuation, infatuation isn't the same as true love. As one teen expressed his opinion about love and marriage:

> *I would like to give a few words of advice. Seek God.*
> *Don't give in to peer pressure. Don't get involved with girls*
> *until you're thinking about marriage.*
>
> Anonymous teen

Peer Pressure

> *I think that the two most important things*
> *we can do as teenagers is to*
> *(1) refuse to be influenced by our friends too much, and*
> *(2) keep our own personalities.*
>
> Erin

> *One of my biggest worries is that I might*
> *someday give in to peer pressure.*
>
> Anonymous teen

> *I really want a boyfriend because*
> *practically everyone else has one.*
>
> Kara

All during your teen years, you'll experience constant pressure from your peers to deny who you really are as a Christian and join them in making unhealthy choices.

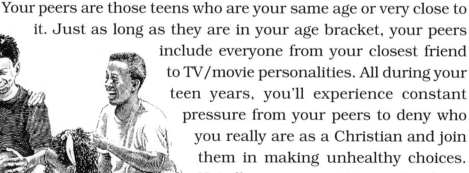

Your peers are those teens who are your same age or very close to it. Just as long as they are in your age bracket, your peers include everyone from your closest friend to TV/movie personalities. All during your teen years, you'll experience constant pressure from your peers to deny who you really are as a Christian and join them in making unhealthy choices. Not all peer pressure is negative, however, it can also be very positive. **Positive peer pressure** is what you feel when others encourage you to do something that gives God glory and is good for you. **Negative peer pressure**

is what you feel when others encourage you to do something that doesn't glorify God and is harmful for you.

God makes it clear in both the Old and New Testaments that you should definitely avoid negative peer pressure. Solomon wrote, "My son, if sinners entice you, don't consent. If they say, 'Come with us....', don't walk in the way with them. Keep your foot from their path" (Proverbs 1:10,11,15). Paul said, "Don't be deceived: 'Evil company corrupts good habits'" (I Corinthians 15:33).

The fact that God wants you to avoid negative peer pressure is clear, but *how* can you do this? Probably the most important step that you can take to learn how to stand alone for the Lord is to develop a good communicating relationship with your parents or a spiritually mature adult. True, it's easier at first to talk to your peers; to someone who's going through the exact same experiences you are. But, talking only to your peers can hurt you. Maybe it already has. Have you ever told your best friend a secret and the next day discovered that everyone in the school knew it? Or, have you ever chosen to take the advice of one of your friends only to discover that it was really 'bad' advice? Have you ever talked with one of your peers and felt like they could relate to your situation, but then found out that they didn't have any practical suggestions for you? Debi shares why she feels inadequate to give advice to her peers:

> *I don't think I can give my friends advice because*
> *I'm probably having the same struggles,*
> *and I still haven't found the answers for myself.*

When you invest in healthy relationships, you surround yourself with the positive influence of good friends. As a result, negative peer pressure won't affect you as much.

When Friendships Change

> *My best friend started to change. She got real boy crazy,*
> *and I didn't like being around her anymore. I became really sad*
> *because we weren't able to be best friends any longer.*
>
> Christina

Guy/girl friendships are not the only kind of relationships that change. All relationships change: best-friend relationships, same-sex relationships, and even family relationships. Have you ever noticed how your own friendships shift over time? The person who's your best friend this year may not have been your best friend last year. Friendships can change even as quickly as one week! A 'breaking up' of any kind can be very hurtful. With every good-bye, there's a sense of separation and loss.

How can you make it through all of these changing friendships and heartbreaks and still be okay? First, remember it's normal to feel sad. Talk about your feelings. Tell someone you trust about them. Ask Jesus to lead you to another good friend. Second, remind yourself of the value of friendships. God brings certain people into our lives at certain times in order for us to become a better Christian, and for us to be able to help someone else to become a better Christian. Third, focus on the good in the friendship. Forgive any bad. Fourth, ask yourself if your friend was becoming a negative influence in your life (or, the other way around). If he/she was, then maybe God wanted to remove him/her from your life for awhile (or, forever) so that you wouldn't be distracted from serving Him in the way that He wanted you to. Though sad at first, maybe the change was the best for you in the long run. Sometimes, it's hard to recognize when a friendship begins to go sour. As you evaluate your present friendships, think about the following qualities that make a good friend.

God brings certain people into our lives at certain times in order for us to become a better Christian, and for us to be able to help someone else to become a better Christian.

Qualities of a Good Friend. Does Your Friend...

- Share the same belief in God as you?
- Encourage you to do things that are the best for you?
- Offer to pray with you about your areas of struggle?
- Encourage you to talk to your parents or other trusted adults when you're having problems?
- Show loyalty to you by standing by you when life gets rough?
- Keep his/her promises?
- Tell the truth?
- Stick up for you in front of others when others try to put you down?

8 • 4 How to Lift Others Up in a "Put-Down" Culture

What is Respect?

What does it mean to show respect to someone? What does being respected by others feel like? Webster defines respect as esteem, admiration, acceptance, or courtesy. It means not intruding upon or interfering with another person's rights. When people say, "You don't respect me", or "Show me some respect", they're expecting to be shown appropriate honor and dignity.

Does everyone deserve respect? The apostle James says "Yes": "With it [our tongue] we bless our God and Father, and with it we curse men, who have been made in the likeness of God" (James 3: 9). When you're trying to build any kind of strong relationship in your life, respect is essential. Can you think of a time when you didn't receive the respect that you felt you deserved? How did it make you feel? When you weren't shown respect, you probably felt put down. Like others, you probably began to feel hurt and angry; maybe even a little fearful and insecure.

Respect for Family

When you show respect to each member of your family, you're strengthening the most important relationships in your life. Your parents need respect because of who they are; the ones who brought you into this world. They care for you unconditionally. You may not feel like showing respect to your parents when you have an argument with them or feel that they're being unfair to you. If you choose to be disrespectful (sarcastic, sassy) to them, it'll put a wedge between you. In a healthy family, however, it's okay for teens to disagree with their parents as long as they do so in a respectful way. Having disagreements with your parents is all a normal part of growing up and forming your own personality and convictions.

When you show respect to each member of your family, you're strengthening the most important relationships in your life.

When family members get emotional, feeling angry or upset is not being disrespectful. It's your *attitude* and how you choose to express yourself that's the most important. How can you respectfully disagree? You "speak the truth in love" (Ephesians 4:15). Some practical responses to use with your parents might be: "May I express my personal opinion about this subject and share with you the reasons that I have for it?" or, "I feel confused because it seems like you and Mom aren't giving me the same message. Can I explain?" or, "I'll do what you ask with as good of an attitude as possible, but I want you to know that I still disagree with you. I hope that's okay with you."

If you get into the habit of showing respect to everyone no matter what their age or position, you'll find it easier to respect adults.

Respect for Adults

Awhile ago, I really disliked writing thank-you notes. They seemed so unnecessary. "Why can't I just thank the person on-the-spot when I receive a gift and leave it at that?" I thought. But, later, I realized that people really like to receive thank-you notes, and I needed to write them for other occasions than just Christmas or my birthday.

Christina

From an early age, you've probably heard the advice, "Respect adults and all of those in authority". If you get into the habit of showing respect to everyone no matter what their age or position, you'll find it easier to respect adults. Some teens have a hard time respecting adults because they may have been hurt by an adult or may not feel like adults really care about them. This is a sad situation because there are some adults who hurt young people, just as young people hurt each other.

Think about how little respect Jesus received—and He was God in the flesh (John 1:1)! After all the good that Jesus did for people, He was treated with the utmost disrespect. The God-man was given an unjust trial and executed as a criminal. Think about it.

Respect for Your Peers

Can you name a few of your peers that you really respect? If so, who are they and why do you respect them? Do you feel that your peers respect you? What makes you feel that they do? If you're like most teens, you have a deep desire to have your peers like and respect you. When teens show kindness and courtesy to others based only on people's looks, clothes, income, career, status, education, or car, they're showing partiality and favoritism. The Scriptures condemn these two attitudes (James 2:1-13). Lots of teens harshly judge others. This attitude isn't God's heart for people. Ask yourself: do you respect one classmate because he gets good grades and then disrespect another who gets lower grades? Are you more polite to your good-looking peers than you are to those who aren't as good-looking? Unconditional respect—with no strings attached—is what God is asking from you. God wants you to respect every human being—Christian or non-Christian—because God made each person in His image and for His own special purpose (James 3:9).

God wants you to respect every human being—Christian or non-Christian—because God made each person in His image and for His own special purpose (James 3:9).

Respect for Yourself

Your reputation is what people think of you. How much does your reputation matter to you? Developing a good reputation is up to you. How you act, how you talk, how you treat others, how

DANGER!

Do you find yourself talking behind people's backs or speaking negatively about others? If you do, you may develop the reputation of being a gossip. Gossips don't have many friends—except for other gossips. When they do get new friends, gossips can't keep them for very long because they don't respect their friend's secrets (Proverbs 20:19). Try something new. The next time you're around your friends, try saying something nice about a person who is not with you and see what the response is. Speaking positively of one another is a part of becoming more like Christ (James 3:1-12).

As you get older, it'll be more difficult to change what people think about you because of all the behaviors and attitudes you will have left behind.

well you keep secrets (versus how much you gossip) will determine much of your reputation.

Do you realize that even though you're a young teenager, you're already developing your reputation? As you get older, it'll be more difficult to change what people think about you because of all the behaviors and attitudes you will have left behind. Right now, however, your future is bright with lots of potential. You have a great opportunity to begin forming a positive reputation for yourself.

Ways to Develop a Great Reputation

- Look for ways to help.
- Defend your friends.
- Be friendly to everyone.
- Keep your word.
- Don't gossip.
- Love God sincerely.

A good name is to be chosen more than great riches.
Proverbs 22:1a

How Do You Show Respect?

Respecting others begins by respecting yourself. Jesus said, "You shall love your neighbor *as yourself*" (Matthew 22:39). If you're having doubts about your worth because of what others have said about you, ask God to help you find security in His unconditional love. There are very practical ways to show respect for others. You won't see these ways shown on most TV programs or movies. In America, entertainers make money by causing others to laugh at those they put down. The following chart demonstrates how the little courtesies that you learn today can really benefit you as you get older.

HOW TO SHOW RESPECT

The first column lists 13 respectful courtesies. The second column describes the typical American attitude toward them and why. The third column explains each courtesy's potential future benefit to you.

The Courtesy	The American Culture	The Future Benefit to You
1. Holding the door for others	1. Considered old-fashioned. Independent women consider it a put-down.	1. Christian girls like it; makes them feel special. Politeness can show you to be a selfless person on the job.
2. Not cutting in front of others whether in line or in a doorway	2. Get where you're going as fast as you can. If others are in your way, it's their fault.	2. Putting others first will cause others to put you first. Will receive more respect both on and off the job. Older people will be inclined to like, trust, and promote you.
3. Saying "Please" and "Thank you"	3. Unnecessary. Demand your own way. Intimidate others to respect you.	3. You'll be shown more kindness. Others will enjoy working with and for you.
4. Pulling the chair out for others	4. Old-fashioned.	4. Adults and girls will appreciate the thoughtfulness. Elderly will notice/be appreciative.
5. Standing when an adult/older person enters the room	5. Unnecessary. Show no special respect for adults/elderly.	5. Bosses will notice how you respect them. Others will respect you more. Parent's friends will like it.
6. Not interrupting others; raising your hand in class to ask a question	6. Talk whenever you feel like it. Interrupt others to keep the attention on yourself.	6. Gain/keep more friends. Receive more respect from others.
7. Being an attentive listener; making good eye contact	7. Wandering eyes. Doesn't matter if you act 'aloof'.	7. Establish more rapport and trust with others at home and in/out of the job.
8. Giving a firm handshake when introduced to someone	8. Doesn't matter. Just be yourself. Old-fashioned.	8. Receive more trust. Make a better first impression. Be considered a gentleman.
9. Sharing your umbrella; helping others on with their coats	9. Unnecessary and sissy.	9. Ladies of all ages like it. People will appreciate your thoughtfulness.
10. Writing thank-you notes	10. Unimportant. Don't do anything special for others.	10. Will be greatly appreciated both in/out of business world. Will impress bosses, customers, clients, and family.
11. Taking dishes over to the sink after meals and washing them without being asked	11. Let Mom or Dad always do it; it's their job. Don't do anything if not first asked. Sit glued to TV.	11. Helpfulness and volunteer attitude will be appreciated by everyone and help job promotions.
12. Using breath mints and deodorant	12. "Accept me as I am."	12. Everyone will appreciate this.
13. Keeping nails/hands clean; washing hands with soap and water regularly	13. Doesn't matter. Go grungy.	13. Everyone will feel more free and friendly around you. People will be more prone to shake your hand; will appreciate cleanliness. Girls like cleanliness in guys.

8 • 5 Learning to Forgive

*I'm very angry with one of my friends. He keeps getting mad at me for
no reason. He continues to bring up my past mistakes.*

Bob

A Replacement for Revenge

Do you know anyone who seems to have a lot of friends? Do you
know anybody who can get along with just about anyone? Being
able to get along with the people around you—whether at school,
home, job, or in the neighborhood—is an essential part of your
social health. No matter how many friends you have or how outgoing or friendly of a person you are, eventually people are going to
hurt you. Some people will hurt you on purpose because they're
jealous of you. Others will hurt you unintentionally. Because of
this inescapable fact, it's a good idea to get prepared with the right
kind of heart attitude that will enable you to process your hurts in
a healthy way. Contrary to our culture, which promotes revenge,
Jesus said that the answer to wanting to "get even" with someone
who has hurt us is showing them mercy and forgiveness.

What is Forgiveness?

*Sometimes, I get mad at my little sister. But, it normally
doesn't last very long. I try to forgive her.*

Lindsey

To "forgive" someone means that you release all of your
desire to punish or get even with those who have hurt or
offended you. **Forgiveness** doesn't mean that you deny
your hurt or how the other person was mean to you. It
simply means that you choose emotionally to release them
from your judgment and put them into the hands of God.
God knows how to deal with the sins of others a lot better than you do because He sees the big picture. He sees
everyone's intentions and motives. To show "mercy" on
someone means to give them what they don't deserve.
When criminals receive mercy, they're released from the
sentences that they had justly coming to them from their

breaking of the law. Jesus said that those who hurt you don't owe you anything compared to how much you owe God for forgiving you of your sins! You should freely forgive others, since the Father has forgiven you through Christ (Matthew 18:21-35).

When Friends Hurt You

Have you ever been hurt by a friend? Have you ever been ignored by a group that you thought were your friends? Others have experienced the same pain of rejection as you have. The psalmist, David, had a very close friend betray him. Some think that the following verse may even refer to his third son, Absalom, who inspired a revolt against him. In his pain, David wrote, "Even my own familiar friend in whom I trusted, who ate my bread, has lifted up his heel against me" (Psalm 41:9). This same verse is applied to Jesus being betrayed by one of his closest friends, one of the original twelve apostles, Judas (John 13:18). One of the hardest experiences in life is "bouncing back" after a good friend has hurt you. Only with God's help can you successfully forgive.

One of the hardest experiences in life is "bouncing back" after a good friend has hurt you. Only with God's help can you successfully forgive.

Can Any Good Come from Being Hurt?

Yes! If you learn genuinely to forgive the person(s) who hurt or abused you. When you realize what it feels like to be hurt, then you're less likely to treat your friends in a cruel way. **Empathy** is when you really feel for a person who's hurt because you've experienced the same hurt (2 Corinthians 1:4).

Why Are Some Teens so Mean?

Why do teens hurt others? That's a difficult question. In an attempted answer, one teenager put it this way:

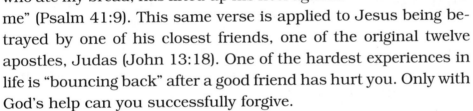

Nobody's perfect. People should let others be their own person because that's all they can be. If you tease others [in a mean way], you're not thinking about their feelings. You really should consider being on the other side and how much it can hurt. The real reason people tease and are mean is because they're insecure about themselves.

David

Do you agree with David when he says that teenagers tease other teens because they're insecure about themselves?

Your Peers May Act Mean to You Because:

•   They're angry about conflicts or pressures at home.

•   They want to be the 'tough', 'cool', or 'macho' person and think it'll gain them respect from their friends.

•   They don't know how else to act. Acting mean is what they've seen at home.

•   They have hurt feelings that are still unresolved.

•   When someone is really irritating them, they don't know how to handle it properly.

•   They're critical of others, always finding fault.

•   They're afraid of being 'uncool' with their mean peers.

Do you see yourself in any of the previous list? It's hard to get along with people when circumstances in your own life are causing you inner frustration.

The Good News

Jesus understands the hurt you feel from being rejected. He experienced the ultimate in betrayal.

The good news is that even if you have hurt others (or have been hurt by others) you can learn and grow from every painful situation. You can choose to change your unforgiving attitude by asking God to help you give them what they don't deserve. You can choose not to punish them—just like God has done for you through His Son, Jesus Christ. Forgiving others is not only the "right" action to choose, it'll also enable you to be a happier Christian. Jesus said,

Blessed [happy] are the merciful, for they shall obtain mercy.
Matthew 5:7

196

Chapter 8 Review

. . . .

Defining the Terms

Social health

Friendship

Relationship

Substitutions

Artificial relationships

Communication

Verbal communication

Nonverbal communication

Walls (between people)

Infatuation

Positive peer pressure

Negative peer pressure

Respect

Disrespect

Reputation

Revenge

Forgive(ness)

Empathy

Recalling the Facts

1. What's the danger in substituting a "thing" for a real person—maybe even a friendship? Give two examples of "things" that can be replacements for friendships.

2. What's the most famous "best friend" relationship in the Bible? What made their friendship so unique?

3. What's meant by the phrase, "Most people can *talk*, but not everyone can genuinely *communicate*"?

4. List the twelve skills of good communication.

5. List the keys to consider before you get emotionally involved with someone of the opposite sex.

6. How can a person avoid negative peer pressure?

Applying the Truth

1. Read Matthew 12:33-37. Explain how this passage can relate to the everyday life of a teenager.

2. The Bible condemns partiality. Read James 2:1-13 and explain how this principle can be applied to your life.

3. Read Proverbs 11:13. Do you find yourself talking behind someone's back or speaking negatively about others? If you do, you may develop the reputation of being a gossip. Why don't those who gossip have many friends? What can a person do to help themselves overcome the temptation to gossip?

"...glorify God in your body and in your spirit, which are God's."

I Corinthians 6:20

THE 7 HABITS OF 9
HIGHLY POPULAR TEENS

What's Coming Up...

9 • 1 The Popularity Predicament

Have you ever felt unpopular? Many teens feel this way at one time or another. Being popular may be extremely important to you right now. If you're a guy, being popular might mean fitting in with the most well-liked guys in your class or youth group. It could also mean being the center of attention for lots of girls. If you're a girl, being popular might mean having certain guys like you, or being a part of the "in" crowd at your school or church.

American culture puts a great significance on outward appearance. Our society promotes looks/glamour, boyfriends/girlfriends, talents/performance, fame/image, and cool fashions. Teen maga-

zines focus on how to use make-up, hairstyle, and the latest designer labels to make you look "hot". This emphasis on what's "hot" is meant to cause you to buy the products that you see advertised. Promoters of popularity want you to believe that if you wear *their* clothes or use *their* make-up, you'll be popular. With all of this pressure to be popular, it can be very difficult to stay focused on what really matters to God.

> *Do not let your beauty be*
> *that outward adorning...*
> *but let it be the hidden person of the heart...*
> **I Peter 3:3-4**

Although God is more concerned about heart issues such as kindness, self-control, purity, and genuine love, He does want you to care for your body through good personal hygiene. Keeping your body clean and properly cared for is an important part of living for Christ since your body is His house.

Why should you take the time to develop good habits of personal hygiene?

With all of this pressure to be popular, it can be very difficult to stay focused on what really matters to God.

- Being clean and attractive will definitely enhance your looks. Try not to fall into the trap, however, of always wanting to "look good" for other people.

- Taking care of yourself makes you feel good about yourself.

- Using good personal hygiene shows respect for others.

- Practicing good body care daily will boost your self-confidence in social situations and positively affect your relationships with others.

You have many good Christian qualities inside of you. Focus on your inner qualities, and then project them through your appearance. Christlikeness on the inside makes a teenager look good on the outside. Is there some part of your appearance that you would like to change? If so, change the areas that are change-

able. Ask the Lord to help you to be content with those aspects you can't change. Your height or type of hair, for example, are both out of your direct control. You can, however, work with what you can change and enhance your natural appearance.

9 •2 What's the Buzz on Skin Care?

· ·

My friend, Jill, has the best looking skin. She never seems to have acne and hardly ever needs to wear make-up. My skin is horrible. How can I have skin like hers?

Sheri

The Importance of Your Skin

Do you think that Sheri could have skin like Jill's? Each member of your family might have different skin types; yours may be more prone to acne while your brother's may be very dry. Although Sheri wants skin like Jill's, her skin type came from her mother and father (or grandparents!). The best Sheri can do is to take good care of the skin she has, exercise regularly, and maintain a nutritious diet.

What's the first feature you notice when you meet people? Is it their clothes, hairstyle, or face? It's usually a person's face. You can tell a lot about a person by looking at his/her skin. By looking at people's skin, you can approximate their age, tell whether they spend much time outdoors, observe whether they like to sunbathe or use the tanning machine, see if they wear a lot of make-up, and tell whether they have acne problems. Your skin is one of the most important elements of your appearance because it's what people see all the time.

It's appropriate in many countries for teens to begin shaving. Girls may shave their legs and underarms while guys shave their faces.

Fun Facts About Your Skin!

What would you say is the largest organ of your body? Would you say that it was your heart, or your lungs, or some other internal organ? No, it's really your skin! The skin weighs between six and ten pounds. If your skin were spread out flat, it would cover an area about three to seven feet!

To gain an appreciation for your skin, take a closer look at how God created it to do a lifetime of work for you. Your skin has three main layers of tissues. The outer is called the **epidermis**, the middle the **dermis**, and the deepest the **subcutaneous layer**. The epidermis has several layers of cells. To keep your skin healthy, new skin cells are produced every day beneath the surface while old skin cells on the top of the skin are dying. Did you know that your outer layer of skin is replaced about every 28 days?

Imagine what your life would be like without your skin. How would your body be held together? How could you feel the warmth of the sun or the coolness of the night air?

Your skin is an amazing organ of your body. It's important to take good care of your skin because it works hard for you fulfilling

It's important to take good care of your skin because it works hard for you fulfilling many important jobs.

The Skin

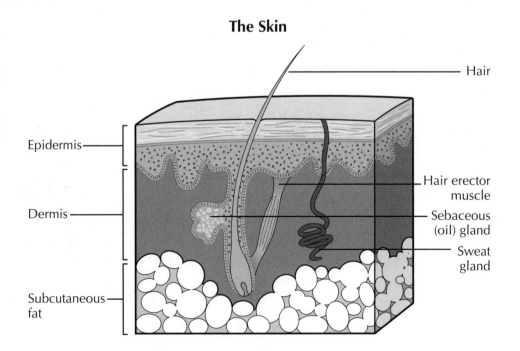

many important jobs. It protects your body against outside water and germs by acting like a shield. Your skin guards your internal organs from heat and cold. When your body temperature is too hot, your skin acts like a major air conditioner. Your skin is also your connection to the world around you. The nerve endings on your skin protect you from danger as well as give you pleasure. By being a sensory organ, your skin alerts you when there's a threat of pain. It also allows you to enjoy someone's touch.

Skin Care

The skin on your face is not the only skin of your body that needs to be cared for. Daily bathing, showering, and washing with a gentle soap to keep your body clean makes you feel and look good. Bacteria on your skin cause body odor. For this reason, it's necessary to use an anti-bacterial soap. During your teen years, it's important to keep your skin clean because of the excess sweat and oil that your changing hormones produce. Sometimes, your skin may seem so dry that it itches. Certain soaps can dry your skin or cause allergic reactions such as flaking or red patches. When you get a reaction from a particular brand of soap discontinue using it. Your skin may be sensitive to some deodorant soaps or those containing perfumes.

It's important to shower after gym class and other physical activities.

The soap you use on your body may not be the best choice for your face. For this reason, some people use a facial cleanser. Choose a cleanser that's the best for your type of skin (dry, oily, combination). It's also important to use a moisturizer on your skin to help keep it from becoming too dry.

Take the Skin Care Quiz.

Do you:

- bathe or shower daily?

- use a deodorant and antiperspirant every day?

- use warm (but not hot) water on your face and body?

The sun's rays are much more intense than they used to be.

- finish your shower with cool water (to help close the pores of your skin)?

- use a washcloth to clean your skin gently?

- make sure to wash your face and remove your make-up before going to bed (girls)?

- exercise regularly to increase the blood circulation to your skin?

- eat a healthy diet of fresh foods?

- drink at least eight glasses of purified water every day?

- get plenty of sleep?

- protect your skin from the elements—especially the sun—by using a sunscreen with at least a SPF (sun protection factor) of 25?

If your answer was "Yes" to all the Skin Quiz questions, you have great skin care habits. Keep it up! If your answer was "No", try to incorporate these ideas into your lifestyle.

DANGER!

You may never think that you could get skin cancer, but how you treat your skin now will help to determine its condition when you're an adult. If you want to reduce your chances of developing skin cancer and premature aging, protect yourself from the dangerous rays of the sun. If you choose to enjoy the outdoors, make sure you take the following precautions:

1. Use a sunscreen at all times—whether it's clear or overcast. Use a sunscreen with a SPF of at least 25; the higher the SPF, the better the protection.

2. Cover up. Wear a wide-rimmed hat as well as loose clothing if you are going to be in the sun. This will help to prevent you from getting sunburn on your scalp or ears.

3. Avoid the intense sun times. The worst time to be in the sun is between 10:00AM-3:00PM.

4. Avoid using tanning beds that use light to tan your skin. They're dangerous to your skin and cause premature aging and wrinkles.

The Zit Files: Is Acne Ruining Your Life?

Most teens, no matter how careful they are with their skin, have to deal with some acne. **Acne** occurs when the pores of your skin become clogged with oil. During adolescence, your body is experiencing so many changes that your elevated level of hormones can increase the amount of oil that's produced in your skin. As a result, an oily substance called **sebum** is produced which even-

tually clogs the pores of your skin. The three general types of acne are whiteheads, blackheads, and pimples.

A **whitehead** is created when oil becomes trapped inside a pore. A pore that's plugged with oil—but is exposed to the air—is called a **blackhead** because of the darkened color of the pore. A **pimple** is a clogged pore that has become infected and filled with pus. Pimples are the most serious type of acne.

If you have acne, it's very important to care for your skin in the proper way so that this temporary condition doesn't cause you more heartache later with scarring or infections. If you get acne, the following Do's and Don'ts may lessen its severity.

Do:

- Wash with a facial cleanser and warm water twice a day.
- Dry your skin carefully with a clean towel. Don't scrub the area.
- Use a mild cleanser suited to your skin type (to help control the excess oil).
- Get plenty of rest.
- Exercise regularly.
- Eat fresh whole foods.
- Drink more than eight glasses of purified water daily.
- Wear oil-free make-up.
- If your condition is serious, see a **dermatologist** (a doctor who treats skin disorders).
- Understand that acne will eventually go away!

Don't:

- Squeeze or pick at your acne. This can cause infection and scarring.
- Use heavy creams or moisturizers on the affected areas.
- Touch your face with your hands or fingers. This can place more oil and dirt on your face.
- Let acne get you depressed or prevent you from having fun!

LOGON!

Different Skin Types

Not all skin types are the same. Take the following quiz to see what kind of skin type you have. Make a note of which of the following statements sound the most like your skin complaints.

- "My acne problem is a major source of stress in my life."
- "The oil on my face seems like it could fill up a McDonald's™ deep-fryer."
- "I don't have any zit problems. My face seems normal."
- "My 't-zone' (forehead, nose, and chin) shines with excess oil, but my cheeks are dry."
- "My skin seems drier than the Sahara Desert."

Based upon your skin type, you can choose products that best suit you. What works for your best friend, may not work for you. There's nothing worse than spending a bunch of money on a product only to discover that it doesn't work. Find something that's strong but safe enough for your skin. Avoid products with perfumes and coloring agents. Some products can even make your skin condition worse!

9 • 3 Choose the Hairstyle That's Best for You

Sometimes, I focus a lot on my hair; something that doesn't really matter and won't really last. I get all upset when my hair doesn't look the way I want it to.

Carrie

A great style can help you to feel very good and confident about yourself.

Have you ever looked in a teen or hairstyle magazine, picked out a "fad" hairstyle that you thought was hot, had your hairdresser cut your hair exactly the same way—only to discover that you looked totally different than the cool photo? Your hair has its own special personality. As much as you may want to look like someone else, God has made you just the way He wanted to. To Him, you're beautiful/handsome. When your hair doesn't seem to cooperate with what you're trying to do, or you just feel it's time for a style change, there are certain factors to keep in mind.

First, try to stay calm. If you've ever changed your hairstyle—or got a "fad" cut—then you know how it can affect your whole outlook on life. A great style can help you to feel very good and confident about yourself. A good line to tell yourself after you get a bad haircut is, "It'll always grow back!"

Second, there are different types of hair. Do you have the same type of hair as your brother(s) or sister(s), or your Mom or Dad? Whether guy or girl, your hair can be thick, thin, wavy, curly, fine, straight, or coarse. It's true that different hair types need different shampoos, conditioners, and cuts to maximize their style, but try not to stop there. Look at the shape of your head and face to help determine what kind of style is right for you.

Third, hairstyles change as often as clothing styles. Try not to pick the "in" cut if it's not the best for you. Find something that makes you feel good and confident about yourself and stick with it. Even a slight highlight in color can lift your spirits without giving you a drastic change. Both guys and girls have the same pressure to have the hottest hairstyles. Usually, the latest hairstyles follow the look of some current movie star(s) or professional athlete. Ask at your local hair salon/barber shop to find a style that is flattering to you. Another good question to keep in mind about any new hairstyle is, "Is this style really practical for me?" If you have a hard time getting up in the morning, for example, try to stay away from a hairstyle that demands a lot of styling time.

LOGON!

"Rapunzel, Rapunzel, Let Down Your Long Hair!"

Do you remember the nursery story of the young girl named Rapunzel who was locked in a high tower? The only way to reach her was to climb up her long hair. Did you know that hair is as strong as aluminum? If you could be like Rapunzel and make a rope out of the strands of your hair, you would not only be able easily to lift a prince to the top of your window, you could also lift a car weighing one ton!

Taking Good Care of Your Hair

The roots of your hair are secured in small pockets called **follicles**. When hair cells die, they are forced out of the follicle and new hair cells take their place. You inherited both the type and

color of your hair from your parents. You may not have the exact color of their hair, but somewhere down the line, your grandparents or distant relatives had hair similar to yours.

Good Hair Care Is as Simple as One—Two—Three.

One: Brush your hair daily. Brushing your hair prevents the build-up of tangles and dirt. Brushing your hair's natural oils through your hair will help make it shine. Brushing your hair too much, too hard, or when you have hair spray on it, however, can damage or pull it out. Choose a good brush that is right for your hair type and hairstyle.

You inherited both the type and color of your hair from your parents.

Two: Shampoo your hair. You may find you don't need to wash your hair every day because it's not excessively oily. However, a good daily shampoo stimulates your scalp, removes styling product residue, removes the daily sweat/grime build-up, and can help you feel clean and fresh.

Use warm—not hot—water to wash and scrub your scalp using the pads of your fingertips. Use cool water to rinse your hair. Cool water closes the pores in your scalp and gives you a clean feeling. Try to let your hair dry by itself without the use of hot hair dryers. If you use a hair dryer every day before school, try to give your hair a break from the artificial drying on the weekends.

Three: Be smart when you choose hair products. If you shop wisely, you won't need to spend excessive amounts of money on them. Find a gentle shampoo that works for your hair type. It should be pH balanced. Hairstylists may tell you to change shampoo products about every two to four weeks to give your hair a rest from that particular brand. If your hair is naturally oily, don't use conditioners just because everyone else uses them. Conditioning your hair once a week would probably be adequate. If you have a problem with **dandruff** (a condition in which the outer layer of skin on the

scalp flakes off), then find a shampoo that is specifically designed to treat dandruff.

DANGER!

Have you ever heard a warning in your school concerning head lice? If you've ever experienced these little creatures personally, you'll never want to have the hassle again. **Head lice** are insects that live in the hair and look very similar to dandruff. Since they're very easy to catch from others, schools can have a lot of problems with them. To prevent catching head lice, always use your own comb and brush at school. Wash your comb and brush regularly. If you catch head lice, use a specially medicated shampoo. Thoroughly clean all bedding, hairbrushes, and household items.

---

9 • 4 Let's See Those Hands and Nails

· ·

I often hide my hands in my pockets because
I don't like the way they look. I also bite my nails.

Jason

Do you have a habit of biting your nails? Do you ever feel like hiding your hands? If so, you know what healthy hands and nails can mean to your self-esteem. Some people can spend a lot of money using a *manicurist* (a person who specializes in caring for fingernails). Manicurists professionally remove cuticles, trim and shape nails, and can apply sets of artificial fingernails. You can also end up spending a lot of money on nail products and services.

Your fingernails and toenails are made of a tough dead material called **keratin** (a hard substance that gives nails their strength). The **cuticle** surrounds the nail and is made of a nonliving skin. The cuticle protects the base of the nail from germs and bacteria.

Taking Good Care of Your Hands and Nails

Have you ever been in a sandwich shop in which the sandwich maker had dirt under his/her fingernails? How did this make you feel about eating there? Have you ever seen the same person who handled your money in a fast food restaurant also fix

Have you ever been in a sandwich shop in which the sandwich maker had dirt under his/her fingernails? How did this make you feel about eating there?

Simple acts like raising your hand in class can draw attention to your hands and fingernails.

your burger? Seeing others with dirty hands and nails can make you lose your appetite. Take a moment right now and look at your own hands. Are they clean? Are your nails trimmed? Do you have noticeable dirt under any of your nails? Although you may not be serving someone food, people do notice the condition of your hands and nails. You may not think that you have time to care for your nails, but healthy hands and nails can play a big part in your outward appearance. Guys, ask the girls you know what they think about a guy who has constantly dirty hands. I think you will find it unanimous—they like to see well cared for hands on a guy! Clean hands also help to prevent you from catching a bacteria or a virus from what you touch or handle during the day.

Keys to Healthy Hands and Nails

1. Wash your hands regularly with warm water and an anti-bacterial soap. Use a mild soap that's not too harsh on your skin. It's healthier to wash your hands with soap from a dispenser than it is to wash with a bar of soap because the bar holds onto people's germs. If your nails are dirty, use a nailbrush to clean underneath them.

2. Try a moisturizer on your hands after washing them. Use one on your feet, knees, and elbows after bathing or showering.

3. Use a fingernail clipper when your nails need to be trimmed. Afterwards, you can use an emery board to shape them. Constant clipping may result in splitting a nail.

4. Shape your fingernails to an appropriate length that's practical for your lifestyle as well as attractive to the length of your fingers.

5. Cut your toenails regularly. If cut too short, a toenail can become infected. An **ingrown toenail** is a nail that pushes into the skin on the side of your toe, and it's very painful. It requires a doctor's attention to prevent further infection.

6. Eat fresh, whole foods. Good nutrition has a lot to do with the health of all of your nails. A poor diet has been linked to weak, hang-, as well as split nails.

7. Use protective gloves whenever you clean or handle any kind of chemical. Moisturize often.

Shape your fingernails to an appropriate length that is practical for your lifestyle as well as attractive to the length of your fingers.

Here Are a Few Tips to Help You Stop Biting Your Nails.

- Take special note of how you feel when you bite your nails. Do you feel bored, nervous, or depressed? If so, the next time the urge hits, try telling yourself, "I need to find something else to do right away so that I don't feel bored, nervous, or depressed".

- The next time the urge to bite them comes, try some of this self-talk: "I really don't have to bite them", or "Biting them isn't really worth it".

- Try doing something else with your hands, for example, getting something to drink.

- Make a decision to stop. Tell someone else who may hold you accountable and ask how you're doing.

- Keep your nails trimmed and smooth so that you won't be as tempted to bite them.

- If you go one month without biting your nails, give yourself a treat. How about your favorite sundae or milk shake? How about a manicure?

- Use a bitter-tasting nail polish.

- If you still have problems, limit your biting to one nail.

9 • 5 Have You Seen Your Dentist Lately?

I'm self-conscious about my teeth, so I don't like to smile.
Jennifer

Do you ever feel embarrassed when you smile? If your teeth are crooked, discolored, missing, or covered with braces, it can affect whether or not you smile. If you have trouble smiling, here are a few thoughts you might want to consider:

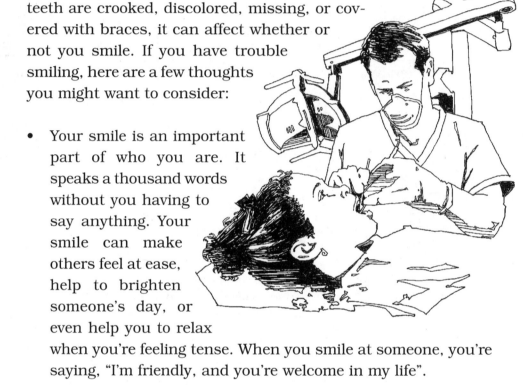

Your smile is an important part of who you are.

- Your smile is an important part of who you are. It speaks a thousand words without you having to say anything. Your smile can make others feel at ease, help to brighten someone's day, or even help you to relax when you're feeling tense. When you smile at someone, you're saying, "I'm friendly, and you're welcome in my life".

- Did you know that it takes more muscles and energy to frown than it does to smile?

- Talk to your dentist about your long-range goals for your smile. He/she will be glad to help you reach them so that you can feel more confident.

- Whenever you begin to feel like not smiling, try this self-talk: "People won't reject me because of my imperfect smile. They just want to know if I'm a friendly person."

- Use your smile as a way of making new friends. Solomon wrote, "A man who has friends must himself be friendly" (Proverbs 18:24a).

How Important Are Your Teeth and Gums?

Have you ever gone to school or went to bed without first brushing your teeth? If so, how did your mouth feel? Brushing your teeth and flossing your gums daily is the single most important part of caring for your teeth. Although you may not notice any serious problem with your teeth and gums as a teenager, you're creating habits now that will affect your teeth as an adult. You may know some adults who have lost their permanent teeth and are now wearing *dentures* (false teeth). If you would ask them, they would probably wish they still had their own teeth. Your teeth and gums benefit you in ways that you probably take for granted. They not only give you self-confidence, they also allow you to chew and digest your food, form a great smile, and give shape to your face. They also help you to speak. Try saying the word "talk" without letting your tongue touch your front teeth!

Brushing your teeth and flossing your gums daily is the single most important part of caring for your teeth.

There are four kinds of permanent teeth in your mouth, each serving a different purpose. Your *incisors* are your front and center teeth and are responsible for cutting and tearing food. They also give people their first impression of you when you smile. The four pointed teeth next to your incisors are your *canine* teeth. Their job is to tear your food and prepare it for chewing. Your *premolars* and your *molars* are located in the sides and the back of your mouth. They grind and chew your food. It's very important not to rush while you're eating. Before you swallow your food, try to **masticate** (chew) it thoroughly. If you can do this, you'll experience a lot less heartburn and indigestion as you get older. You'll feel healthier since the process of digestion will have had a great start.

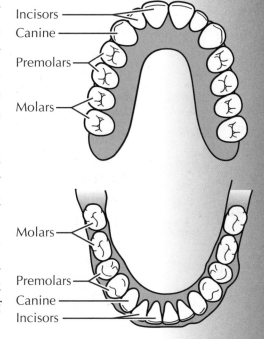

In order for you to prevent yourself from getting tooth decay and/or gum disease, it's important to learn about the various parts of your teeth and gums.

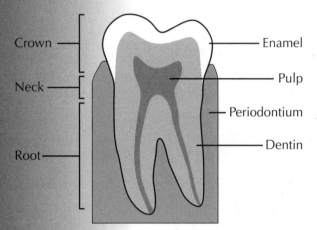

Crown

Neck

Root

Enamel

Pulp

Periodontium

Dentin

Periodontium is the name of the bone, tissue, and gum that support your teeth. Each of your teeth has four parts: the crown, the neck, the root, and the pulp. The *crown* is the part of the tooth that you can see. It's covered with the hardest substance in the human body (*enamel*). The *neck* of the tooth is the part between the crown and the root. The *root* is the part of the tooth that is below the gum and is made up of *dentin* (a material about the hardness of bone surrounding the pulp of the tooth). The *pulp*, the inside of the tooth, is composed of blood vessels, nerves, and connective tissue.

What Can Go Wrong?

Do you know how many fillings you have in your mouth? Unless you've already spent a lot of time in the dental chair, you may not be aware of all of the problems that can result from a lack of consistent tooth and gum care. A **cavity** results when bacteria combines with sugary foods and forms an acid. This acid not only destroys your protective tooth enamel, it also irritates your gums. To prevent tooth decay, you must keep the bacteria from remaining on your teeth. The best way to do this is to cut back on eating sugary foods and brush and floss after every meal.

Plaque is a grainy, sticky coating that is constantly forming on your teeth. It consists of saliva, bacteria, and food particles. Plaque should be removed with daily brushing and flossing. If the plaque is not removed, it can harden into a substance called *calculus* or **tartar**. Place your tongue on the back of your lower front teeth. Do you feel a rough substance? If so, this is the formation of tartar. Brushing cannot remove tartar, but regular dental cleanings can. If plaque and tartar are not removed on a regular basis, they will irritate your gums and promote gum disease.

To prevent tooth decay, you must keep the bacteria from remaining on your teeth.

Getting a cavity is not the only concern you should have about your teeth. **Gingivitis** is a gum disease caused by a build-up of plaque and tartar on your teeth. Food that is caught between your teeth can cause the bacteria to attack your gums. Signs of gingivitis include gums that are dark red at the gum line, swelling, and bleeding. Visiting your dentist regularly will help to spot gingivitis before it turns to **periodontal disease** (more advanced gum disease).

Orthodontics (braces) can treat severe irregularities.

Are you self-conscious because your teeth are crooked? Do you have an under- or an overbite? When your upper and lower teeth don't line up properly, it's called a **malocclusion**. Slight malocclusions are common. **Orthodontics** (braces) can treat severe irregularities. When overcrowding is the cause, some teeth may need to be extracted (pulled).

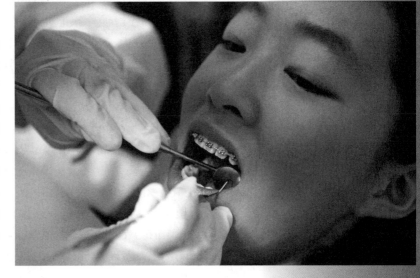

How to Take Good Care of Your Teeth

When good dental care becomes a daily routine, it won't seem to be such a hassle. You'll reap the long-term benefit of keeping your own good-looking teeth and smile if you develop good habits now! Here's what to do:

- **Brush your teeth after each meal.** If you can't, rinse your mouth out with water to remove surface food. Buy a toothbrush with soft bristles and use gentle, circular strokes on your teeth and gum line. A hard toothbrush and/or pressing too hard on your teeth can irritate your gums and cause them to recede (be pushed away from your teeth).

- **Brush your tongue.** Much of the bacteria and film in your mouth rests on your tongue. It can contribute to bad breath. When you give your tongue a good scrub before ending your brushing routine, your mouth will feel even more refreshed.

- **Change your toothbrush.** How long have you been using your present toothbrush? It's a good idea to replace your toothbrush regularly—especially after you've been sick. Germs and bacteria can remain on your brush and re-infect you.

- **Floss at least once a day.** You can buy either waxed or unwaxed string to clean between your teeth. Waxed floss makes it easier to clean between teeth that are very close together.

- **Use fluoride.** Many communities have added fluoride to their water system. Health authorities, however, are still undecided about whether fluoride is totally fit for human consumption. On the positive side, fluoride has been found to strengthen teeth and help prevent tooth decay. It's a good idea to use a toothpaste that contains fluoride.

- **Eat healthfully.** Although eating sweets may seem harmless at the time, the sugar you consume is slowly and silently destroying your teeth. To help prevent tooth decay, try to make a special effort to brush your teeth after eating sugary foods.

- **Visit your dentist twice a year.** Regular visits to the dentist help in the prevention and early detection of gum and tooth problems. A professional tooth cleaning is followed by an exam.

Do You Have a Dragon Living in Your Mouth?

Have you ever talked with someone who had bad breath? If so, you know what a turn-off bad breath can be! Some of the causes of **halitosis** (bad breath) include: poor brushing and flossing habits, mouth infection(s), poor digestion, body dehydration (lack of water), tobacco us-

age, coffee drinking, and eating strongly flavored foods like garlic or onions. If you have good health habits but still worry about bad breath, you can use sugarless breath mints.

Putting the "Squeeze" on Toothpaste

Have you glanced down the toothpaste aisle lately? There's a lot of hype about different kinds of toothpaste. Is there a "perfect" toothpaste? Toothpaste manufacturers continue to increase their selections. Crest™ has seven kinds of paste or gels. Colgate-Palmolive™ offers more than twelve! Another brand combines three different kinds of colors in one tube. What should you look for in good quality toothpaste? Try to avoid toothpaste with artificial ingredients because most of the time you do end up swallowing some of the paste as you brush. Make sure the toothpaste contains fluoride. If you read the labels carefully, you'll find that many brands of toothpaste contain the same ingredients with just a different dispenser or multiple-color combination to dazzle you. I use a "natural" toothpaste that claims to have no saccharin, preservatives, dyes, or animal ingredients. It also claims low abrasion for teeth.

9 • 6 Protecting Your Eyes and Ears

· ·

The hearing ear and the seeing eye,
the Lord has made both of them.
Proverbs 20:12

God created a beautiful world for you to enjoy. Two of the major ways you connect with His wonderful creation is through your abilities to see and to hear. Unless your own vision or hearing has been impaired in some way, you can't truly relate to those who are blind or deaf. It's very common to take God's gifts of seeing and hearing for granted and to underestimate their importance. By gaining more information not only about your vision but also your hearing, maybe you will begin to appreciate them a little bit more.

Your Eyes

*The lamp of the body is the eye. If therefore your eye is good,
your whole body will be full of light.*
Matthew 6:22

The Bible uses the natural illustration of the eye to illustrate a spiritual truth. What did Jesus mean when He described your eye as the "lamp" of your body? God created your physical eyes to gather information. Your eyes, however, can receive both negative as well as positive input. It's important to protect yourself from the damage caused by negative influences. How might this spiritual truth relate specifically to a teenager like yourself?

God created your physical eyes to gather information. Your eyes, however, can receive both negative as well as positive input.

The ability to see requires the proper function of several important parts of your anatomy. Your eyes rest in bony sockets in your skull called *orbits*. The muscles surrounding your eyes control their movements. Your *eyelids* protect your eyes. You use them automatically to squint when the sun is too bright and to blink when a foreign object gets too close. Even your *eyelashes* and *eyebrows* help to keep small particles and dust from blurring your vision.

The eye itself is made up of seven parts. The tough outer covering is called the *sclera*. You notice this as being the white of the eye. This area protects the inside of the eye. The part of the eye that lets light in is called the *cornea*. The color you see from the outside of your eye is called the *iris*. In the center of the iris is the *pupil*, a dark opening that controls the amount of light that enters. Try an experiment. Go into your bathroom, close the door, turn off the light, and wait for a few moments. Then, get close to the mirror, look straight into it, and turn on the light. Do you see your pupils changing shape? Your pupils enlarge

when it's dark to allow as much light in as possible. When it becomes light again, however, your pupils shrink to screen out some of the brightness.

Once light has entered your pupil, the *lens* behind it allows the light to come into the inner part of your eye. After the light rays pass through the lens, a group of nerves called the *retina* change the light into electrical messages and send it by way of your *optic nerve* to your brain which then creates the image.

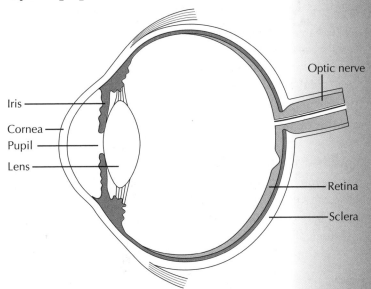

What Can Go Wrong with Your Eyes?

If you have problems with your vision, an eye doctor may prescribe corrective lenses (glasses) to help you to see better. Do you know anyone who uses glasses only for reading or for seeing things close up? These people suffer from a condition called **farsightedness**. If your father or mother has a difficult time seeing traffic signs far away, but they can see close objects very distinctly, they suffer from **nearsightedness**. **Astigmatism** is a condition in which a person's vision is distorted due to the irregular shape of the cornea or lens.

Eye irritations can be very painful. Have you ever suffered from pink eye? **Pink eye** is a very contagious condition caused by a bacterial infection. The thin tissue of the eyelid becomes inflamed, red, and weepy. A sty is different than pink eye, but it's still extremely uncomfortable. A **sty** results when one of the small glands in your eyelid gets infected and swollen. It may look like a pimple but don't touch or pick at it. Place warm compresses on the infected eye, and if it doesn't clear up, see your doctor.

How Well Can You See?

Have you ever had an eye exam? If not, it would be a good idea to have your eyes checked regularly. If you experience frequent headaches, blurred vision, squinting, red or watery eyes, you need to see your eye doctor (*ophthalmologist* or *optometrist*). During your exam, the doctor will:

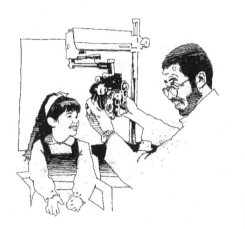

- Examine each eye to make sure the structure and condition of each is healthy.

- Check for early signs of glaucoma (an eye disease).

- Check your vision by having you read an eye chart to determine if you need corrective lenses.

- Check for cataracts (clouding of the lens of the eye). Cataracts need to be surgically removed.

How to Take Good Care of Your Eyes

- Have annual eye exams.

- Eat healthy foods.

- Wear protective eye gear when working with wood or metal.

- Wear protective eye gear in appropriate sporting activities like umpiring baseball or playing racketball.

- Watch television at a good distance and in a well-lit room.

- Read with good light.

- When working on your computer, keep the screen brightness at least three times brighter than that of the room light.

- Keep your eyes a comfortable distance from your computer.

Wear protective eye gear in appropriate sporting activities.

Your Ears

Listen very carefully to the sounds you're hearing right now. Do you hear people talking, birds chirping, lawn mowers running, or cars driving? Did you know that your ability to interpret noises would not be the only benefit that you'd lose if you experienced problems with your ears? You would also lose your sense of physical balance. Your ears are the organs of both hearing and balance.

Recognizing sounds and analyzing their meaning is a very complex process. To enable you to do so, God has given you two ears. Have you ever wondered why God gave us *two* ears but only *one* mouth? Maybe His intention was reflected in the words of the apostle James when he wrote, "Be quick to hear and slow to speak" (1:19)!

Your ears are the organs of both hearing and balance.

There are three parts to each of your ears: the outer, middle, and inner ears. Your outer ear is the part that you see on the outside of your head. Its shape reflects its function of collecting sound waves. When you put an ocean shell up to your ear, you're not hearing sounds of the inside of the shell. Rather, you're hearing the sounds of the blood flowing through your outer ear using the shell as an amplifier. Your *middle ear* is made up of the *eardrum* that separates your middle ear from your outer ear. An important part of each of your ears that stretches from the back of your nose to your middle ear is the *Eustachian tube*. This tube is a small canal that helps to equalize the air pressure in your ear. When you yawn or swallow on an airplane and your ear(s) pops, your Eustachian tube is working for you.

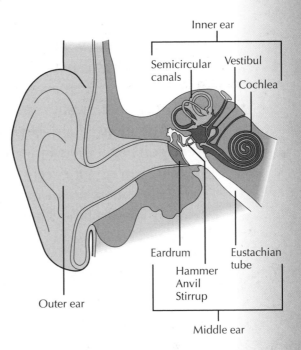

Three tiny bones lie behind your eardrum. They're the *hammer*, *anvil*, and *stirrup*. These small bones connect your eardrum to your inner ear. Your eardrum vibrates from the sound waves that

221

When you yawn or swallow on an airplane and your ear(s) pops, your Eustachian tube is working for you.

hit it. This causes the three small bones to move. The sound then travels to your inner ear. The *inner ear* contains two parts related to hearing (*vestibule* and *cochlea*) and one that aids in balance (*semicircular canals*). The nerves and hair cells in the cochlea carry messages to your brain. The semicircular canals within the inner ear are filled with fluid and lined with hair cells. Each movement you make moves the fluid and the hairs, which then send messages to your brain. Your brain receives the messages and tells your body how to adjust to counteract the movement and maintain balance. If the balance center in your ears wasn't functioning, you'd be continually falling down when you tried to move.

What Can Go Wrong with Your Ears?

Have you ever experienced ear problems? Unless you have, it would be difficult for you to understand the intense pain and distraction that can be caused by improper ear functioning. Imagine being on a plane when your left ear begins to act up. At first, your hearing sounds a little fuzzy, but you attribute it to the altitude. You've flown before; it'll go away soon. Next, your left ear feels plugged. You yawn and swallow many times but nothing seems to help. Then the plugged ear begins to hurt—a dull, throbbing at first. Next, you begin to hear a crackling and ringing in your ear....what next? If you're not careful, you could permanently damage your ear. This can occur in one or both ears and can be the result of flying in an airplane when you have a cold or neglect taking care of an earache.

The most common form of ear trouble is an ear infection. A viral or bacterial infection of the nose, throat, or Eustachian tubes can cause intense ear pain. Unlike a middle-ear infection, swimmer's ear occurs in the outer ear. You're most likely to get swimmer's ear on a hot day when you spend hours in the water. You can help to prevent swimmer's ear by trying earplugs or ear drops and using a hairdryer (on low) to dry out your ears after you swim. Medication is usually prescribed to treat ear infections.

Have you ever spoken extra loudly to a senior citizen because you falsely assumed that all older people were hard of hearing? It was rather embarrassing, wasn't it? Whether old or young, you may know someone who has experienced some hearing loss. It's true that age can contribute to it, but whether partial or complete, hearing loss can be caused by several factors. Ear infections, excess wax build-up, nerve damage caused by loud noises, and injuries can all cause hearing impairment. What do you think would be the number one cause of damage to a teen's hearing? If you guessed loud music, then you were right!

Listening to loud music can cause damage to the eardrum and result in a loss of hearing.

How to Take Good Care of Your Ears

Here's how to care properly for your ears:

- Protect your ears from loud noises. Wear earplugs when mowing your lawn or working with loud machinery.

- Use headphones with care. Keep the volume low; especially if you're going to use them to listen to music, television, or speaking tapes.

- Keep all sharp objects out of your ears. Nothing smaller than your elbow belongs in your ear!

- Cover your ears during high wind or cold. This will help to protect your ears from frostbite as well as infection.

- Keep your ears clean. Use a washcloth on the outer ear. If you have a wax build-up problem, see your physician about ear drops. Don't stick a Q-tip™ into your middle or inner ear.

9 •7 How Do You Stand?

Do you know teens who don't stand up straight or always walk with their heads bent over? If you didn't already know them, a lack of good posture could give you a negative impression about them. How's your *posture*? It's hard to think about whether you're standing tall, walking upright, sitting straight, or properly carrying yourself. Even so, just as good posture enhances your physical appearance, so poor posture can take away from it. Not only is posture important for the way you present yourself to others, it's also important for your good health.

The Benefits of Good Posture

Good posture:

Just as good posture enhances your physical appearance, so poor posture can take away from it.

- makes you more physically attractive,

- opens others to meeting you and becoming your friend,

- improves your breathing efficiency by strengthening the muscles and ligaments you use in breathing,

- reflects a more confident mood and positive self-image to others,

- keeps blood flowing to your brain and helps your circulatory system and internal organs function properly,

- strengthens your bones and muscles, and

- improves your ability to stay alert when sitting for long periods of time like in class.

When you stand, sit, or walk, having good posture makes a statement about who you are and what your attitude is. As taught in self-defense classes, when a young lady walks confidently with a purpose, she is much less likely to be the target of a stranger.

Oftentimes, people who work on a computer or sit at a desk in class tend to sit with their neck projected forward. To examine your own posture, stand in front of a mirror, turn sideways and notice your profile. Are your head and neck falling for-

ward? Is your stomach pushed out? Do you look like you are slouching? Do a "posture check". When you drive in a car, sit in your desk at school, watch TV, eat at a table in a restaurant, or play a computer game, occasionally remind yourself, "Posture check!" When sitting down, always try to have your seat and lower back pushed up against the back of the chair. This will help to prevent undue stress on your lower back muscles and prevent lower back pain.

Have you done a "posture check" lately? How do you sit in class?

How can you improve your posture? Imagine a string with a helium balloon connected to the crown (the very highest part) of your head. Pretend the balloon is pulling straight upward. How does this change your posture? Your chin should go down and your neck come back into proper alignment with your shoulders.

At first, it might feel odd or uncomfortable to change your posture, but it'll be well worth the effort. People will notice something is different about you even though they may not be able to put their finger on it. Good posture changes the way people look at you and how you feel about yourself.

DANGER!

Do you carry a heavy backpack to and from school? Do you swing it over the same shoulder all the time? Although this may seem like a convenient way to carry books, it's possibly damaging your posture. Try to wear the backpack evenly over both shoulders or trade shoulders. Better yet, lighten up and don't carry such a heavy load; finish your homework at school!

Chapter 9 Review

Defining the Terms

Epidermis

Dermis

Subcutaneous layer

Acne

Sebum

Whitehead

Blackhead

Pimple

Dermatologist

Follicle(s)

Dandruff

Head lice

Keratin

Cuticle

Ingrown toenail

Masticate

Periodontium

Cavity

Plaque

Tartar

Gingivitis

Periodontal disease

Malocclusion

Orthodontics

Halitosis

Farsightedness

Nearsightedness

Astigmatism

Pink eye

Sty

Recalling the Facts

1. Why should you take the time to develop good habits of personal hygiene?

2. What is the worst time for your skin to be exposed to the sun during the day? Why?

3. If you get acne, what are five Do's and three Don'ts of caring for your skin?

4. What are the three factors to keep in mind when your hair doesn't seem to cooperate with what you're trying to do, or you just feel it's time for a style change?

5. List the ways to take good care of your teeth.

6. What part of the eye is responsible for controlling the amount of light that enters the eye?

7. What is the most common form of ear trouble?

8. How might a person do a "posture check" on him/herself?

9. What might you tell a friend who wants to stop biting his/her fingernails?

Applying the Truth

1.   *The lamp of the body is the eye. If therefore your eye is good,*
      your whole body will be full of light.

                        Matthew 6:22

   The Bible uses the natural illustration of the eye to illustrate a
   spiritual truth. What did Jesus mean when He described your
   eye as the "lamp" of your body? How might this spiritual truth
   relate specifically to a teenager like yourself?

2. Read James 1;19-20. Why do you think the Bible addresses the
   issue of anger? What might listening and speaking have to do
   with getting angry?

3. Read Proverbs 20:12. God has made both your eyes and ears.
   How do you think that you can use your eyes and ears the most
   to please God?

"...and do not be drunk
with wine...but be filled
with the Spirit."
Ephesians 5:18

LIVING THE SUPERNATURAL HIGH 10

10 • 1 Why Some Christian Teens Abuse Substances

Tim was raised in a Christian home, attended a private school, and was involved in his youth group. His parents were ordained ministers, and his family was well-respected in the church. Tim was outgoing and popular with the other students but distant and aloof with his teachers. He earned excellent grades and seemed to say and do all the "right" things. Many of Tim's friends, however, were concerned about him. They said he would joke about how much he disliked his parents and the school. "I can't wait to get outta here..." he would tell his buddies. People who really knew Tim described him as a "walking time bomb—ready to explode". After graduation from high school, Tim rejected all of the boundaries that his parents, church, and school had tried to teach him for his own safety and happiness. He abused his new found freedom. He thought that exercising his independence was

the answer to all of his inner frustrations. He began to "do his own thing". Tim became involved with premarital sex, drugs, and alcohol.

How do you think this could happen to a teenager who had godly parents and a strong youth group? What do you think happened to all of the Christian teaching that Tim received as a young person? No one knew what was going on in Tim's mind and heart all those years as he was growing up. What was his relationship like with his parents? How did he feel toward God? How did he really feel about the Bible? Could what happened to Tim possibly happen to you or to one of your friends? Sometimes, teens make dark and dangerous choices. Many have to hit rock-bottom before they look up and ask God to help them change the course of their lives. Unfortunately, some don't ever make it back.

What do you think are some of the reasons that even some Christian teens choose to try drugs, alcohol, or tobacco?

What do you think are some of the reasons that even some Christian teens choose to try drugs, alcohol, or tobacco? Many factors influence a teenager's decisions. A teen's lack of personal convictions makes him/her extra vulnerable to curiosity and negative peer pressure. For most teens, listening to lectures from their parents or memorizing Scripture verses just aren't enough. Many young people experience incredible stress, abuse, neglect, and a lack of quality relationships. They don't feel accepted or affirmed as they are. They haven't been able to feel God's love. In an attempt to feel better about themselves, they try addictive substances. Teens use them to try to escape or "fit in".

The following are eight reasons why some teens may choose to use addictive substances. See if you relate to any of the teen comments made by your peers.

1. Freedom Without Responsibility

When I grow up, I'm looking forward to my freedom.

John

Many teens look forward to the ever-increasing freedoms they'll have as they get older. This is a normal and natural desire. It's a healthy aspiration because it's an essential part of your transition into adulthood. Did you know that God has a "Freedom Formula"? It is: show responsibility, gain freedom; show more responsibility, gain more freedom. According to this "Freedom Formula", freedom is something that a teen *earns*, not demands.

Which of the following statements best describes what gaining freedom means to you?

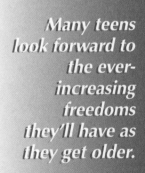

- Doing what you want as long as it's legal.

- Doing what you want as long as you don't think that it hurts anyone else.

- Doing what you want just so you don't get caught.

- Doing what your friends feel is okay.

- Doing what your conscience allows.

- Doing what you want as long as it's in the privacy of your own home.

- Doing what is right with the desire and power to live within God's boundaries?

One reason why your parents have such a hard time with your transition into adulthood is because they must "let go". Since they feel that most of the choices that they've made for you up to this point have kept you safe and happy, they struggle with giving you the reins. They don't want you to make a serious mistake or hurt yourself. One mother put it this way when her son received his driver's license on his sixteenth birthday, "David, it's not that I don't trust you, I don't trust the other drivers on the road." In giving her son the freedom that comes with driving, this mother struggled with relying on the trust that she had built with her son as well as her trust in God's protection for him.

Many teens look forward to the ever-increasing freedoms they'll have as they get older.

How can teens' increasing sense of personal freedom contribute to their desire to try dangerous substances? First, teens' increased freedom gives them more time and exposure to learn about addictive substances. Some teens wonder, "What would drugs be like? How could just one time hurt me?" It's natural for you as a teen to have a general curiosity about life. It motivates you to learn more about the world that God created. But, a curiosity without spiritual and moral boundaries can be very dangerous (Genesis 3:6). Second, more freedom gives teens a greater opportunity to discover and express their own individuality. While many teens choose "way out" clothing styles or haircuts, some experiment with the more serious "forbidden fruit" and find themselves being trapped by drugs, tobacco, or alcohol. They find that the substance trap is more than just losing control of their lives to an addictive chemical. They discover that they are being dragged into the lifestyle of an addict; a cycle of *shame, secrecy,* and *loss of control.* The sad fact is that they lose the very freedom that they sought in the first place.

> *The sad fact is that the teens who experiment with drugs lose the very freedom that they sought in the first place.*

As you mature, God will give you the freedom to think any thought, harbor any feeling, or make any decision you want. You must be willing, however, to experience the consequences of each of your choices.

2. A Lack of Personal Convictions

The hardest thing about being a Christian is the rules.

Ashley

Ashley feels that the Christian life is difficult because of the "rules". Do you ever feel tired of always having other people tell you what

DANGER!

Try to remember:

- Freedom requires responsibility.
- Responsibility involves accountability.
- All choices have consequences.

to do or not to do? Think about Tim. He had strong Christian parents who thought that the rules they were enforcing at home were going to be enough to prevent their son from experimenting with drugs and alcohol.

Once Tim left home and graduated from high school—once the boundaries were lifted—there was nothing *inside of him* to stop him from making hurtful choices. Tim never formed his own convictions about his parent's or teacher's rules. That is why it's so important that you begin to form your own personal **convictions** (strong beliefs) about different issues now. The rules that your parents or school set for you are to help guide you while you're strength-

ening your biblical convictions. Your personal convictions about drugs, alcohol, and tobacco may have already been tested. If you resisted, good job!

The rules that your parents or school set for you are to help guide you.

To make it through all of the temptations in today's culture, you must (1) "own" your own faith, (2) develop your own personal relationship with God, and (3) begin to make your own decisions about the issues that confront you according to your Christian convictions. Hopefully, you will draw from your parent's wisdom and the Scriptures as you grow.

3. An Attempt to Reduce Stress

I am so stressed out about my friends, schoolwork, and my parents.

Angie

Do the pressures from your friends, family, and school ever over-whelm you? Today, many teens face similar stresses as those of adults: family responsibilities, consequences of divorce, death of loved ones, culture's pressure to conform to a fast-paced lifestyle, high expectations, and even some financial pressures. As a re-sult, many teens turn to drugs and alcohol to escape the stress. Even though it may seem that drugs and/or alcohol lessen the

stress load, the relief is only superficial and temporary. Very quickly, chemical substances create a whole new set of problems and pressures in a teen's life.

Sin is packaged very appealingly in our culture, and it carries a promise of immediate satisfaction. That is why so many choose sin—it offers instant gratification. Right choices, on the other hand, often require postponing immediate satisfaction for better long-term benefits. Truth has a tough time competing with counterfeits for this reason. But, a counterfeit is still a counterfeit— a substitution for the original. And far too many of our youth are suffering the consequences of choosing harmful substitutes.[1]

To whom can you turn when life's pressures get too great? You can share your struggles with:

Do the pressures from friends, family, or school ever overwhelm you? Try to talk about your stresses with someone you trust.

- Your parents. It might seem hard right now, but they used to be teenagers themselves. If you're honest with them about your needs, they'll probably become more sensitive to you.

- Your pastor or youth pastor. He/she has probably been through similar experiences. He/she can be a good friend by listening to you, calling you, and praying for you.

- A professional Christian counselor. You might need to talk to a counselor at one time or another. Have your parents help you find the "right" one to help you and your parents communicate effectively.

- An adult you trust. Find a solid Christian adult who is mature and understanding.

- A school counselor. Some school counselors can really help because they're aware of the different stresses that are unique with a school environment.

- Your favorite teacher. A teacher at school whom you trust might really be handy to talk to when you need to vent your frustrations and receive encouragement.

- Jesus. To a lot of teens, Jesus is far, far away. But, if you'll turn to Him, you'll find Him right inside of your heart. As you share your feelings with Him, He'll share His thoughts with you, too. He loves you more than you can imagine. He simply wants a re- lationship with you. You don't have to spend a lot of time "praying"; just start talking to Him briefly here and there during the day. Ask Him for His help, advice, encouragement, and comfort—whatever you need. He is say- ing to you,

> *Come to Me…you who labor and are heavy laden, and I will*
> *give you rest…[With Me], you'll find rest for your souls.*
> Matthew 11:28, 29

Be brave! Take the natural opportunities of vacations, sports activities, and fishing trips to bring up sensitive issues with your parents.

4. Not Seeing the Bible as a Practical Guide

> *Just because the Bible says things are wrong,*
> *that doesn't mean I won't do them.*
>
> Megan

How do you feel about what the Bible says is good and moral? It's during this intense time of your life that the Word of God in your heart will be tested. Are you tired of people quoting Bible verses at you? Do you ever get frustrated when some Christians avoid talking about issues but instead just repeat, "Because the Bible says so…"? Even when everything that people tell you is abso- lutely true, rules enforced from the Bible, without you having a *loving relationship* with God, can lead you to rebel against your faith and everything you've been taught. This was part of Tim's problem. His parents and teachers had told him what the Bible said to do and not to do, but Tim never accepted it for himself. To him, the Bible was just an irrelevant book of harsh rules from a legalistic God enforced by overly-strict parents.

Many teens have a hard time believing that the Bible contains very workable and practical answers for their lives, but it does. The Bible gives you such practical advice as how to:

Many teens have a hard time believing that the Bible contains very workable and practical answers for their lives, but it does.

- avoid an argument with your parents (Proverbs 17:14);

- have lots of friends (Proverbs 18:24);

- earn money for a bike or car (Proverbs 10:4-6);

- choose the best boyfriend (Proverbs 22:24); and

- choose the best girlfriend (Proverbs 19:14; 31:10-31).

How practical is the Bible to you? Do you ever find yourself doubting that God's promises are for you? Doubts can actually be your friends when you bring them sincerely and honestly to God. He understands your doubts, and because He's much bigger than all of them put together, He will show you the answers that you honestly seek. It's easy, however, to focus only on all of the negative aspects of your life and not see the "whole picture" as God sees it. It can be difficult to believe that He always has your best in mind. God's desire is that you become like Christ. Sometimes, this goal leads you down a difficult, character-developing road. God isn't as concerned about what you're experiencing as much as He's concerned about how you respond to it. He's always there to give you the strength that you need to make it.

5. Negative Peer Pressure

What if you get dared to do something dangerous, but you don't want to do it? What if others laugh at you? What do you do?

David

The pressure you feel from your peers to take dangerous risks can be very strong. Many teens give in to their first drink or their first cigarette because they wanted to "fit in" with their friends. Their need to be "cool" or accepted can become a major hindrance to their Christian life. It's a pressure that won't go away—even after you graduate from high school. The pressure to conform to your social group is called by a name out of the animal kingdom; it's called the "herd mentality". As individual animals unthinkingly follow their flock or herd, so teens are tempted to imitate their social group in clothes, haircuts, music, language, and values. Many teens claim that they're trying to express their individuality while all they're doing is thinking, looking, and acting exactly like everyone else in their group.

God created you unique. He made you with your own special personality, tastes, gifts, and opinions. True, it's harder to stand up for yourself and be different than the "herd". If being like others, however, means you must lower your Christian standards or go against you own convictions, then you're allowing others to lead your life for you. If some of your friends actually encourage you to do activities that you don't feel comfortable doing, then ask God to bring better friends into your life.

6. Greedy Culture

I enjoy reading teen magazines and like to keep up on what's "hot".

Jenny

Our culture has a very strong influence upon the choices you make. The billboards, TV commercials, movies, radio spots, newspapers, and teen magazines, are all trying to lure you into a particular lifestyle; a lifestyle that will require you to buy their particular products and services. The next time you see an ad, ask yourself, "What kind of value-message is this ad trying to communicate to me? What kind of 'cool image' or 'fun' does this ad promise me if I

The next time you see an ad, ask yourself, "What kind of value-message is this ad trying to communicate to me?"

buy their product?" Since our society is based upon meeting the needs of the consumer by getting people to buy products and services, anyone who tries to expose the negative consequences of such purchases as tobacco, alcohol, or pornography is going against the financial flow. How often, for example, have you seen lung cancer patients on TV experiencing the negative side effects of chemotherapy or radiation? The sad fact is that companies purposely hide the unhealthy consequences of their products and services because they're more interested in your money than in your health!

LOGON!

It's About Time!

The government has begun to get tough with the tobacco industry for promoting a product that causes addiction and death among its users. This took years of people suing the tobacco companies for false advertising and for increasing the addictive chemical (nicotine) in tobacco rather than decreasing it. You've probably seen the "tough and cool" image portrayed by the Marlboro™ cowboy who used to sell that brand of cigarettes. Did you know that the original Marlboro™ cowboy has emphysema? This is why the "Bob, I've got emphysema" billboard has replaced the pro-smoking ad.

7. Overly-Critical Parents

My parents hold too high of a standard for me. I can never seem to reach it. They're always disappointed in me.

Patrick

Do you think that your parents sometimes put too much pressure on you? Do you feel that some of your parent's expectations of you are too high? Although some parents are intentionally hard on their teens, many parents can't see the negative results of their harsh parenting style. Unfortunately, many teens experiment with drugs and alcohol just to hurt—or get the attention of—their parents. Some hang around the wrong crowd in an effort to make an unspoken statement to their parents about their rules. In the end, this hurts the teen the most, because it's their life that is being directly damaged by the behavior. Do you think that your relationship with your parents is so tense that it's causing you to seek out drugs, alcohol, or tobacco?

Do you ever feel that the arguments and misunderstandings at home are unbearable? One reason you might feel this is because of all of the physical and emotional changes that you're now experiencing. Whenever anyone is physically tired, their capacity to get along with others greatly decreases. Even when getting along with those at home gets difficult, try not to give up. Overall, parents can be a big help to you during your teen years. When you feel that your parents don't really seem to understand you, still attempt to maintain the relationship with as much open communication as possible. All quality relationships require hard work!

Do you ever feel that the arguments and misunderstandings at home are unbearable? One reason you might feel this is because of all of the physical and emotional changes that you're now experiencing.

> *I used to hate my parents and think they were trying to make my life miserable. Now, I know they were doing it because they loved me.*
>
> Amy

I'm sure Amy still has some "heated" moments of disagreement with her parents, but somehow she has worked it out so that her outlook toward them is more positive. It might be good to ask yourself the following question every now and then, "Have I said or done anything to hurt my parents? If so, how can I resolve it?" Apologize whenever you're disrespectful, ungrateful, aloof, or demanding toward your parents. If you feel you've let them down because you have not met their high expectations, even though you were doing your best, don't apologize, but communicate honestly about how you feel. Your parents want to enjoy a good relationship with you, but they don't always know how. Try to understand that a parent's inability to relate to their children many times comes from the way their parents (your grandparents) related to them.

8. Wrong Concept of God

My relationship with God is the hardest thing for me right now. I feel like whatever I do, I can't have a strong walk with Him. I've messed up so many times, I feel like I'm taking advantage of the words "I'm sorry".

Jasmine

Close your eyes for a moment. How do you see God? Do you see Him as a mean policeman who's standing over you with a big club in His hand ready to belt you whenever you make a mistake? Do you view God as being so disappointed in you that He's purposely withholding His love or presence from you? Or, do you see God as so full of love that He'd love you the same no matter what your struggles (Romans 8:35,38,39)?

The way you perceive God has much to do with the choices you make. Just because God may not be pleased with some of your attitudes, thoughts, or actions, it doesn't mean that He doesn't deeply value you. It's true that nothing can separate you from the love of God, but your choices can help or hinder your personal relationship with Him. When Adam and Eve sinned in the garden, they tried to hide from God. Although God was not pleased with them, He called for them and wanted to help them. God even took the initiative and sent His own Son, Jesus, to suffer death on a cross, to pay the price for your sin, in order to restore your relationship with Him which Adam and Eve had destroyed. God does care for you and wants you to know that He desires that you tell Him all of your failures and temptations, and ask for His strength to overcome. When you're real with Him, He'll be real with you.

One time when I was praying, I didn't feel open to talk to God. Then, I realized that I was keeping something from Him. I thought He would think it was stupid, so I didn't bring it up. Finally, I said, "God, I really want to win the lottery!" After I was honest with God about this, I felt totally free inside, and that God didn't think I was stupid for asking. I went on to pray about lots of other concerns, and I felt close to God again.

John

10 • 2 Alcohol: A Depressing Story

• •

What's the Big Deal?

Mary had a lot of friends and seemed to be an out-going, popular teenager. She was the middle child in a large family where fearing God and "doing right" was very important. "When we were your age, we never even thought about doing some of the things that you kids do today", was a common response from her parents. Mary felt that talking to her parents about her drinking was out of the question. Besides, drinking seemed harmless and made her feel more accepted and popular with her friends. Mary chose to drink because it lowered her inhibitions and made her feel more outgoing. "I can stop drinking whenever I feel like it", she reasoned. After a few years of social drinking, some of the consequences of her habit began to surface. One night at a party, Mary had too much to drink. She wasn't thinking straight and couldn't physically protect herself from a young man. Mary lost her virginity that night to a guy she didn't even care about. The next morning she woke up with a hangover and a deep emptiness inside. Mary didn't tell anyone about losing her virginity. She didn't seek help for her drinking problem either. She just kept drinking to try to escape her disappointments and hurts.

Unfortunately, Mary's story is common among teenagers who drink alcohol or use drugs. Teens don't intentionally drink so they'll have an "excuse" to do something they'll regret later. The results of drinking, however, easily result in participation in activities that are dangerous and harmful. Some teens start drinking by thinking, "What's the big deal? I'm not going to get drunk or become an alcoholic". In the following section, we look at some of the reasons why it *is* a big deal if you start drinking alcohol.

> ## DANGER!
>
> Conservative estimates show that there are over five million persons in the United States with a severe alcohol problem. Such statistics mean that alcohol abuse is among the foremost health problems of this country and the world. Although very few adolescents report signs of alcohol dependence, approximately 31% of 10th through 12th graders report drunkenness at least six times a year. Studies show that the incidence increases dramatically on college campuses.[2]

The Negative Effects of Alcohol

No matter what a person's original intention concerning alcohol is, the immediate effects of alcohol on the body are obvious when a person drinks too much. They include slurred speech, inability to walk straight, forgetfulness, and acting obnoxious. Others who drink might endanger themselves and others by driving drunk, assaulting someone, or, at the very least, embarrassing themselves in front of others.

When she drank, Mary found herself doing things she would not normally do.

The health problems that begin to result from drinking alcohol are not as visible as the outward behavior problems. Ethyl alcohol (ethanol) is the active ingredient in alcoholic beverages. When a person drinks alcohol, the ethanol is absorbed rapidly into the bloodstream. It stays in the bloodstream until the liver removes it from the body. The liver, however, can't handle the constant duty of removing this toxin. With too much drinking, a chronic disease of the liver occurs which is called **cirrhosis**. In cirrhosis, fibrous tissue invades and replaces normal tissues in this vital organ, disrupting digestion and detoxification (cleansing).

Alcohol also damages the central nervous system by acting like a depressant. Although people think that alcohol makes a person laugh and feel happy, it actually depresses one's system. Mary learned that her drinking lowered her inhibitions. The outgoing behavior you often associate with people who drink results from the blocking of the center of the brain that controls a person's degree of self-control and shyness. This is known as the **inhibitory effect** of alcohol. As a result, some people who are normally shy "come out of their

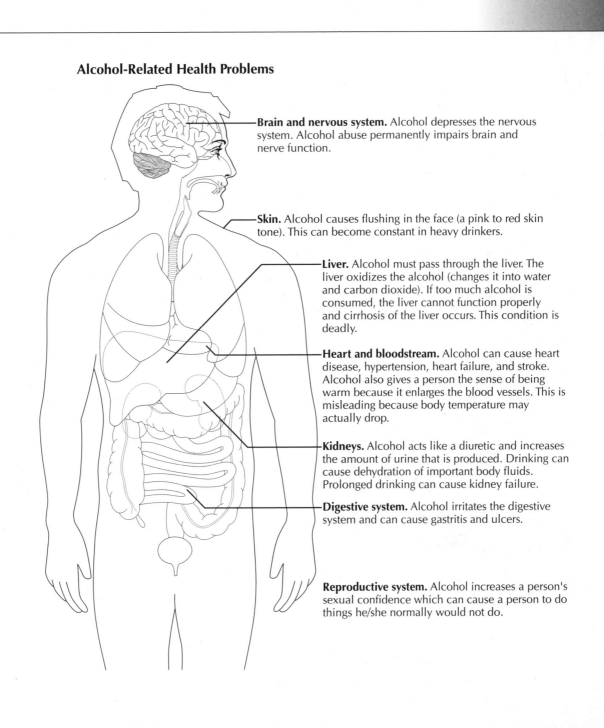

Alcohol-Related Health Problems

Brain and nervous system. Alcohol depresses the nervous system. Alcohol abuse permanently impairs brain and nerve function.

Skin. Alcohol causes flushing in the face (a pink to red skin tone). This can become constant in heavy drinkers.

Liver. Alcohol must pass through the liver. The liver oxidizes the alcohol (changes it into water and carbon dioxide). If too much alcohol is consumed, the liver cannot function properly and cirrhosis of the liver occurs. This condition is deadly.

Heart and bloodstream. Alcohol can cause heart disease, hypertension, heart failure, and stroke. Alcohol also gives a person the sense of being warm because it enlarges the blood vessels. This is misleading because body temperature may actually drop.

Kidneys. Alcohol acts like a diuretic and increases the amount of urine that is produced. Drinking can cause dehydration of important body fluids. Prolonged drinking can cause kidney failure.

Digestive system. Alcohol irritates the digestive system and can cause gastritis and ulcers.

Reproductive system. Alcohol increases a person's sexual confidence which can cause a person to do things he/she normally would not do.

shell" and act in ways that they would not normally behave. When she drank, Mary found herself doing things she would not normally do. Due to over-drinking, Mary lost her virginity, a part of herself that she could never regain. The use of alcohol not only

destroys your physical body, it also damages your relationships with others, your view of God, and your self-respect. Next time you're tempted to experiment with alcohol, ask yourself, "Is it really worth it?"

Alcohol and the Bible

Alcohol has been used and abused since the time of its earliest recorded history. Until about five hundred years ago, alcoholic drinks were made primarily by the fermentation of fruit juices. Although fermented alcohol could alter an individual's mood, it wasn't until the process of distillation was invented that alcohol became more potent and more destructive. Drinks containing distilled alcohol have a much higher alcohol content than drinks containing fermented alcohol.[3]

Today, drinking is often associated with being sophisticated and "cool." This false image often causes teens to try their first drink.

In the Bible, drinking wine (fermented grape juice) was not a sin. But, drinking too much of it was. Throughout the Bible, God warns us about the dangers of drinking in excess. Noah, for example, got drunk and took his clothes off in his tent. His sons had to come in and cover him up (Genesis 9:21-23). Hundreds of years later, God judged drunkenness in His people in the prophet Joel's day (Joel 1:5). Jesus, too, warned the people about how drunkenness would make them unprepared for the Last Day (Luke 21:34-36).

King Solomon gave the best description of the various consequences of drinking too much wine in Proverbs 23:29-35. Read this entire passage and list how many more consequences of drunkenness you can count besides the ones included in the partial quotation below.

Who has woe? Who has sorrow? Who has contentions? Who has complaints? Who has wounds without [knowing the] cause? Who has redness of eyes? Those who linger long at the wine.... In the end, it will bite like a serpent and sting like a viper. Your eyes will see strange things, and your heart will utter perverse things.

Knowing what the Bible says about drinking may not be enough to keep you from trying alcohol. Be sure to remember, however, that

244

DANGER!

You may not be aware of it, but there's alcohol in many of the medicines people use today. Many cold medicines and cough syrups contain various levels of alcohol. Make sure you read the label before taking any medication. Alcohol in any form should not be mixed with any medications. Never take more than the recommended dose on the label.

God's warnings are always for your own spiritual and physical benefit. Because God loves and cares for you so much, He doesn't want anything to hurt you or to cause you to waste your life.

Paul, the apostle, gave the spiritual alternative to alcohol consumption when he wrote:

...be not drunk with wine, in which is dissipation [degradation/ easy excess], but be filled with the Holy Spirit.
Ephesians 5:18

When Christians focus upon being filled with the Holy Spirit, they don't feel the need for any other stimulus to bring excitement or fulfillment to their lives.

Although you may not intend to become a "drinker", studies show that people who begin drinking alcohol at an early age are more likely to become addicted to alcohol later in life.

What about Alcoholism?

Some view **alcoholism**, or alcohol dependence, as an *illness* characterized by habitual, compulsive, long-term, and heavy drinking. You may only think of a bum on skid row as being an alcoholic, but two criteria determine a person's alcohol dependence: tolerance and withdrawal. When people drink alcohol for awhile, their bodies build up a resistance to its effects. This resistance is referred to as a **tolerance level**. For example, the person who can drink ten beers and not show signs of intoxication has a higher tolerance level than a person who starts slurring his words after drinking two beers. **Withdrawal** refers to the physical disturbance that results when the individual does not consume the alcohol. "Morn-

ing shakes" and DTs (delirium tremens) are the worst well-known forms of withdrawal.[4]

For many teens, drinking alcohol is a social activity. Lots of teens don't even enjoy the taste of liquor. They just drink to "fit in", be accepted, or look "cool". Although you may not intend to become a "drinker", studies show that people who begin drinking alcohol at an early age are more likely to become addicted to alcohol later in life. Research also connects alcoholism to some individuals who have a history of alcohol abuse in their family. If you feel that you may be susceptible to developing a drinking problem—whatever the contributing factors—the safest choice for you to make now is not to take that first drink. If you'll say a clear "No" to alcohol, then you can live the rest of your life worry-free from this deadly addiction.

Alcohol and the Media

Dennis spent the night at Nick's house. After he woke up, Dennis spent the whole morning with his head hung over the toilet vomiting. From outside the bathroom door, Nick exclaimed, "Wasn't the party last night great? Let's do it again tonight!"

The media rarely shows you the negative effects of alcohol. The reason is simply because the media is driven by its financial sponsors (the companies who pay them to promote their products to consumers). The next time you see alcohol linked with fun, popularity, or happiness, remember the sad fact that advertisers don't care about your health or sanity, they only care about your money!

Have you ever seen a movie that accurately showed an alcoholic go through an alcohol treatment program? Does Hollywood make a point to report how many car accidents and deaths drunk drivers cause each year? **MADD** (Mothers Against Drunk Driving) began by mothers who had lost their own children from those driving under the influence. True, society encourages you not to drink and drive. But

True, society encourages you not to drink and drive. But it doesn't encourage you to stay away from alcohol altogether.

it doesn't encourage you to stay away from alcohol altogether. The advertiser-driven image that still remains in the minds of many teenagers is: "It'll be okay to drink when I'm old enough, just as long as I have a designated driver to take me home."

Before you decide to drink a beer or a glass of hard liquor, think through your decision very carefully. Don't allow society to lure you into believing that it's cool or socially acceptable to get drunk— or to start a habit that can destroy your health, job, and marriage.

Before You Decide to Take Your First Drink, Consider the Following:

- Alcohol claims the most lives in the 15-24 year age group (22,000 deaths per year).
- The average beginning age for alcohol consumption is 12-12.5 years old.
- The decision to drink alcohol is made two years prior to the first drink.
- Five out of seven who try alcohol will abuse it.
- One out of seven who try alcohol will become dependent (14-17%).
- One reason alcohol abuse is such a problem is because alcohol isn't viewed as a drug, which it is. In reality, when people get drunk, they've had a drug overdose. When people are alcoholics, they have a drug addiction.

Where Can a Person Get Help?

You don't need to be an alcoholic to experience the turmoil that alcohol dependence brings to a family. When any family member suffers from this addiction, it adversely affects everyone else in the family. If you have an alcoholic Dad, Mom, friend, or relative, you may be afraid to invite your friends over to your home out of fear of embarrassment. Every time you're around your alcoholic relative, you may also feel like you're "walking on eggshells". You don't want to say or do anything that will set off an emotional eruption. If the alcoholic (and the close relatives of the alcoholic) don't get help, the drug dependency can destroy the entire family.

There are support groups specifically designed for alcoholics and their families. **Alcoholics Anonymous** ("AA") helps alcoholics beat their addiction. **Alateen** is a group designed to help children of

alcoholic parents. **Al-Anon** is another group that helps the husbands, wives, and friends of alcoholics. Don't be silent if you suspect that someone in your home or a friend suffers from alcohol dependence. Confiding in a safe adult and attending meetings on your own will help you to deal with the problems that often follow the families of alcoholics.

10 • 3 Drugs: A Substitute for the Real Thing

I would never use drugs!

Jay

I asked hundreds of Christian teens the question, "How do you feel about taking drugs?" All of them responded like Jay: "I would never use drugs!" If I asked Jay the same question ten years from now, what do you think are the chances that he would give the same response? It's good to know that many Christian teenagers say "No" to drugs. There are, however, some teens who are already experimenting with drugs or who will choose drugs when they get a few years older.

When referring to drugs, most teens think of illegal drugs. There are also, however, drugs that are legal. Where would the health care establishment be without antibiotics and immunizations? Whenever you suffer from an ear infection, you can be very grateful to **Alexander Fleming** who discovered penicillin in London (1928) and ushered in the "antibiotic age". **Drugs** are substances that alter the function of one or more body organs, the mind, or the process of a disease. Many foods contain small quantities of substances that are considered drugs. Coffee, some teas, and cola drinks contain caffeine, which is both a stimulant and a diuretic (a drug that increases urination). A drug can also be considered a medicine. **Medicines** are drugs that are meant to relieve pain, cure diseases, or prevent other illnesses. Any legal drug can be dangerous if a person doesn't use it correctly. **Drug abuse** occurs when a person uses an illegal drug or misuses a legal one.

Prescription and Nonprescription Drugs

You may be very familiar with **prescription drugs** (drugs that are to be sold only with a written order from a doctor). **Nonprescription** drugs or "over-the-counter" drugs are medicines that can be sold without a doctor's written permission. Over-the-counter drugs are generally weaker in strength but still should be taken carefully by the consumer. Before a drug can "get on the market" or be sold to the consumer, it must be approved by the FDA (Food and Drug Administration). The FDA tests these drugs to make sure they're safe. What's scary is the fact that even after FDA approval and years of consumer usage, some drugs have had to be taken off the market after serious dangers were observed about their effectiveness or safety.

To be a wise consumer and a responsible individual, make sure you read the entire label of both prescription and nonprescription drugs. Follow the directions carefully. Never take more of a drug than is directed. If you experience any **side effects** (any reactions to a drug other than the intended effect), stop taking the drug and contact your doctor. Negative side effects such as upset stomach, headache, extreme drowsiness, or dizziness, may indicate that you're allergic to the medicine; in which case, you'll be given an alternative medicine.

To be a wise consumer and a responsible individual, make sure you read the entire label of both prescription and nonprescription drugs.

DANGER!

- Never share prescription drugs.
- Never mix drugs (either prescription or nonprescription).
- Never leave drugs out on the counter or with the lids off.
- Never use a drug after its expiration date. Flush pills down the toilet.
- Never mix drugs with any kind of alcohol.
- Never take a medication without first carefully reading the label.

Stimulants can speed up the nervous system in such a way that the body cannot handle the stress.

The Roller Coaster Ride of Stimulants and Depressants

Do you ever drink too much coffee, tea, or cola? If so, other than having to use the restroom a lot more, you'd also have experienced some stimulation of your body's nervous system. Although you wouldn't think of coffee or cola as being drugs, they do contain **caffeine** which is considered a stimulant.

Stimulants are drugs that speed up the body's nervous system. They cause the heart to beat faster, blood pressure to rise, and breathing rate to increase. Amphetamines, cocaine, crack, and caffeine are all stimulants. After drinking too much coffee, you may feel jittery, agitated, or excited. Abuse of stimulants can cause damage to your body and even result in death.

Like any drug, a person can become addicted to a stimulant. That means that it's possible for you to get addicted to coffee, tea, or cola. An **addiction** is a physical and/or mental need for a drug or other substance. You may mistake an addiction to the caffeine in cola or coffee with having a strong craving for it. Your craving is really an addiction if you always "feel better" after you drink it.

Being addicted to a drug can be both a mental as well as a physical experience. First, let's look at the mental aspect. Think for a moment about the class you have just before lunchtime. What do you think about? Are you able fully to concentrate upon what your teacher is saying, or are you thinking about what kind of pop you're going to drink with your lunch? Let's imagine…

When the clock hits noon, you spring to your feet. You run to your locker to put your books away. You dash to the pop machine, shove the coins down the slot, and make your selection. As you take your first few gulps, how do you feel? All of your anxieties disappear—temporarily, that is, until your mind wants another cola. For a few moments, you're able to enjoy your cola as something familiar and comforting.

This is an everyday example of a mental dependence. Your mind and emotions are so connected to this substance that you now have a drug habit!

Next, let's look at the physical aspect of such an addiction. Imagine that it's midafternoon and…

You're getting bored in class. You haven't had any pop since lunch. You start to feel a dull, throbbing headache. Your whole body begins to feel weak and tired. You can't wait for school to get out. When the final bell rings, you speed to the cafeteria, pump in the quarters, and grab another cola. After all, it's your favorite flavor. You guzzle it down. Your headache disappears, and you have a new burst of energy!

Many people find it too difficult to give up coffee or cola. This dependence is really a physical and mental addiction.

You just experienced physical dependence. Your body showed signs of withdrawal as it needed more caffeine. When you satisfied your body's craving, you experienced relief—temporarily, that is—until your body needs another "fix".

Although this cola scenario might seem trivial to you, it's good to remember that your body will adapt to caffeine just as a drug user's body will adapt to harder and harder substances. On any level, the degree of withdrawal symptoms that you experience are directly related to the strength of the drug and how much you use it. The more cola, tea, or coffee you drink, the greater will be your body's demand. To keep yourself sober from a "caffeine high", stop drinking it for a couple of months and see if your body feels any healthier. If it does, it might be worth it to you to "kick" the caffeine habit.

Depressants are drugs that tend to slow down your body's nervous system. They cause your heart to beat more slowly, your blood pressure to drop, and your breathing rate to decrease. If you took a medication that contained a depressant, you would experience drowsiness and sleepiness. Barbiturates, sedatives, and tranquilizers are depressants. Some depressants are prescribed by doctors for people who have a hard time sleeping (insomnia). In an attempt to increase their energy level, many who become addicted to depressants also become addicted to stimulants. Such an up-and-down cycle is very dangerous for the nervous system and puts a great strain on the body.

Narcotics are depressants that induce sleep or decrease feeling. Many doctors prescribe the narcotics **morphine** and **codeine** to patients as painkillers. Because these narcotics are highly addictive, they're not available over-the-counter but only through a doctor's prescription. **Heroin** is an illegal drug that is extremely dangerous. It's a depressant because it's made from the same source as morphine. Heroine is often mixed with other substances such as cornstarch and strychnine (poison). A heroine user will easily become addicted and experience intense withdrawal symptoms.

Even "one try" of an illegal drug can result in addiction or death.

Marijuana, Hallucinogens, and Inhalants

The most commonly used illegal or "street drug" is marijuana. Marijuana is made from the hemp plant. It's used in the form of a tobacco, but its ingredients are far more dangerous than regular tobacco. Marijuana contains over 400 different chemicals. It has four to five times the number of toxins as tobacco. Some of the States are legislating that terminally ill patients be able legally to use marijuana to reduce their level of pain.

Marijuana's Negative Effects on Users:

- Causes irregular heartbeat

- Increases hunger

- Slows down the body's rate of development

- Lowers body temperature

- Impairs perception and response time

- Damages the immune system

- Hurts the reproductive system

- Injures brain cells

- Distorts reality

One marijuana joint contains 421 poisons!

LOGON!

Marijuana Facts

- One marijuana joint contains 421 chemicals (poisons). The one chemical that causes the "high" effect is THC (tetrahydrocannabinol).
- The marijuana today has 10-20 times more THC than the marijuana of ten years ago.
- The average beginning age for marijuana use is eleven to twelve years old.
- Four out of ten twelve-year-olds who try marijuana once are still using it in their twenties. This fact shows how important it is not to try it "just this once".
- The use of marijuana twice per week for a period of four months will lower the critical energy of each cell in the body. In the brain, the critical energy is lowered 20-25%.

Hallucinogens

Hallucinogens are a group of drugs that cause the brain to form unreal images. **PCP** (phencyclidine) and **LSD** (lysergic acid diethylamide) are two dangerous hallucinogens. The negative effects of PCP (angel dust) can last a long time. Some of their side effects include a false feeling of super power, a loss of muscle control and coordination, and a loss of the feeling of pain. The combination of these effects can cause a PCP user to participate in dangerous and high-risk behavior.

LSD (acid) is an extremely unpredictable drug. Even after the drug hasn't been taken for awhile, the user can still experience flashbacks (reoccurring effects of the drug). Because the dangers of LSD and PCP have been well-advertised, their use has dropped.

Inhalants

Some young people have experimented with harmful inhalants. **Inhalants** are substances whose fumes are breathed in to give the user a high-like feeling. One of the reasons that teens have tried these drugs is because of their availability and ease of use. The inhalation of paint thinner and airplane glue are two examples. If you've ever glued a plastic model together or painted a room without adequate ventilation, you may have felt the beginning effects of these drugs. Any prolonged inhaling can cause permanent brain damage and even death.

Where Can A Person Get Help?

If you—or a friend of yours—wants help with a drug problem, it's important to talk to someone right away. The more often you use drugs, the higher your risk of addiction or overdose. *Even "one try" can result in addiction or death.* Drug users can get help from support groups and treatment centers just as alcoholics can.

Communication channels in families, schools, and sports teams need to be kept open so that those who need help will seek it rather than go into denial. **Denial** is refusing to acknowledge the existence of a problem (issue). Many families deny the existence of drug problems due to ignorance, fear, uncertainty, or trying to maintain a positive social image (pride). Parents may deny the drug problem of one of their teenagers by saying, "Oh my son/daughter would never take drugs!" Many times, family members deny their parent's drug-use problems because they fear their parent's reaction if confronted. Learn to come out of denial. Find a safe person with whom you can share your problems and concerns. Remember, showing unconditional love to people who are struggling with drugs doesn't mean that you accept their behavior.

Communication channels in families, schools, and sports teams need to be kept open so that those who need help will seek it rather than go into denial.

10 • 4 Tobacco: A Deadly Habit

• •

Why would anyone poison his or her own body?
Beth

The Truth About Tobacco

From the careful cultivation of tiny tobacco seeds that look like finely ground pepper, a gigantic enterprise has emerged. The tobacco industry is a multi-billion dollar business. With its huge size and prevalent advertising, it's important to remember that money (greed) is the driving force behind the production and marketing of all tobacco products (cigarettes, cigars, pipes, and chewing tobacco). Tobacco manufacturers aren't the least bit concerned about you maintaining your good health. They only want your money.

Government reports have clearly stated that smoking is the number one *preventable* cause of lung disease and death.

Studies show that over 390,000 deaths each year are directly linked to smoking. What an unnecessary tragedy! Tobacco-related deaths are so high that health organizations have banned together to try to fight the production of tobacco. Since they haven't been able to stop the manufacture of the product, they've at least been trying to educate society about its deadly effects.

Most of the fifty million smokers in the United States started smoking when they were teenagers. They got hooked on the drug nicotine.

Each time you puff on a cigarette, you unleash over 3,000 chemicals into your body. Your body isn't designed to handle the toxins contained in tobacco. The most deadly and addictive drug in tobacco is nicotine. **Nicotine** is a colorless, oily, water-soluble, highly toxic, liquid alkaloid obtained from tobacco. It poisons your body to death—even though cigarette manufacturers claim that cigarette filters screen out much of the nicotine and that the amount you inhale isn't fatal. When smokers try their first cigarette, they experience dizziness, nausea, and an increased pulse rate. These physical reactions are signs that the individual is being *poisoned*. After smokers consume more cigarettes, however, these initial physical symptoms decrease, but the nicotine poisoning continues within their bodies—slowly and silently killing them.

Tar is a thick, dark sticky liquid that's formed when tobacco burns. With the use of each tobacco product, tar enters the lungs. Over a period of time, the tar build-up in the lungs causes disease. Because cigars, pipes, and chewing tobacco use no filtration system, tar is a real danger. Its particles drastically affect the lining of the mouth and throat. For this reason, oral cancer is very high among pipe, cigar, and chewing tobacco users.

Imagine placing your mouth over the exhaust pipe of a running car and taking a deep breath! If you ever did this, you would inhale a lungful of carbon monoxide. **Carbon monoxide** is a poisonous gas that's produced not only by car engines but also by burning tobacco. The inhalation of carbon monoxide is deadly because it cuts off the body's ability to absorb and carry oxygen. Because of this, smokers often have trouble jogging around a track, playing a game of basketball, walking up a flight of stairs, or having a great laugh with their friends. Carbon monoxide also hinders the proper functioning of the heart and brain as well as contributing to cardiovascular disease.

A Changing Message

A handsome man pulls out his pack of cigarettes in front of a beautiful young lady and asks, "Do you mind if I smoke?" The young lady replies, "Do you mind if I die?"

If you have seen this advertisement, you would agree that it has a powerful message. This type of "anti-smoking" billboard is a lot different from the ones you used to see lining the freeways. People are waking up to the deadly effects of smoking. The government is getting involved and forcing the tobacco industry to make some changes.

In 1984, the U.S. Surgeon General, Dr. C. Everett Koop, began a campaign to warn our nation about the dangers of smoking. His goal was to have a smoke-free society by the year 2000. Because of his noble efforts, the government now requires the Surgeon General's warning about smoking to be on every cigarette package. It also places a limitation on advertisements that are directed to young people. In 1998, for example, one tobacco manufacturer had to stop using cool Joe Camel™ in its appeal to youth. Furthermore, it's now common to see signs like "This Is a No Smoking Establishment", or "No Smoking" in restaurants, airports, planes, businesses, and on public transportation.

A Deadly Habit

Most of the fifty million smokers in the United States started smoking when they were teenagers. They got hooked on the drug

People who smoke or who live with smokers often live with impaired health or smoke-related illnesses.

nicotine. Now, as adults, their nicotine addiction controls their lives. People who smoke or who live with smokers, often live with impaired health or smoke-related illnesses.

Cancer

The continual exposure to tar and other chemicals in smoke poisons the lungs. Although not everyone who smokes develops lung cancer, all smokers definitely damage their lungs. Smokers are more susceptible to chronic bronchitis because their bronchi, the passages that bring oxygen to their lungs, become damaged from the tobacco's poisons. The deep-throated, hacking cough that most people call "smoker's cough" is from diseased bronchi.

Cancer from tobacco, however, isn't just limited to the lungs. People who smoke pipes allow the thick smoke to remain in their mouths and throats. Although these smokers don't always inhale the poisons (as do cigarette smokers), the chemicals and tar cause cancer of the mouth and throat.

People who use chewing tobacco (also called smokeless tobacco), place a wad of tobacco, or snuff, between their cheek and gum. From their mouth, the nicotine goes directly into their bloodstream. Users also swallow the poison-filled tobacco juice that can cause stomach ulcers.

Emphysema

Emphysema is an irreversible lung disease that's primarily caused by smoking. The tiny air sacs in the lungs become damaged after constant exposure to toxic poisons. A person who suffers from this disease always feels short of breath. Normal walking may cause smokers with emphysema to feel as if they're suffocating.

Danger to the Unborn

Years ago, pregnant women didn't consider smoking to be dangerous to their growing fetuses. Today, however, doctors encourage those who do smoke to quit. Studies have shown that smoking while carrying a child increases the chance of miscarriage, premature birth, stillbirth, birth defects, and low birthweight.

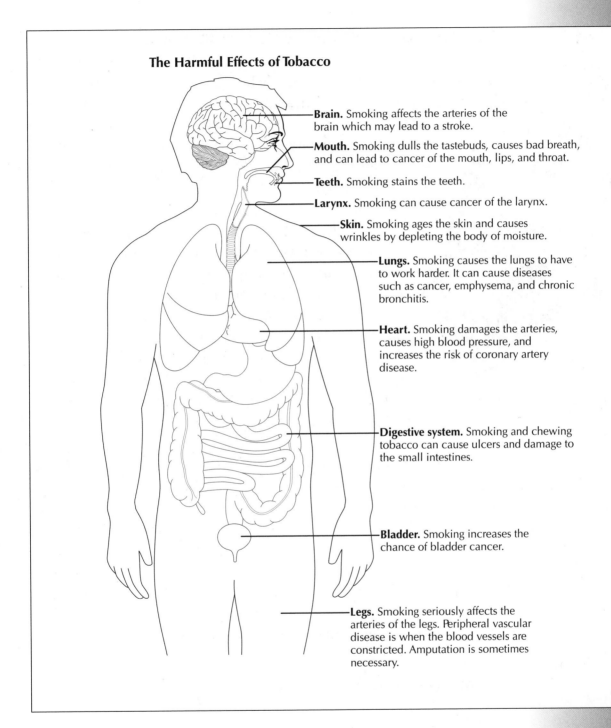

The Harmful Effects of Tobacco

Brain. Smoking affects the arteries of the brain which may lead to a stroke.

Mouth. Smoking dulls the tastebuds, causes bad breath, and can lead to cancer of the mouth, lips, and throat.

Teeth. Smoking stains the teeth.

Larynx. Smoking can cause cancer of the larynx.

Skin. Smoking ages the skin and causes wrinkles by depleting the body of moisture.

Lungs. Smoking causes the lungs to have to work harder. It can cause diseases such as cancer, emphysema, and chronic bronchitis.

Heart. Smoking damages the arteries, causes high blood pressure, and increases the risk of coronary artery disease.

Digestive system. Smoking and chewing tobacco can cause ulcers and damage to the small intestines.

Bladder. Smoking increases the chance of bladder cancer.

Legs. Smoking seriously affects the arteries of the legs. Peripheral vascular disease is when the blood vessels are constricted. Amputation is sometimes necessary.

Death by Fire

Smoking contributes to many deaths due to fire. People who smoke while in bed may fall asleep with a burning cigarette in hand. Sometimes, forest fires start as a careless smoker tosses a burning cigarette to the ground. Innocent people—as well as nature—suffer because of this dangerous habit.

Second-Hand Smoke Still Means First-Hand Death

Although society is headed in the right direction concerning the dangers of smoking, many people have lost their lives to the deadly habit—without even smoking a cigarette! Researchers have found that non-smokers who are regularly exposed to cigarette smoke can die from the exposure, too. The following commercial shown on national television depicts this tragedy:

> *My wife used to get so mad at me for smoking. Sometimes, she would refuse to kiss me because she wanted me to quit. She would say, "You're going to lose your life someday because of this habit". In response, I would say, "It's my life, I'm not hurting anyone else". Last year, I did lose my life to smoking, but the life I lost was not my own but my wife's. She died because I chose to smoke. If I had known that my smoking was killing her, I would have stopped. My wife was my life.*

Researchers have found that non-smokers who are regularly exposed to cigarette smoke can die from the exposure, too.

If you've ever been in a restaurant where someone was smoking right next to you, you may have experienced itchy/burning eyes, scratchy throat, irritated nasal passages, headache, or loss of appetite. The smoke you breathe that comes from another person's cigarette is called **second-hand smoke** (also called passive smoke). To better understand it, tobacco smoke is grouped into three categories:

1. **Mainstream smoke** is the smoke that is inhaled and then exhaled by the smoker.

2. **Sidestream smoke** is the smoke that comes out of the end of a lit cigarette.

3. **Environmental smoke** is the smoke that stays in the air where smokers have been smoking.

What kind of smoke would you most likely breathe in a restaurant that had both smoking and non-smoking sections? How do you feel about the controversial issue of smokers' vs. non-smokers' rights?

Best Defense: Never Light-Up!

After learning the facts about the dangers of tobacco, why do you think that thousands of teenagers still light-up? Could it be that teens have the feeling of being indestructible? Have you heard any of your friends who smoke say:

* *I'll never get lung cancer. Look at the actor George Burns. He lived to be in his 90's and always smoked a large cigar.*

* *I know that smoking isn't that good for me. I plan to quit when I get older.*

* *I'm not going to get a disease from smoking. I get plenty of exercise and stay really healthy.*

* *Smoking makes me feel 'tough' and 'cool'.*

Fortunately, smoking doesn't have such a "cool" image anymore. Increased cigarette taxes put a bite on smokers' pocketbooks. Some legislators believe that the higher the cigarette tax, the more difficult it'll be for teens to smoke. When you choose not to smoke, you'll be choosing not only to save yourself a lot of money; you'll also be deciding to save your own life as well as the lives of others. How much is saving your life worth?

Although the effects of smoking may not be evident until a smoker is an adult, the smoking habit is more difficult to break than most people think. Nicotine is a strong addictive drug. As with other drug dependencies, the uncomfortable withdrawal symptoms that a person trying to quit will experience, may discourage them from quitting. Your strong craving for chocolate, cola, or pizza can't even compare to your body's intense craving for more nicotine once you start smoking. Many smokers feel that it's impossible to quit. Some rationalize that they would rather die happy smoking than live longer and be miserable trying to quit. There's no denying the fact that quitting is hard. But, when it comes to a person's own life, isn't it worth the fight?

After learning the facts about the dangers of tobacco, why do you think that thousands of teenagers still light-up?

Where Can A Smoker Get Help?

There are many groups that help people stop smoking. The American Lung Association, the American Heart Association, as well as the American Cancer Society all offer programs to help smokers quit. You may have seen advertisements for the nicotine-containing "patch" or chewing gum. These helps are designed to break the nicotine addiction slowly while preventing a person from inhaling the poisons.

Many people, however, find that the actual habit of smoking is a real part of their addiction. Having a cigarette "first thing in the morning" can be similar to coffee drinkers needing their morning java. To many smokers, smoking a cigarette after a meal provides them with more pleasure than eating something sweet. Many smokers need more than just a substitute for their addiction. They need the support of people who are willing to encourage them as they break this deadly habit.

How Can I Quit?

If you (or someone you know) have already started smoking and really want to quit, here are a few suggestions:

- Tell a non-smoker you want to quit. Be accountable to someone who will encourage you. It won't work to tell a friend who still smokes!

- When you feel the temptation to smoke, do something different and think of all the benefits of quitting.

- Toss all of your smoking-related items away: the ashtrays, matches, cigarette boxes (full or empty!), lighters, pipes, and tobacco cans/pouches (chewing, too!).

- Wash and dry clean all your clothes that smell of smoke.

- Change your habits that remind you of smoking. For example, did you always sit in a certain chair or smoke with your friends in a certain location?

- Set reasonable goals for yourself.

- After you've reached your small goals, reward yourself with something special. Avoid using food as a reward or replacement for smoking, however, because you'll soon gain weight and become discouraged.

- Make exercise a part of your daily routine.

- Begin to eat healthy foods and drink lots of pure water. This will help your body recover from tobacco poisons and will give you a healthy feeling.

There's no denying the fact that quitting is hard. But, when it comes to a person's own life, isn't it worth the fight?

10 • 5 Jesus: The Supernatural High

· ·

> *If we live in the Spirit, let us also walk in the Spirit.*
> **Galatians 5:25**

Have you ever seen a movie that made you feel scared or excited? Many teens watch suspense movies because they want to "feel scared". Some doctors who study the way people think and act (psychologists) feel that most people have a need for a "natural high". They believe that human beings have a real need to escape the way they feel in their daily routines in order to experience deeper, more intense feelings of excitement and exhilaration. Athletes, for example, who invest their time and energy into their sport enjoy an "adrenaline rush" (produced by the release of endorphins in the body) when they workout. Although your faith in God is not based on your feelings, God has created you with an inner desire, literally, to feel and experience His supernatural love, power, and presence.

God wants you to be "high"—supernaturally high on Him!

The more you are in love with Jesus, the less room there is in your heart to love unhealthy addictions.

Everyone needs to feel loved, wanted, needed, appreciated, worthwhile, and excited about life. Even though teens' needs are basically the same, some teens seek to fulfill their needs in different ways. Some turn to alcohol, tobacco, drugs, sex, gangs, pornography, and non-Christian music to try to fulfill them. What they find, however, is that each of these areas only gives them a temporary escape from the reality of the pain and longing deep inside that only God can fill. The great-sinner-turned-saint, Augustine, put it this way to God: "Our hearts are restless until they find their rest in You." You have a choice. You can either try to get your spiritual and emotional needs met through pursuing the addictions of your culture, or you can begin to seek to get your needs met by God Himself. The more you are in love with Jesus, the less room there is in your heart to love unhealthy addictions.

John, the close friend of Jesus, put it this way:

> *Do not love the world or the things in the world. If anyone loves the world, the love of the Father is not in him.*
> **I John 2:15**

Many teens don't want to follow Jesus with their whole heart because they think that Christianity is dull, boring, unexciting, and unemotional. Their picture of following Jesus is simply to memorize Bible verses and go to church services or youth group. Even though it's good to memorize the Word of God and be involved in a strong church, God wants you personally to feel Him for yourself. It's okay to *experience* God because He made you a human being with emotions. Do you have a need to experience more of God? If so, sensing your need is the first step. Jesus said, "Blessed are the poor in spirit, for theirs is the kingdom of heaven" (Matthew 5:3). If you're "poor in spirit", you're very aware of your need for God. When you're aware of how much you need God, you can experience part of the "kingdom of heaven" right here in your own life. You can touch God's presence and power! Realize that:

264

- Since God is love (I John 4:16), He wants you to feel His love so that you can show it to others.

- Because one of the fruits of His Spirit is joy (Galatians 5:22) and, as David wrote to God, "In Your presence is fullness of joy" (Psalm 16:11), He wants you to feel His joy inside of your heart so that you can share it.

- Since another fruit of the Holy Spirit is peace (Galatians 5:22), God wants you to experience His deep rest whenever you're full of anxiety. "Let your requests be made known to God" (Philippians 4:6), so that you can experience "...the peace of God that surpasses all understanding [which] will guard your hearts and minds through Christ Jesus" (Philippians 4:7).

- Because Jesus has all supernatural power at His disposal (Matthew 28:17), He wants you to encounter some of His power so that you can help a hurting and dying world.

Have you ever felt God's presence? If so, what did He feel like? Warm? Loving? Accepting? Forgiving? Motivating? If you haven't experienced His presence, do you want to? If you really want to, you can!

You won't ever be totally happy or fulfilled until you experience God for yourself.

Jesus said that when you experience His truth, it will "set you free" (John 8:32). Even though God does give you certain boundaries, He gives them to you for your own good, happiness, and fulfillment. *There's no deep or permanent good, happiness, or fulfillment in an addiction to alcohol, tobacco, drugs, sex, gangs, violence, pornography, or non-Christian music.* God is in love with you! He created you to have an intimate relationship with Him. You won't ever be totally happy or fulfilled until you experience God for yourself. God will probably ask you to give up some habits in your life, but He will replace them with blessings that are much better. By sending the Holy Spirit (Acts 2), Jesus gives you the opportunity to experience a real supernatural high!

Chapter 10 Review

Defining the Terms

Cirrhosis
Inhibitory effect
Alcoholism
Tolerance level
Withdrawal
MADD
Alcoholics Anonymous (AA)
Alateen
Al-Anon
Alexander Fleming
Drugs
Medicine(s)

Drug abuse
Prescription drug
Nonprescription drug
FDA
Side effects
Caffeine
Stimulants
Addiction
Depressants
Narcotics
Morphine, codeine
Heroin
Hallucinogen

PCP or angel dust (phencyclidine)
LSD (lysergic acid diethylamide)
Denial
Nicotine
Tar
Carbon monoxide
Emphysema
Second-hand smoke
Mainstream smoke
Sidestream smoke
Environmental smoke

Recalling the Facts

1. What is God's "Freedom Formula"?

2. How can teens' increasing sense of personal freedom contribute to their desire to try dangerous substances?

3. List five immediate effects of alcohol on the body when a person drinks too much.

4. Explain the meaning of the phrase, "Advertisers don't care about your health, they only care about your money!"

5. Explain how coffee, tea, and certain soda pop, can be considered drugs. What are some of the withdrawal symptoms people might experience when going without these products?

6. List five of the nine negative effects of using marijuana.

7. Explain the importance of not trying a drug, like marijuana, not even once.

8. Why do you think young teens still smoke even though they know it's dangerous?

Applying the Truth

1. What is meant by the phrase, "You must 'own' your own faith"?

2. Give four examples of how the Bible gives you practical advice for today. List the verses.

3. How can teenagers experience part of the "kingdom of heaven" right now in their own lives?

Unit 4 • Spiritual Health

" Jesus said, 'You shall love the Lord your God with all your...mind'."
Matthew 22:37

"TELL ME WHY..." 11
TEENS & THEIR QUESTIONS

What's Coming Up...

11•1 Building Your Bridge to Maturity

• •

> *Brethren, do not be children in your thinking...*
> *but in your thinking be mature.*
> I Corinthians 14:20, NAS

When Paul told the Corinthians, "in your thinking be mature", he was encouraging the Corinthians to think wisely. He meant for them to "keep on becoming adults" in their minds.[1]

If you want to "keep on becoming an adult" in your mind, then you need to start pursuing answers to all of the different kinds of questions you have. No doubt you have many questions about God, life, friendships, and other issues, too. Good questions don't always have to start with a "Why?". They can also begin with a "How?", "When?", "Who?", or "Where?". The following three questions represent the kind of concerns that many of your peers have:

* *How do I begin to talk to my parents about dating?* Mike

* *Why did my parents get a divorce?* Jason

* *When will I know that I'm in love with the right person?* Amy

Does reading the questions of Mike, Jason, or Amy remind you of any questions that you have? What are some of the questions that are important to you right now?

These three questions about dating, divorce, and falling in love are just a few of the many questions that will begin to form in your mind the more you read, learn, live life, go to school, talk to people, search your heart, and grow in maturity. As you mature, you'll probably have more questions next year than you did this year.

Good questions don't always have to start with a "Why?". They can also begin with a "How?", "When?", "Who?", or "Where?"

When you have a question, who is the first person you go to for an answer? God? Your parents? Your teachers? Your youth pastor? Your best friend? Actively seeking answers to your questions from those that God has put into your life is actually one of your bridges to maturity and adulthood. Maturing teens ask good questions.

The Road to Invention and Discovery

God allows you the freedom to ask questions so that you can enjoy the exciting journey of discovery and invention. What do you think are the most important scientific discoveries in the world? Space flight? Computers? Electricity? No great discovery or invention would ever have been made if someone hadn't asked a question. Though some great discoveries have been by 'accident', it was usually a question of some kind that a curious person was trying to answer that provided the key insight or breakthrough. Use your imagination for a moment. Try to go back into the minds of some of the great thinkers and inventors of the past. Maybe some of the inner questions that drove them to discover and invent went something like this:

- *How can I make my harmonic telegraph work? Why can't I make voices travel over a telephone line?* (Alexander Graham Bell)

- *Is lightning energy? If so, how can I harness it for mankind's use?* (Benjamin Franklin)

- *How can I put a personal computer on everyone's desktop?* (Bill Gates)

- *Why can't we put a man on the moon in the next ten years?* (John Kennedy)

- *How can we make man fly like the birds?* (Orville & Wilbur Wright)

- *If the world is round, why can't I sail around it and end up in the same place that I started?* (Magellan)

How can we make man fly like the birds? (Orville & Wilbur Wright)

God doesn't want you to "blow" your mind with drugs or alcohol. He wants you to "grow" your mind with good questions. God also doesn't want you to waste your mind by becoming addicted to electronic media that could, if overused, make your brain turn into a non-thinking vegetable. He wants to develop your mind into one of a mature, thinking adult mind. God desires you to train your mind and use it to do what He's called you to do. Good questions make you think and develop your mental skills.

11 • 2 Developing the Leader Within You

Many of the greatest leaders in Church history have been those who have been thinkers and asked tough questions. Luther, Calvin, Wycliffe, Finney, and Wesley were all well-educated men. Fortunately, none of these leaders were distracted by any form of electronic entertainment from applying their minds to studying and communicating God's Word to others. Some of the questions that motivated these Church leaders were:

God desires you to train your mind and use it to do what He's called you to do. Good questions make you think and develop your mental skills.

- *Doesn't the Bible say that we are saved by faith and not by works?* Martin Luther, church reformer

- *How does the biblical doctrine of God's sovereignty apply to our daily lives?* John Calvin, church reformer

- *Why can't I translate the Bible into the language of the common man?* John Wycliffe, church reformer, Bible translator

- *How can true revival be maintained?* Charles Finney, evangelist

- *What kind of method can we use to teach Christians to be holy and disciplined?* John Wesley, founder of Methodism

There's a leader inside of you, too. In order to cause that leader to develop, you must continue thinking and questioning. When your thoughts and questions are directed according to God's Word, then you'll be able to lead many others into knowing, loving, and serving God with "all their minds".

Leaders as Readers

Blessed is he who reads [this book]...
Revelation 1:3

[With electronic entertainment], you don't have to worry about getting really bored because it's happening; and you don't have to do any work to see it, to have it happen. But you have to work to read, and that's no fun. I mean, it's fun when it's a good book, but how can you tell if the book will be good? Anyhow, I'd rather see it as a television program.[2]

Amy

Like Amy, do you find most reading boring? Or, does it all depend on the book that you're reading? Would you rather watch a television show, see a movie, or play a video game rather than read a good book? Many teens would. One of the foundations to all of your leadership skills is your reading and **comprehension** (understanding and remembering what you've read). You wouldn't be able to earn good grades in school unless you were able to read, understand, and learn information from books. Abraham Lincoln, a former Christian President of the United States, is just one example of a great leader who loved to read books. Readers are leaders!

One of the foundations to all of your leadership skills is your reading and comprehension.

In order to increase your reading skills, you can do the following.

- The next time you watch a movie, look at the credits and see what book the movie was taken from. Many—if not most— movies come from already-published books. Read the book upon which your favorite movie was based. Compare the book with the movie. Watching the movie made from a book instead of reading the book itself is, many times, unfortunate because the book will have a lot more exciting details in it than the movie.

- Tell yourself that you're going to spend just as much time reading as you do watching TV or movies.

- Try not using any electronic entertainment for a day, a week, or more. In that time, see if you get better grades, develop more friendships, have fun learning something new, or get more good books read. Teens use electronic entertainment the more it's available to them. John was fourteen and Christina was twelve when their mother let each of them have a television in his/her room. Because he had a TV and VCR in his own room, John didn't spend as much time with his family. His Mom didn't like that.

Because Christina had her own TV, she watched it a lot more. Consequently, their Mom soon gave both of their TVs away and allowed there to be only one in the living room. John began to spend more time reading.

You can help to make your home an environment that is favorable to reading.

• Find a friend who likes to read the same kind of books that you do. Greg, a young Christian teen, likes to read science fiction. He sometimes reads as many as two sci-fi books a week. Greg really didn't know of anyone else who liked the same kind of books that he liked, so he asked his Dad if he would like to read some of the same novels. His Dad said, "Yes". So far, John's Dad has read two of Greg's favorite sci-fi novels. They both had fun talking about them. They not only talked about the plot and characters of the books but also the Christian meanings—or lack thereof—in each novel.

• Use a Bible translation that you really understand and like. Sometimes, you may want to look into different "graphic" Bibles (Bibles with lots of pictures and illustrations). Reading is one of the reasons why God had His Word captured in print. He tells us to read His Word so that our thoughts can be filled with His thoughts. Out of good thoughts come good behavior. David tells us that when a believer meditates in God's Word, he will find success in his life (Psalm 1:2-3).

• Help to put together a home environment that is favorable to reading. Is your home filled with lots of good books? Does your family own some Christian books that address issues that are important to you? If not, you may want to talk with your Dad and/or Mom about what you could do together to make your home a place that strongly encourages the reading of good books.

Followers Who "Veg Out"

Leaders are thinkers, questioners, and readers. But, not every teen wants to be a leader. Some teens choose not to think, question, or read. They spend most of their time "vegging out" and letting their minds go dead. Teens who spend most of their time "vegging out" in front of the TV, or other forms of entertainment, may have the same habit when they get older. Unfortunately, they probably won't develop the leader that God has put inside of them. They'll remain followers. Furthermore, when a teen fails to develop his/her mind as a young person, the opportunities for quality education and fulfilling employment decrease.

If you want to be a leader instead of a follower; if you want to begin to control your TV and movie viewing time so that you can develop your mind, here are a few suggestions:

- Always do your homework before you watch TV. Limit your TV viewing time. God wants you continually to develop the mind that He gave you. This will be a challenge in our media-dominated culture because researchers have found that as TV viewing, for example, has increased ever since its introduction in the 1950's, the SAT (Scholastic Aptitude Test) scores for high school students' entrance into college have dramatically decreased.

- Learn how to lengthen your attention span. As you're developing your mind through reading and thinking—don't rush! Learn to focus longer on one of your own thoughts or a scene in a good book, and you'll give yourself more time personally to think about what you're reading.

- When you watch TV or movies, try to analyze what you're watching. Making comments like, "I didn't like that..." "That took

Teens who spend most of their time "vegging out" in front of the TV, or other entertainment, may have the same habit when they get older.

Electronic entertainment decreases your attention span because of the fast-paced image changes.

too much time..." "What's the point here?" and "What is this saying about God?" will help you to think more clearly about what you're watching. Similarly, whenever you read a book, try to (1) draw your own conclusion, (2) form  your own opinion, (3) give an interpretation, (4) create some new ideas, and (5) compare what you're reading with what you know so far about God and the Bible.

- Whenever you notice that you're feeling (1) withdrawn from other people, (2) a "don't care" attitude, or (3) like escaping from "real thinking", turn to other forms of fun—other than electronic.

- Develop your writing skills. As you learn how to express yourself in writing, you'll automatically develop your thinking skills. You'll force yourself to think in order to express your thoughts on paper. Luther, Calvin, Wycliffe, Finney, and Wesley were all writers, too. Learning to write is hard, but writing is how you'll learn to form and express your thoughts. Remember that "Learning to write is the hardest [but] most important thing any [student] does. Learning to write is learning to think."[3]

11 • 3 Coming Closer to God

I really want to get closer to God, but I don't know how.

Mark

The Bible and Questions

How do you think God feels about your questions? Do you think that He feels fearful or insecure about them? Or, do you think that He welcomes them and loves to answer them?

Let's look at how many questions there are in the Bible, God's book about Himself and us. How many questions do you think there are in the Bible altogether? According to one source, there are a total of 3,294 questions in the Bible (2,272 questions in the Old Testament and 1,022 questions in the New Testament).[4]

Now, that's a lot of questions! All of these questions actually make very interesting reading in themselves, but if God was against you asking questions, why would He allow so many questions in the Bible?

How did God respond to people in the Bible who asked a lot of questions? The Bible describes king David, the writer of many of the psalms (songs) in Scripture, as a "man after God's own heart" (Acts 13:22; I Samuel 13:14). In dozens of the songs David composed, he asked God many questions. His questions included the most difficult kind: "Why?" questions (Psalm 10:1; 22:1; 74:1). Not feeling ashamed of his own impatience, he also asked, "How long?" questions (Psalm 6:3). Sometimes, he'd examine the depths of his own heart with questions like, "Why am I so depressed?" (Psalm 42:5). Being very open and honest, David also inquired of God with questions like, "Why have You forgotten me?" (Psalm 42:9). Sometimes, David even asked questions about God's seeming lack of involvement in his as well as others' lives (Psalm 88:14). If David was a "man after God's own heart"—a believer who very much pleased God—how could we consider his asking of questions to be "wrong", "lacking faith", or "non-Christian"? Furthermore, if it was perfectly okay for David to ask questions, then why wouldn't it be okay for you to ask questions, too?

Jesus and Questions

How did Jesus respond to people who had honest questions—even doubts—about Him? Did He get defensive, rebuke them,

Jesus is interested in what you think. He wants to develop your mind by asking you questions about your own opinions and feelings.

and 'pull rank' with words such as, "Don't question Me because I'm God!"? No. Do you remember the story of "doubting" Thomas? After Jesus rose from the dead, some of the disciples told Thomas, "We have seen the Lord." When they told him this, Thomas had doubts and questions. To those disciples he replied, "Unless I see in His hands the print of the nails, and put my finger into the print of the nails, and put my hand into His side, I will not believe." Eight days later, Thomas was again in the upper room with the other disciples when Jesus appeared to them and said, "Peace to you!" Jesus singled Thomas out and personally said to him, "Reach your finger here, and look at My hands; and reach your hand here, and put it into My side. Do not be unbelieving but believing." Thomas answered and said to Him, "My Lord and my God!" Jesus replied, "Thomas, because you have seen Me, you have believed. Blessed are those who have not seen and yet have believed" (John 20:25-29). Even though Jesus did bless those who had believed that He had risen from the dead without having first to touch or see Him, Jesus didn't criticize, reject, or make fun of Thomas' question or request. Instead, Jesus showed Thomas the "evidence" for which he was honestly seeking. Jesus "answered" his sincere question.

Jesus is interested in what you think. He wants to develop your mind by asking you questions about your own opinions and feelings. The "question approach" was one of the main teaching methods that Jesus used when He was on earth. When a lawyer asked Jesus what he had to do to gain eternal life, Jesus responded by asking him two questions. The first question was, "What is written in the law?" and the second one, "What is your reading of it?" (Luke 10:25-26). When Jesus taught His disciples about taking care of people, He asked them, "What do you think?" (Matthew 18:12). When He discussed a tax question with Peter, He asked, "What do you think, Simon?" (Matthew 17:25). He also asked the opinion of the masses (Matthew 21:28) as well as the Pharisees (Matthew 22:42).

Adults and Questions

My sixth grade teacher was presenting information to the girls about maturity and reproduction. When she finished the thirty-minute lesson, she turned to the class and asked, "Are there any questions?" Upon realizing that no one was quickly raising her hand, she responded, "Good, then let's all open up our math books to page..."

Susan

As Susan discovered, some adults feel uncomfortable about the questions teens sometimes have. They may even act impatient or defensive with you. Adults may not have the perspective that "growing teens are thinking teens". Questions are good—not bad—when they come out of a sincere heart that is simply seeking the truth. Thinking biblically and asking intelligent questions are signs of the following good, biblical qualities:

- **Knowledge**. Mature teens ask questions to seek for the facts. Knowledge humbles Christian teens rather than puffing them up in pride. Paul the apostle said, "If anyone thinks that he knows anything, he knows nothing yet as he ought to know" (I Corinthians 8:2).

- **Wisdom**. Wise teens ask questions to find the truth about how God wants them to understand the world He created and how He wants them to live. When certain simple answers no longer were sufficient for some thinkers in the Bible because those answers didn't go along with what they actually observed in real life, they wrote books. These books included many important questions. These books were put into the Bible. They're called "Wisdom Books" and they include Job, Psalms, Proverbs, and Ecclesiastes. King Solomon, who was involved with writing these last two books, saw thoughts and questions as actual encouragers of faith. He didn't see them as evil—as long as people had a genuine fear of God in their hearts.

Questions are good— not bad— especially when they come from a sincere heart that's simply seeking the truth.

King Solomon saw thoughts and questions as actual encouragers of faith. He didn't see them as evil— as long as people had a genuine fear of God in their hearts.

- **Humility**. Realizing their own limitations, humble teens admit that they don't know everything. They're open to hearing the other side of issues because they're not only open-minded but also secure in themselves. Paul wrote, "I say...to everyone who is among you, not to think of himself more highly [not to 'over-think'] than he ought to think, but to think soberly ['to be in one's right mind'], as God has dealt to each one a measure of faith" (Romans 12:3).[5]

11 • 4 Talking with Your Parents

*I want to talk to my parents about sex,
but how can I bring up the subject?*
Tim

One day in a junior high class, a teacher asked the question, "How many of you feel that you can ask your parents tough questions?" Instantly, one girl responded, "One day I asked my Mom a question, and she said,

"When I was your age, I never asked questions like that!"

Has an adult ever said something like this to you? Most young people have a difficult time asking parents or adults hard questions. Why? Teens are afraid of the adult's response. The adult might get mad or put them down for asking such a question. They also think that adults would probably never understand.

If, for whatever reason, you find that you aren't able to talk to your parents very well, then it's important to find a trusted adult with whom you can talk. You may feel more comfortable talking feelings over with your friends. Unfortunately, in most cases, your friends can't tell you anything that you don't already know.

Do you ever feel guilty for some of the questions you have? Do others try to make you feel afraid of asking certain questions? Have you ever not asked a question in class because you didn't want to look "dumb"? Everybody has. Even though you might feel embarrassed at times in class, it's good to know that in life, as long as you're sincerely seeking the truth, there are no dumb or stupid questions. Every sincere question will help you mature into adulthood.

Every sincere question will help you mature into adulthood.

With all of the changes that you're presently experiencing, some of the most important changes are your mental (**intellectual**) ones. As you mature, you will be asking more and more questions. You'll be using the mind that God has given to you more often. The attitude you take toward the questions that you ask will have a lot to do with whether your questions allow you to mature or to **regress** (go backward).

Tips on Talking with Your Parents and Safe Adults

Parents want to talk with their teens and have their teens talk to them. Some parents, unfortunately, just don't know how. Do you want to have a better relationship with your Dad/ Mom? If so, try to put into practice the following two suggestions.

When parents and teens don't know how to talk to each other, many unnecessary hurts and struggles arise.

1. Ask Open-Ended, Honest Questions.

Start asking your parents open-ended questions. Open-ended questions are those which start a good discussion in which both sides participate. Sincerely ask your parent(s) to share about their own lives. This can really help to open up the avenues of communication between you. When your communication improves, everything in your relationship (and in your life) will get better. When parents and teens don't know how to talk to each other, many unnecessary hurts and struggles arise. Each person tends to overreact to the other rather than calmly listening. Both need to show respect to the other. Some parents make the false assumption that teens don't have any valid thoughts or feelings for themselves. Too many teens, on the other hand, don't show respect for their parents. They too easily forget that their parents were once teens, too.

Here are a few questions that you could ask your parent(s). Can you think of any others?

- What was it like when you were my age?

- What jobs did you have when you were a teen?

- Do you have any ideas of what kind of job(s) I could get?

- I know that I'll be making my own decision, but what kind of career do you think that I might be good at?

- What kind of relationship did you have with your Dad or Mom? Did you ever get into any struggles or arguments with them? If so, about what? How did you resolve them?

- If you were to relive your teen years, what would you do the same? What would you do differently?

- Did you ever struggle with your faith in God?

Adults appreciate being asked honest questions. What's an "honest" question? It's a question you ask in which (a) you sincerely want a response, and (b) you're open to a truthful reply (whether it's what you want to hear or not). What are your motives when you ask adults questions? Are you trying to embarrass them? Are you attempting to get them upset? Are you trying to pit one parent against another? Jesus liked people to ask Him honest questions, too. Certain people, however, asked Jesus dishonest questions. They had wrong motives behind their asking. On one occasion, the Pharisees and Sadducees asked Jesus to show them a sign from heaven to put Him on the spot and have Him perform something like a "magic show". Because He had already done many supernatural signs, and they still didn't follow Him, He knew that another sign wouldn't have made any difference. Since their words and their hearts were miles apart, Jesus called them **hypocrites** ("two-faced"). After that, He told them that He would show them no sign except the sign of His resurrection (Matthew 16:1-4).

2. Show Respect to Your Parents.

Speak respectfully to your parents. Everyone desires to be spoken to with common decency and respect. It doesn't mean that you must think that your parents are perfect. They aren't. But your parents will open up more to you if you show them respect. Showing respect to your parents can be summed up in two phrases: *good manners* and *good attitude*. Good manners means being polite to your parents. Being polite and showing them respect includes:

- looking at them when they're talking to you;

- acknowledging what they've said to you by repeating it back to them, or saying "Yes, Mom/Dad";

- asking them to reconsider by giving them a good reason if you are struggling with what they've just asked you to do;

- saying "Please" more often; and

Your parents will open up more to you if you show them respect.

- showing a grateful spirit toward all that they have done for you by sincerely saying "Thank you" more often.

Having a good attitude means showing regard for your parents in your spirit and on your face (or **countenance**). Having warm feelings toward your parents in your spirit (or heart) will require you to learn how to resolve hurts and offenses. You'll be able to do this by learning how to share with them when they hurt you. You can use words like, "I felt hurt when…" or, "I don't feel good when…". Yelling, screaming, door-slamming, or name-calling don't help. Once you have a good feeling in your heart toward your parents, you'll usually show that on your countenance. Your parents won't respond well if you get sassy, sarcastic, or demanding with them. One way to check to see how your inner attitude is toward your parents is by answering the following question:

What do you say to your friends about your parents when your parents aren't around?

One of the ways that you can show respect for your parents is in allowing them to "save face". As you mature, you're going to make some mistakes, and so are your Dad and Mom. Your parents have a lot of pressure on them to "be right" and "do right" most of the time. Because of this pressure, they usually won't appreciate it if you expose their mistakes in an embarrassing or disrespectful way.

Having a "good attitude" means showing regard for your parents in your spirit and on your face (or countenance).

Thinking, questioning, reading, and writing are all bridges to you becoming a mature adult. Each of these skills will help you to become a leader rather than a follower. The more you learn to think and to read, the more that you'll be able to develop into a capable Christian leader. As you learn respectfully how to ask adults honest, open-ended questions, you'll be able to feel free to express yourself within acceptable limits. Whenever you face a crisis or struggle in life, always try to remember that God isn't afraid of your tough questions.

Chapter 11 Review

Defining the Terms

Comprehension	Regress	Hypocrites
Intellectual	Humility	Countenance

Recalling the Facts

1. What famous church leaders may have asked the following questions:

   - Doesn't the Bible say that we are saved by faith and not by works?

   - How does the biblical doctrine of God's sovereignty apply to our daily lives?

   - Why can't I translate the Bible into the language of the common man?

   - How can true revival be maintained?

   - What kind of method can we use to teach Christians to be holy and disciplined?

2. One of the foundations to all of your leadership skills is your reading and comprehension. List five things you can do in order to increase your reading skills.

3. If asking questions is good, when does it become wrong or bad?

4. List five ways to show respect to your parents (or anyone!).

5. What does it mean to allow your parents to "save face"? Why is this a sign of respect?

Applying the Truth

1. After reading this chapter on questions, think of five sincere questions you have for God and write them on a piece of paper. The next time you're alone with God in prayer, share with Him one or two of these concerns. Keep an open mind and heart as you listen for Him to speak to you. He may not answer right away, and His response may not be the answer you were hoping for, but He will meet with you if you seek Him sincerely.

2. Set up alone time with your Dad or Mom. Ask him/her two of the questions on page 280. As they begin sharing with you, also ask them two of your own questions. Evaluate the quality time you shared, and see how you can improve your communication.

"Behold, I stand at the door and knock."

Revelation 3:20

ME, MYSELF, AND GOD 12

What's Coming Up...

12•1 What's Your View of God?

. . . .

> *God is my closest friend and my father.*
> Rebecca

> *As I need a friend, I can go to God*
> *because I know He's always listening.*
> Paul

> *My Dad left when I was younger,*
> *so God is my Dad now.*
> Sara

As you think of God, what picture comes into your mind? Is it a picture of an angry father who is disappointed in you? Is it an illustration of a detective spying on you to try to catch you making your next mistake? Or, is it a portrait of a close friend talking with you; an understanding Dad who is stretching out his arms toward you? Rebecca, Paul, and Sara all picture God as a close friend or a loving father. Why do you think that they picture God in such positive terms? Sara sees God as her very own Dad because her biological Dad abandoned her. Sara was able to turn a potentially negative view of God ("He'll abandon me just like my Dad did!") into a very positive one ("My Dad left when I was younger, but God is my Dad now!").

There are several factors that influence your view of God. What your parents, teachers, and pastors have taught you about God is likely to be the same way that you think about Him. If your parents are easy to talk to and very understanding, you'll probably see God in that way, too. But, if your parents are distant, or too busy for you, you might begin to think that God is the same way—even though He isn't.

God wants you to view Him as a caring, loving Father who wants to spend time with you.

How does God want you to view Him? He wants you to see Him as a caring father. As your father, He wants you to picture Him as kind, loving, patient, and forgiving. As a father who genuinely cares about your personal well-being, He wants you also to include in this picture the fact that He cares enough for you that He provides certain boundaries to protect you from hurting yourself. His sincere care for you motivates Him at times even to feel jealous over your life. Such a jealousy would cause Him to get very angry at the devil and any form of evil that would try to destroy you. Would you see a father who allowed his son or daughter—without any driver education—to drive a car on the

freeway at 80mph to be a truly caring father? Probably not. In the same way, God knows what limitations are needed in your life to get you to the destination that He has for you; one of happiness and fulfillment, doing His will.

If you see God as overly-strict and a "kill-joy", you probably won't be interested in having a close relationship with Him. If, however, you see Him as one who is truly interested in your personal growth—like a coach—then you probably would really like to get to know Him better. If you feel that you have a false picture of God in your mind, you can always change it. After you change it, you may find a new door opening up inside of your heart that says, "Now, I really do want to get to know Him, but how?

12 • 2 What Kind of Relationship Do You Have with God?

I want to get on the right track with God, but it's hard for me because I don't know how to have a closer relationship with Him.

Ryan

My relationship with God is like a roller coaster. I admit some days I really want Jesus, but other days I forget that He's the center.

Janie

If you talked to your peers, you would find that many struggle in their relationship with God.

Bible Reading

Do you want a closer relationship with God? If so, do you know how to develop one? When we asked some of your peers how to get closer to God, one of their most common answers was "Read the Bible". Sounds kind of easy, doesn't it? But, it's really not. Look at some of the reasons that many of your peers gave for their reply of "No" to the question, "Do you regularly read your Bible?"

- *It's too boring.* (Karen)

- *I'm trying to start.* (Tim)

- *I haven't yet, but I'm going to start.* (James)

- *I don't have time.* (Joe)

- *I want to try to make it a habit.* (Megan)

- *I'm lazy.* (Michael)

- *I always say, 'I'm going to read every day', but I never get to it.* (Tony)

- *I always forget.* (Carolyn)

- *I don't have time, and it's kind of boring.* (Katy)

- *I can't understand it.* (Tim)

- *It makes me fall asleep.* (Karen)

"Reading my Bible, especially in the morning, helps me with my attitude."
Megan

The good thing about the above list is the fact that Karen, Tim, and the other teens were honest with their responses. They weren't trying to appear more "spiritual" than they really were. Actually, openness and honesty is really the only way to have a good relationship with God. All teens can relate to the struggle of spending time in the Word. As John put it: "I try to read the Bible regularly, but it's really hard because I'd rather do other things." Some teens read their Bible on a regular basis, but it's not because they choose to read it for themselves. When asked whether she read her Bible regularly, Elizabeth replied, "Yes, but only during Bible class." In response to the same question, Dale remarked, "Yes, but only because my teacher tells me to." How about you? Do you read your Bible only when it's given to you as a homework assignment, or do you ever read it because you really want to?

Do you know any teens who have a close relationship with Jesus and really want to read His Word on their own? You might be one of them. Reading the Bible can be much like reading many exciting letters from God. Do you ever get excited to find a letter from your best friend in your mailbox (including email)? Andy knows Jesus and loves to read the Word. He said, "Yes, I read God's Word every day. It keeps me going through life." Chrissy takes it a step fur-

ther and encourages other teens to use their Bibles to answer some of the questions or problems they have. She exclaimed, "Yes, if you're having problems in your life, look at the back of your Bible. In the back of your Bible, there should be different verses for different problems. So, if you're having a problem, look up the verses that will help you."

Teens read the Bible because it does something for them. Andy told us that he reads the Bible because it "keeps him going through life". When we asked other Christian teens why they read the Bible, this is what they shared:

- *It makes me feel good.* (Mandy)

- *It gives me more understanding of God.* (Ted)

- *It encourages me.* (Carolyn)

- *It strengthens my relationships.* (Ellyn)

- *It perfects my mistakes.* (David)

- *It gives me hope.* (John)

- *It helps me to understand why God does things.* (Dale)

- *It helps me to see how the world works.* (Andy)

Talking about specific verses in the Bible with a parent or other Christian adult can help you apply God's Word to your life.

If reading the Bible doesn't do any of the above for you, there are several questions you might ask yourself:

- Do you have a personal relationship with God, the author of the Bible? (A book always makes more sense when you know its author.)

- Are you involved with any teen Bible study so that you can hear practical teaching from the Word?

- When you have a question about a verse of Scripture, do you write it down and ask your parents or your youth pastor?

Are you involved with any teen Bible study so that you can hear practical teaching from the Word?

If you continue struggling with reading the Word, John has some good news for you. He said, "Yes, I read the Bible, and it's neat because the Bible gets more interesting to me the older I get."

If you try to be "perfect" in your Bible reading or Scripture memorization, the following thoughts may help you to relax and enjoy your relationship with God a lot more.

- If you feel confused about the style of language used in some Bibles, did you know that there are many different translations and teen study Bibles available for you today?

- If you're reading through the Bible using a formal reading schedule—possibly even a "chapter a day" plan—are you also asking the Holy Spirit to make certain verses that you really need "jump out at you"?

- While you're memorizing verses of Scripture, are you also asking God to make the truths that they contain change your life and deepen your relationship with Him?

Bible reading has three basic goals. First, it's to help you to love God more by developing a closer relationship with Him. Second,

it's to show you how to love people more like Jesus loves them. Third, it's to make clear what God expects of you.

Prayer

When we asked many teens how to get closer to God, one of their most common answers was "Pray". Do *you* ever pray? What do you think that **prayer** really is? It's simply talking to God—and listening to hear what He would say to you. In this way, you get closer to Him. Prayer is like you talking to your best friend and then he or she responding back to you. Even though prayer sounds so easy, many teens still struggle with it. Prayer, for example, doesn't seem to "work" for Carolyn. She put it this way:

Even though prayer sounds so easy, many teens still struggle with it.

I don't feel like I'm really close to God. I want to be so badly that it's driving me insane. I don't know how I can get closer. I pray and pray to God for help. I try everything, but I still feel isolated...

Carolyn said she "prays and prays" to God for help but still feels "isolated". Have you ever felt that your praying hasn't brought you closer to God? Among other possibilities, it could be that God wants Carolyn to do something other than pray in order to get closer to Him. He might want her to join a youth group, break off a friendship that is a negative influence on her, or go and talk to her parents or school counselor about her struggles.

Is it easier for you to pray with others than it is to pray by yourself? If so, you're not alone. David also struggles with praying alone. This is the way that he described it:

I feel that I need to get closer to God, but something's holding me back. I want to get closer to Him. I try to pray alone, but it's like I'm talking to myself.

If you often feel like David does when he's trying to pray, you probably won't pray very much. David's desire to get closer to God, however, is to be greatly admired. His difficulty praying could be due to several other factors besides a lack of prayer. His life could be suffering the consequences of an unhealthy relationship with his parents, arguing with his siblings, moral impurity, lying, or having bad friends.

When we asked your peers the question, "Do you pray regularly to God?", lots of them said "Yes". When we then asked them, "What kinds of things do you talk to God about?", this is what they said:

- *I ask Him to fill me with love and the Holy Spirit. I ask for His strength so I can keep going towards Him.* (Sue)

- *I share with Him the bad things that I do.* (Cathy)

- *When I'm having an awful day, I talk to Him and tell Him about it.* (Vera)

- *I talk to Him about whatever is on my heart.* (Mary)

- *I talk to Him about my life and my parents.* (Cathy)

- *I pray about my friends and what I should do in certain situations.* (John)

- *I ask Him for help where I need it, and I also thank Him.* (Barbie)

- *I pray before meals and before I go to bed. I ask for more patience along with safety, good grades on tests, and for me to get my homework done before a certain time.* (Janelle)

- *I talk to Him about my friends, siblings, and parents; anything that's bothering me.* (Cora)

- *I talk to Him about my Dad who lives in Alaska, the girl I like, and my friends.* (Ray)

- *I ask Him about how I can help the people who are suffering.* (Enrique)

Praying is like using your own internal spiritual hot line to talk to God. When teens ask God to forgive them of their sins and dedicate all of their lives to Jesus Christ as their Savior, God sends His Holy Spirit to live inside of them. Anytime they want to, Christians can "look within" to the Lord in their hearts and have a conversation with Him. Prayer is an opportunity for you to have a continual conversation with God throughout the day; from the classroom to the basketball court...from choir practice to youth group...from church to the privacy of your own bedroom...anytime, anywhere. You can "look within" and talk to Jesus when you've made a mistake, when you need help, when you're being tempted, or when you're happy and want to thank Him for something.

It's your choice. The Bible says, "Draw near to God, and He will draw near to you" (James 4:8). Take the initiative. All you have to do is to come near to Him by sharing your thoughts and feelings with Him. The more you do this, the more comfortable you'll feel with sharing deeper and more personal areas of your life with Him. Just remember: He already knows about all of your struggles and loves you, anyway.

Anytime they want to, Christians can "look within" to the Lord in their hearts and have a conversation with Him.

Sometimes, God will answer your prayers right away; other times, He will answer them later. He's always listening and ready to understand and comfort you whenever you turn to Him. Now and then, God will give you exactly what you ask for. On other occasions, He'll give you something else He knows will be better for you in the long run. Either way, He cares for you and will provide for all of your needs.

At times, the way you hear others pray can make you feel that you have to pray in the same way in order for God to hear you. You might think that you have to pray as loud or as long or with the same words or emotions as someone else. This simply isn't true. God will answer your prayers when you are simply:

- being yourself,

- honest and sincere (about what you ask),

- believing and trusting (in Him for the best and final results),

- pure in your motives (for His glory and someone else's genuine good),

- genuinely repentant for your mistakes, and

- humble and open (admitting your needs and/or desires).

Do you find yourself really busy— too busy to spend time in prayer? God understands.

Do you find it hard to set aside time to pray? Many teens do. But the quality of your prayer hot line with God is not just when you can be all alone somewhere; it's really whether you choose to "abide" in Him throughout the day. As you find your day really busy, God understands. There might be many days that the only words you can say to Him are when you go to sleep at night. That's okay. You'll be joining other teens like Ryan who doesn't pray very much on his own, but just before he goes to sleep at night, he's able to say, "Good night, God!" Remember, you can always choose to talk to Him more the next day.

An Invitation to Prayer

Maybe you don't have a personal relationship with God, and, therefore, you don't like the idea of "praying". Maybe others have told you that prayer is "sissy" or "stupid". But, did you know that you don't have to be a Christian in order to talk to God? Were you aware that you don't have to know that you're going to heaven to have God listen to you? God loves you just as you are. He proved His love for you by sending His Son, Jesus, to the earth to pay the penalty of death for all of the wrongs that you have done. Jesus paid the full price for all of your mistakes and anytime you want to ask Him to forgive you and dedicate your life to Him, you can. He's always there, just waiting for you to come and talk with Him.

Maybe you don't know whether you're a genuine Christian or not. When we asked some more of your peers why they felt that they had a personal relationship with Jesus, these are some of the reasons they gave:

- *I talk with Him a lot.* (Jeremy)

- *I know that I can tell Him everything.* (Cathy)

- *I sometimes have conversations with Him.* (Daniel)

- *I accepted Him in my heart, and He's my best friend. I know that I can always talk to Him about anything. I know He always knows what I did or how I feel.* (Jessa)

- *I can feel His presence.* (Jasmine)

- *He comforts me in bad situations.* (Sue)

- *I have asked Him into my heart.* (Joe)

- *I have felt Him touch my heart.* (Tom)

Can you relate to what Jeremy, Cathy, or the other teens above have said about their relationship with Jesus Christ? If not, maybe you feel like Cora who said that she didn't find it hard to talk with God except when she had "sinned". Have you sinned and now feel the need to ask God for His forgiveness? He's willing to forgive you right now if you'll turn away from your sin and ask Him for His mercy. The Bible says that if you'll confess your sins, God will be faithful to forgive you of all of your sins and to cleanse you from all of your unrighteousness (I John 1:9). Do you feel afraid about where you'll spend eternity when you die? Amy was very open about her **fears** (concern or anxiety about something real or imagined) of death:

God sent His Son Jesus to pay the penalty of death for all of the wrongs that you have done.

I'm struggling with fear with where I'm going after I die. I know that if I have Jesus in my heart, I'll go to heaven. It's just that I'm not sure He's there. I'm trying to grow in my walk with God, but it's so hard.

If you're not a Christian as yet, or if you have serious doubts about being one like Amy does, Ted would like to encourage you:

Young people of America! I think you should all become Christians! To do this, you must read God's Word! Ask someone who knows about God, and they will help you if they are true Christians.

Similarly, Sue shares her personal conviction in these words:

Become a Christian. You might think you are, but maybe you're not. I know a lot of hypocrites (without judging). Remember, God loves you when things aren't going well. He loves you when you sin. He'll help you to change. I'll pray for all of you…

Do you feel far away from God? Then you feel like many teens who know Jesus but admit that their relationship with Him "needs

to improve". If you feel like this, God wants you to know that He loves you very much and that He's waiting for you to take one step toward Him so that He'll take three steps toward you. The Prodigal Son finally became sick of living away from his father, came to his senses, and said, "I will return to my father's house" (Luke 15:11).

Or, maybe you feel like Vera who said: "At times, I feel He's near. At other times, He seems farther away." Did you know that God will withdraw His presence from you sometimes so that you will run after Him more intensely? Maybe you feel like the Lord is drawing you to a greater commitment to Him. If so, your deeper dedication can all start with a single prayer. As you genuinely connect with God, your whole life can be changed forever.

12 • 3 What Are You Allowing To Influence Your Life?

· ·

It seems that the world reaches toward me harder and harder.

David

*I just want to say that I know it's hard being a teenager
and a Christian at the same time because of all of the temptations
that try to influence me: sex, drugs, crime, back-talking,
dating too soon, and pressures to drop out of school.*

Lindsay

What Kind of Friends Do You Have?

"…sex, drugs, crime, back-talking…", there are so many influences that try to destroy teens' lives today, aren't there? The influences that Lindsay has listed are only the beginning. Friends, for example, don't always help. As some more of your peers put it: "My friends are always cussing rather than talking about God" (Vera). "When my friends do things that are wrong, I end up doing them, too" (Katrina). What do you think that these teens should do about all of these pressures from their friends? Carolyn began to see that there was a difference between her and many of her peers, and it didn't make her feel very good: "I don't feel very secure because my relationship with God isn't very good, and I don't quite fit in with my peers".

What do you think that teens should do about all of the pressures from their friends?

Tim admitted that a big part of his problem was "spending more time with my peers than with God". Because of the negative influence that his friends were having on him, Jeremy made a bold decision. He found new friends: "I used to be friends with people who made bad decisions but not anymore". What do you think about Jeremy's decision?

DANGER!

One of the subtle ways that the enemy will use to try to get you to compromise your standards is to get you involved with friends who have a negative influence upon you. Andy, Megan, and Ted expressed the pressure in this way:

- *My friends pressure me toward sexual immorality.*

- *My peers pressure me into going out with guys and making the wrong choices.*

- *My friends make it uncool to be nice.*

When you feel pressured to make unhealthy choices because of the influence of some of your friends, try to remember what Paul told the Corinthians:

> **Do not be deceived. 'Evil company corrupts good habits.'**
> **(I Corinthians 15:33)**

Making positive changes in your life can be very difficult. As you struggle, you're likely to make a few mistakes. Unfortunately, some of your mistakes might be "big" ones. Maybe you've already made a few big mistakes. If you feel you have "blown it"—what would you say was the biggest mistake that you've ever made? Here's how some of your peers answered that question:

- *telling someone I hated them* (Jenny),

- *drinking alcohol* (Sue),

- *obeying Satan* (Steve),

- *having sex* (Ann),

- *stealing and then lying about it* (Daniel),

- *yelling at my parents* (Ryan),

- *cussing out God* (Karen),

- *going off campus with a friend to look for a cute guy's house* (Janet),

- *watching a certain movie* (Tom), and

- *talking badly about someone behind her back* (Kim).

Can you relate to any of these mistakes? If not, your mistakes may be totally different than theirs. How would you advise one

of your friends to handle their mistakes? Whatever your advice to them might be, a more important question is how do *you* handle the mistakes that *you* make? When you make a mistake, do you feel like Sheena: "unclean and a little sick to her stomach" or, like Carolyn: so "miserable that she wants to lay down and die"? Whatever your bad feeling when you "blow it", it's there to motivate you to ask God and others to forgive you.

When You Sin, How Do You Think God Feels About You?

Some of your peers shared that God feels "disappointed" (Elise), or, "He thinks that I'm an imposter because I sin so much, like I don't really mean it when I say 'sorry'" (Janet), or even, "Sometimes, I think He cries" (Emily). John's reply was simply, "God doesn't like it."

Even the computer that can be educational has the potential of becoming a negative influence.

Saying that God doesn't like your sin is true. But, do you ever take that statement one step further and conclude that God doesn't like *you* when you sin? Some teens do. Apparently, this is how Jamie feels whenever he makes a wrong choice: "Whenever I make a mistake, I think that God feels very poorly about me. I don't think that He appreciates me". Jamie is sadly mistaken. The fact is that you could never make a mistake big enough to change God's deep feelings of love and care for you. David has discovered this. These are his words about God's love:

> *You can't do anything to make God <u>not</u> love you.*

Mistakes have consequences, some being worse than others, but God will never leave you alone as you are trying to correct your situation. Sometimes, teens feel ashamed about their actions or attitudes and stay away from God. Unfortunately, this is one reason why Satan loves to get you to sin. He knows that if he can make you feel so bad about yourself, you won't tell anyone and you will stay away from your loving Father. You can expect opposition from Satan if you really want to make things right. He will lie to you about how bad you are and how disappointed God and

You can expect opposition from Satan if you really want to make things right. He will lie to you, but don't listen to him!

others are in you. Don't listen to him (James 4:7)! Humble yourself and go directly to God and those whom you have offended. As a result, you will grow in spiritual maturity and feel like a brand new person!

Looking to Others for Strength

When you are trying to make some positive choices as a Christian, it helps to have some positive role models. Who would you consider to be a good role model in your life? When we asked some of your peers who their greatest spiritual role model (or hero) was and why, this is what they said:

- *Esther—because she showed loyalty and courage in a bad situation.* (Elise)

- *My Dad—because he reads the Bible, and he usually understands me.* (John)

- *Mark, my youth pastor—it's just the way he preaches.* (Ben)

- *My Bible teacher—she's really cool.* (Sara)

If you don't think you have anyone you feel you respect in this way, pray that God will bring special people into your life. You will also find it encouraging as you read about the lives of many Bible characters who also struggled to make wise choices. Make an effort to learn about the spiritual patriarchs of the Christian faith. Their lives of faith will encourage you.

12 • 4 Will You Count the Cost of Being a Christian?

• •

*In the Bible, Job is my spiritual hero because everything
was taken from him, and he still stayed with God.*
David

If you're a Christian, what do you like the most about being one?
When asked what they *liked* the most about Christianity, some
fourteen-year-olds said:

- *I can be forgiven.* (Michelle)

- *I never feel totally rejected. I'm at peace. I can go to God anytime.*
  (Carolyn)

- *I have someone to turn to.* (Ted)

- *I know that God will always be there for me.* (Katrina)

- *I get to go to heaven.* (Amy)

- *I like serving someone who truly loves me.* (Megan)

- *I know that I have someone on my side no matter what.* (Matt)

- *I can talk to God like a friend.* (Allison)

- *I don't have to worry about death.* (Arista)

- *I like others wondering what it is that I have that they don't.* (Lindsey)

- *I can still have fun.* (Ron)

If there are so many benefits for serving God, why do you think
more teens aren't Christians? One reason is that teens find other
aspects about being a Christian they don't like. When asked what
they most *disliked* about being a Christian, these are some of the
answers that other students gave:

- *being made fun of* (Joe);

- *having to set a good example* (Ted);

*If there are so
many benefits
for serving
God, why do
you think more
teens aren't
Christians?*

303

- *people thinking you're a perfect angel with no mistakes, but, as you can see, I make plenty of them* (Megan);

- *always trying to follow the rules* (Mandy);

- *It's hard to follow God all the time.* (Amy);

- *the commitment* (Jan);

- *It's hard for me to sit through church services.* (Joe);

- *I often feel guilty.* (Andy); and

- *people thinking that I'm dumb for believing in something that I can't see* (Lindsey).

All of these aspects that teens don't like about being a Christian make following Jesus challenging and sometimes difficult. Some teens decide that becoming a Christian is too hard and choose not to serve Jesus. Others may pretend to love and serve God on the outside while inside they really don't want to pay the price. Consequently, they know how to "act" spiritual, yet lack a true, life-changing relationship with Him. Angela put it this way, "Some teens try to 'fake' serving God because inwardly they're really scared of becoming true Christians." How many teens do you know who are "pretenders"?

There are many reasons why some teens try to "fake" their Christianity. Here are some of the reasons that your peers gave as to why some put on such a front:

- *to impress their teachers* (Candace);

- *so as not to lose friends* (Lindsey);

- *so that they can fit in* (Emily);

- *because they don't have a healthy self-esteem* (Lindy);

- *in order to please their parents* (Ted);

When "image" is everything, some teens try to put on a front that everything is okay.

304

- *so that they won't get into trouble* (Jenee);

- *because they go to a Christian school and they have to appear 'spiritual'* (Debi);

- *because they think it'll get them into the kingdom of God* (Arista);

- *to get a really fine Christian girl* (Dale);

- *so that people will think that they're a good person* (Shelly);

- *to gain privileges* (Stephanie);

- *to protect their reputation* (Andy); and,

- *to fool their youth pastor and do things behind his back because they don't really care about being a Christian* (Annie).

If you don't want to be a Christian "pretender", then ask the Lord to help you to know and love Him so much that you become willing to accept the things that you don't like about Christianity. In doing this, you'll be counting the cost of being a true follower of Jesus Christ.

12 • 5 What Does Your Future Hold?

· ·

I'm drifting further away from God. Actually, I go back and forth. But, either way, I don't know what to do. There's no one I want to talk to.

Andrew

Maybe I need help in my life, but I don't really want it. Sorry.

Janie

> **Your future is going to be filled with both the good and bad of your personal choices.**

Andrew and Janie have the same basic problem. What do you think it is? They both *need* help, but they both don't *want* help. "There's no one I want to talk to", Andrew says, and "I don't really want help" Janie admits. Just as Andrew's and Janie's futures will reflect whether they choose to get help or not, so your future is going to be filled with both the good and bad of your personal choices.

Do you want to grow spiritually? Your future will be determined by whether you choose to change spiritually or choose to stay the same. Fortunately, many teens your own age have a deep desire for spiritual growth. When asked, "How do you wish your spiritual life would be different?", this is what some of them said:

- *I want to be closer to God in a personal way.* (Aaron)

- *I wish that the Holy Spirit would preach through me.* (Perry)

- *I wish I would shut up and just listen to God.* (Cora)

- *I want to be more open about Jesus in public.* (Ellie)

- *I wish I could hear God.* (Ann)

- *I wish I was more on fire for God.* (Emily)

- *I wish that God would talk to me more.* (Ray)

- *I wish that nothing would pull me back from Him.* (Sue)

- *I wish I could pray aloud more easily.* (Rachel)

The spiritual future for Rachel and the rest of these teens looks bright because they're choosing to desire more of God. How about you? Do you want to hear from God personally? You can learn to hear God's voice. God uses many different ways to speak to people. Here are some of the avenues He uses to communicate with some of your peers.

- *God speaks to me through the Bible and my friends.* (David)

- *God points out the things I need to work on.* (Mandy)

- *He speaks to me through the Holy Spirit.* (Lindy)

- *He uses other people to talk to me.* (Ted)

Some people think it is "luck" when something good happens, while others believe God is ultimately in charge of every detail in their life. What do you think?

- *God speaks to me by giving me strong convictions about certain things.* (Rebecca)

- *He uses worship to communicate with me.* (Karen)

- *God talks to me through prayer.* (John)

- *He speaks to me through my conscience in every decision I make.* (Andy)

- *Through dreams and whispers, He makes His thoughts known to me.* (Christiana)

- *He sends people or experiences to me and speaks to me through them.* (Lindsey)

Recognizing when God speaks to you is only half of the point in "hearing from God". The other half is obeying what you hear. As one Christian put it, "I pray and then obey." Choosing to listen to God and then doing what He says will help you stay close to God and help you never to be haunted by what Kyle said was his worst fear about growing up: "falling away from God".

Do you have a sense of personal **destiny** (the main purpose for which God has created you)? Your future will be happy and fulfilled if you choose to follow the personal destiny that God has planned for you. If, however, you choose to "do your own thing" without consulting Him, then you'll be unhappy in the end. At this point in your life, you might feel like Annie, who said that she didn't feel that God had made her for any special purpose. If you feel like Annie, you can choose to begin seriously to ask God to show you what He created you to be and to do. He will gradu-

As you develop your talents, gifts, and uniqueness, you will feel more secure about your future.

"I love to read and learn new things—Do you think this might have something to do with my future?"
Suzanne

ally begin to unfold it to you. If you don't feel like Annie, you might feel like Ryan and Rachel who both said that they "didn't know" what God's special purpose for them was as yet. At your age, not knowing your special purpose is normal and natural. As you seek to know what your destiny is, however, God will gradually begin to show it to you. As you develop your talents, gifts, and uniqueness, you will feel more secure about your future. Having a divine destiny can make you feel very secure. Your future is in the best hands!

If you feel like Ryan and Rachel, there are a few hindrances that could presently be blocking you from seeing your special purpose in life. One hindrance is not feeling good about yourself as a person who God has created in His own image. Vera describes the connection between her self-image and sense of destiny this way: "When I'm feeling good about myself, I feel that God has a plan for me". It would also follow from Vera's remarks that when you're feeling badly about yourself, you don't feel that God has a plan for you.

Another obstacle to feeling that God has a special plan for you might be how often you feel that you "get into trouble". Mary has felt that way: "When I get into trouble a lot, I don't think there's anything out there for me". Do you think that Mary is right in thinking that there's nothing out there for her because she gets into trouble so much?

Did you know that even adults don't always know for sure what their futures hold? Many of them only take one step at a time. This is the way the characters in the Bible lived, too. Abraham, the father of faith, is a good example. God called him to leave his home town of Ur (Mesopotamia), where the people worshipped the moon god. When God called him to leave, He didn't tell him exactly where He was leading him. Abraham "...went out, not knowing where he was going" (Hebrews 11:8). Abraham had to depend on God each step of the way. Why doesn't God show you a complete picture of your life all at once? It's because He wants

you to learn to live by faith; to trust Him to put together each piece of your Life Puzzle in His own time and in His own way.

> *Everybody has a purpose. Everyone's life is like a puzzle.*
> *One piece doesn't mean anything, but if you hook all*
> *of the pieces together, they form a picture.*
> Perry

If you're having trouble finding the next piece of your Life Puzzle, you might want to consider taking Jessica's advice: "...call on God to help you, because He will".

There are, however, many teens your age who are already recognizing their special purpose:

- *I sometimes think that my special purpose is working with children because people say that I'm really good with them.* (Ashley)

- *A lot of pastors have prayed for me, and they said that I'm going to be a leader in God's kingdom.* (Ben)

- *I think that basketball is my purpose in life because I'm very good at it.* (Danny)

- *My purpose is to be kind to others and make them feel good.* (Jeremy)

- *I know that I'm supposed to witness to my friends.* (Jasmine)

- *I think that God wants me to teach the Word to others.* (John)

- *God has told me to help save the lost.* (Barbie)

- *I have wanted to be a missionary.* (Luke, Sue)

- *My special purpose is going to be through my future job which might also mean being a pastor.* (Bill)

- *I hope marriage is in my destiny.* (Ryan)

"I love science class. Maybe someday I will find a cure for cancer."
Donald

From playing basketball to being a missionary, from wanting to get married to evangelism, God's special purpose for you will be different from everyone else's. It will be very exciting for you to find your divine destiny and fulfill it. I can tell you right now what the most important part of your destiny is—having a close, loving relationship with Jesus! If you're not sure what your next step is in fulfilling your special purpose, then start asking Him and He'll begin to let you know! God's more anxious for you to discover His unique plan for you than you are to discover it.

Do you remember Eve's choice that we mentioned to you at the beginning of this book? Do you recall how she allowed herself to become distracted from God's plan by the subtle and deceptive thoughts of the Evil One? Do you recall how all of the sin, sickness, and struggle in the world could have been prevented—if only she had made the right choice? As it was with Adam and Eve, so it'll be in your life. Your future will be a giant unfolding of the results of all of your personal choices. God bless you on your journey.

Your future will be a giant unfolding of the results of all of your personal choices.

Chapter 12 Review

· ·

Defining the Terms

Prayer

Fear

Destiny

Recalling the Facts

1. What factors influence your view of God?

2. What are two main goals of Bible reading?

3. What does it mean to "abide" in God throughout the day?

4. How is your life like a puzzle?

Applying the Truth

1. I Corinthians 15:33 says: "Do not be deceived. 'Evil company corrupts good habits'." How might this verse apply to your own life?

2. The Bible says that Satan is the "father of lies"(Read John 8:44). How might knowing this help you to recognize his schemes against you? Apply James 4:7 to your life: "Submit to God. Resist the devil and he will flee from you".

3. What does it mean for a teenager to "count the cost" of being a Christian? What does it mean to "fake" your Christianity? Why might teens act this way? How do you think this makes God feel?

4. You can learn to hear God's voice—personally. How might God speak to you?

NOTES

Chapter 1

1 Rick Joyner, *There Were Two Trees in the Garden* (Pineville, North Carolina: Morning Star Publications; New Kensington, Pennsylvania: Whitaker House, 1992), 9.

Chapter 2

1 Dr. Paul Brand and Philip Yancey, *Fearfully and Wonderfully Made* (Grand Rapids: Zondervan Publishing House, 1980), 27-28.

Chapter 3

1 "Why are Hamburgers called Hamburgers?" *Parade* (February 28, 1999).
2 Karen Catchpole, "What is Fit?", *Jump* (April, 1998).
3 Dr. James Dobson, "The Ultimate Child Abuse", *Dr. James Dobson's Bulletin* (Focus on the Family, March, 1999).

Chapter 4

1 Karen Catchpole, "What is Fit?", *Jump* (April, 1998).
2 Ibid.
3 Ibid.
4 Roger Rapoport, "Blasting Away at Body Fat", *Running* (March/April, 1982).
5 Bob Anderson, *Stretching* (Bolinas, California: Shelter Publications, 1980), 11.

Chapter 5

1 Kristen Drenten as told to Michelle Sullivan, "I'm Living With Cancer", *Teen,* (January, 1998).
2 Susan Boe, *Total Health: Choices for a Winning Lifestyle* (West Linn, Oregon: RiversEdge Publishing Company, 1995), xv.
3 Dr. Paul Brand and Philip Yancey, *Fearfully and Wonderfully Made* (Grand Rapids: Zondervan Publishing House, 1980), 59.

4   Dr. James F. and Phyllis A. Balch, *Prescription for Nutritional Healing,* 2nd Edition (C.N.C. Avery Publishing Group, 1990), 228- 229.

5   Ibid., 228.

Chapter 6

1   Francis Frangipane, *The Three Battlegrounds* (Cedar Rapids, Iowa: Arrow Publications, 1996), 13-14.

2   Ibid., 15.

Chapter 8

1   Marie Winn, *The Plug-in Drug* (New York: Penguin Books, 1985), 67.

2   Ibid., 54-55.

Chapter 10

1   Josh McDowell and Bob Hostetler, *RIGHT FROM WRONG: What You Need To Know To Help Youth Make Right Choices* (Dallas, Texas: Word Publishing, 1994), 20.

2   David G. Benner,ed., *Baker Encyclopedia of Psychology* (Grand Rapids: Baker Book House, 1985), 37.

3   Ibid., 35.

4   Ibid., 37.

Chapter 11

1   A.T. Robertson, *Word Pictures in the New Testament* (Nashville: Broadman Press, 1930), 184.

2   Marie Winn, *The Plug-in Drug* (New York: Penguin Books, 1985), 67.

3   Ibid., 88.

4   F.J. Dake, *Dake's Annotated Reference Bible* (1961), 319, 931.

5   A.T. Robertson, *Word Pictures in the New Testament* (Nashville: Broadman Press, 1930), IV, 403.

BIBLIOGRAPHY

Devotional References

Arnott, John. *What Christians Should Know About the Importance of Forgiveness.* Tonbridge, Kent TN11 OZS, England: Sovereign World Limited, distributed by Renew Books, a ministry of Gospel Light, Ventura, California, 1997.

Brand, Dr. Paul and Philip Yancey. *Fearfully and Wonderfully Made.* Grand Rapids: Zondervan Publishing House, 1980.

Dobson, Dr. James. *Focus on the Family Bulletin.* Carol Stream, Illinois: Tyndale House, November, 1998.

Frangipane, Francis. *Holiness, Truth and The Presence Of God.* Cedar Rapids, Iowa: Arrow Publications, 1986.

Frangipane, Francis. *The Three Battlegrounds.* Cedar Rapids, Iowa: Arrow Publications, 1996.

Joyner, Rick. *There Were Two Trees In The Garden.* Pineville, North Carolina: Morning Star Publications; New Kensington, Pennsylvania: Whitaker House, 1992.

McMillen, S.I. *None of These Diseases.* Grand Rapids: Fleming H. Revell, division of Baker Book House, 1984.

Smith, Wendell. *Dragon Slayer.* Portland, Oregon: Generation Ministries of Bible Temple, 1978.

Smith, Wendell. *Roots of Character.* Portland, Oregon: Bible Temple Publishing, 1979.

White, Jerry. *Honesty, Morality and Conscience.* Colorado Springs: Navpress, 1979.

Health References

Anderson, Bob. *Stretching.* Bolinas, California: Shelter Publications, 1945.

Balch, Dr. James F. and Phyllis A., *Prescription for Nutritional Healing.* C.N.C. Avery Publishing Group, 1990.

Bicycle Helmet Safety Institute. *A Compendium of Statistics from Various Sources.* http://helmets.org/webdocs/stats.htm

Boe, Susan. *Total Health: Choices for a Winning Lifestyle.* West Linn, Oregon: RiversEdge Publishing Company, 1995.

Brand, Paul. *You Are Wonderful.* Tape Series: Norlynn Audio Media Services, 1994.

Great American Smokeout FAQ's. American Cancer Society, 1999. http://www.cancer.org/smokeout/faq.html

Minirth, Dr. Frank, et al. *Love Hunger: Recovery From Food Addiction.* Nashville: Thomas Nelson Publishers, 1990.

"Protecting Your Heart." The Meridian Newsletter. Portland, Oregon: Legacy Health Systems, 1999.

Walker, Norman, W. *Colon Health: the KEY to a VIBRANT LIFE.* Prescott: Norwalk Press, 1979.

ABC's of The Human Body: A Family Answer Book. Reader's Digest Editors. Pleasantville, NY: The Reader's Digest Association, 1987.

The Complete Manual of Fitness and Well-Being. Reader's Digest Editors. Pleasantville, NY: The Reader's Digest Association, 1988.

Ubell, Earl. *"The Deadly Emotions: They Can Shorten Your Life If You Let Them."* Parade (Feruary 11, 1990), 4-6.

Vredevelt, Pam. *Walking A Thin Line: Anorexia and Bulimia, The Battle Can Be Won.* Portland, Oregon: Multnomah Press, 1985.

MADD. Mother's Against Drunk Driving. http://www.MADD.org/stats/youth

Marijuana: Facts Parents Need to Know. National Institute on Drug Abuse, 1998.

Teen Drug Use Doubled Since 1992. Roberto Suro. Washington Post, 1996. http://www.washingtonpost.com

Teenage Drug Use. Frank's Case Book. Frank Monaldo, 1996. http://home.us.net/~fmm/teens.htm

Medical References

Guidelines for Effective School Health Education To Prevent the Spread of AIDS. Center for Disease Control.. MMWR 1988;37 (suppl. No. S-2) (inclusive page numbers).

"HIV/AIDS PREVENTION." Center for Disease Control. (September, 1992).

Home Medical Encyclopedia, The American Medical Association, Vol. Two, I-Z. Clayman, Charles B. (Medical Editor). New York: Published by The Reader's Digest Association, Inc., with permission of Random House, Inc.

Hole, John W. Jr. *Human Anatomy and Physiology.* Second Edition. Dubuque, Iowa: Wm. C. Brown Company Publishers, 1981.

Roy, Steven and Richard Irvin. *Sports Medicine: Prevention, Evaluation, Management, and Rehabilitation.* Englewood Cliffs, New Jersey: Prentice Hall, Inc., 1983.

"AIDS PREVENTION GUIDE: The Facts About HIV Infection And AIDS." U.S. Department of Health and Human Services. (1992).

Teen References

"A Gift No One Can Take Away." Rosemary Zibart. Parade Magazine. Portland, Oregon (November, 1998).

Anderson, Neil T. and Dave Park. *The Bondage Breaker, Youth Edition.* Eugene, Oregon: Harvest House Publishers, 1993.

Dobson, Dr. James. *Preparing for Adolescence.* Ventura: Regal Books a Division of Gospel Light, 1989.

McDowell, Josh. *How To Help Your Child Say "NO" To Sexual Pressure.* Dallas: Word Publishing, 1987.

McDowell, Josh and Bob Hostetler. *"Help Your Teen Make the Right Choice."* Focus on the Family (November, 1994), 3-4.

McDowell, Josh and Bob Hostetler. *RIGHT FROM WRONG: What You Need To Know To Help Youth Make Right Choices.* Dallas: Word Publishing, 1994.

McDowell, Josh and Dick Day. *Why Wait? What You Need To Know About the Teen Sexuality Crisis.* Nashville: Thomas Nelson Publishers.

Talley, Scott. *Talking with Your Kids about the Birds and the Bees.* Ventura: Regal Books, a division of Gospel Light Publications, 1990.

"The New Sexual Revolution." Focus on the Family Newsletter, "Plugged In" special insert (October, 1997).

Winn, Marie. *The Plug-in Drug.* New York: Penguin Books, 1985.

Biblical References

Elwall, W.A.,ed. *Evangelical Dictionary of Theology.* Grand Rapids: Baker, 1984.

Dake, F.J. *Dake's Annotated Reference Bible.* 1961.

Douglas, J.D, ed. *The New Bible Dictionary.* Grand Rapids: Eerdmans, 1962.

Nave, Orville, J. *Nave's Topical Bible: Original Edition With Index.* Grand Rapids: Baker Book House, 1981.

Robertson, A.T., *Word Pictures in the New Testament.* Nashville: Broadman Press, 1930.

Vincent, Marvin, R. *Word Studies In The New Testament.* Grand Rapids: Eerdmans, 1980.

Standard References

Benner, David G., ed. *Baker Encyclopedia of Psychology.* Grand Rapids: Baker Book House, 1985.

Random House Dictionary. New York: Ballantine Books, 1978.

Webster's New Collegiate Dictionary. Springfield, Massachusetts: Merriam-Webster, 1977.

GLOSSARY

Acne. A skin condition that occurs when the pores of your skin become clogged with oil.

Addiction. A physical or mental need for a drug or other substance.

Adrenal glands. Release hormones in response to certain types of stress. Responsible for the "fight or flight" response.

Aerobic. When your muscles demand more oxygen than normal during an activity.

AIDS. Acquired Immunodeficiency Syndrome. A result of HIV.

Alateen. A group designed to help children of alcoholic parents.

Al-Anon. A group designed to help the husbands, wives, and friends of alcoholics.

Alcoholics Anonymous (AA). A support group specifically designed for alcoholics.

Alcoholism. An illness characterized by habitual, compulsive, long-term, and heavy drinking.

Alexander Fleming. The individual who discovered the drug penicillin in London in 1928.

Alimentary canal. A long muscular tube that extends from the mouth to the anus.

Anaerobic. Short bursts of activity without the use of much oxygen.

Anemia. A condition which occurs when a person has an inadequate supply of red blood cells.

Anorexia. A self-induced starvation resulting in extreme weight loss and characterized by an intense fear of gaining weight and becoming fat.

Antibodies. Produced by your white blood cells to fight off germs.

Arteries. Blood vessels that carry oxygenated blood away from the heart.

Arteriosclerosis. A disease caused by the hardening of the arteries.

Arthritis. A condition when joints become inflamed.

Artificial relationships. Bonding with someone or something that doesn't really exist instead of with an actual living person.

Asthma. A condition in which the bronchi swell and constrict breathing.

Astigmatism. A condition in which a person's vision is distorted due to the irregular shape of the cornea or lens.

Atrophy. A condition which occurs when a long period of time lapses between workouts and the muscles decrease in size and strength.

Bacteria. Single-celled tiny organisms that attack your body. Strep throat, pneumonia, and some STDs are caused by bacteria.

Balanced diet. Making food choices that include a wide variety from all that God has given to you in nature.

Blackhead. A pore that's plugged with oil—but is exposed to the air.

Blood pressure. The force that your blood puts on the inside walls of your blood vessels.

Body composition. The relationship between your fat and lean (muscle) body weight.

Boundary. An invisible line that separates you from everyone and everything else. Like a fence with a gate that you control between you and the outside world.

Bronchitis. A swelling or inflammation of the bronchi.

Bruise. (see *hematoma*).

Bulimia. A pattern of "bingeing" (eating large amounts of food) and "purging" (self-induced vomiting or laxative abuse), with or without weight loss.

Bursitis. A condition where the bursa becomes inflamed.

Caffeine. A stimulant found in many products such as coffee, tea, cola, some diet aids, and chocolate.

Calorie. A unit of heat that your body uses for activity.

Cancer. A disease which occurs when abnormal cells grow out of control.

Capillaries. The smallest blood vessels.

Carbohydrates. Sugars and starches that the body uses for energy.

Carbon monoxide. A poisonous gas that is produced by car engines and burning tobacco.

Carcinogen. Any substance that tends to produce cancer. They are both natural and man-made.

Cardiac muscle. The heart muscle.

Cardiovascular fitness. The condition of the heart.

Cardiovascular system. Portion of the circulatory system that includes the heart.

Carrier. A person who is carrying the germ but doesn't seem to be suffering from the illness.

Cartilage. Strong elastic material on the ends of the bones.

Cavity. When bacteria combines with sugary foods and forms an acid.

Cells. The basic building blocks of the body from which all larger parts are formed.

Central nervous system (CNS). The main control center of the body that includes the brain and spinal cord.

Cerebral palsy (CP). A condition in which the cerebrum of the brain is damaged.

Character. Who you are on the inside, what you do when no one is watching.

Cholesterol. A fatty substance in the blood which increases the risk of heart disease.

Chronic overeating. The habit of eating more food than your body needs.

Cirrhosis. A chronic disease of the liver that often results from a long-standing addiction to alcohol.

Codeine. Highly addictive narcotics that are prescribed as pain killers.

Communication. The act of expressing thoughts, feelings, information, or beliefs easily or effectively through speech, writing or signs.

Comprehension. To have an understanding and memory of what you've read.

Intellectual. Having to do with your mind; mental.

Confident. To have no feelings of inferiority.

Congenital. A condition occurring at birth.

Connective tissue. The tissues that bind structures together providing support and protection.

Consequences. The effect, outcome, or result of something.

Constipation. A condition which occurs when the feces are hard and dry making a bowel movement very difficult.

Contagious period. (see *incubation period*).

Convictions. A person's strong belief on a particular issue.

Countenance. The expression of your face.

Cramp. A condition that results when a muscle doesn't relax.

Cuticle. Surrounds the nail and is made of a nonliving skin. The cuticle protects the base of the nail from germs and bacteria.

Dandruff. A condition in which the outer layer of skin on the scalp flakes off.

Deception. The act of misleading by false appearance or statement; to trick.

Degenerative. Diseases where the body's tissues break down, don't grow, or malfunction.

Denial. Refusing to acknowledge the existence of a problem.

Depressants. Drugs that tend to slow down your body's nervous system.

Dermatologist. A doctor who treats skin disorders.

Dermis. The middle layer of skin.

Destiny. A purpose for which God has created you.

Diabetes mellitus. A condition which occurs when the body cannot properly utilize sugar.

Diabetes type I. A condition which results in a person being insulin-dependent where the pancreas produces little or no insulin.

Diabetes type II: A condition that results in a person being non-insulin dependent where the pancreas does not produce enough insulin to meet the body's needs or the body can't use it correctly.

Diaphragm. A large muscle that separates the chest from the abdomen.

Diarrhea. A condition which occurs when there is too much water in the bowels causing loose and watery stools.

Diet. All the foods you choose to eat on a regular basis.

Digestion. The process by which food is broken down and made useful for the body.

Disease. Any condition that negatively affects the healthy and normal functioning of your mind or body.

Dislocation. When the end of a bone is pushed out of its joint.

Disrespect. To show a lack of courtesy by being rude; to insult; to be sarcastic, sassy.

Distract. To divide the mind.

Drug abuse. A condition that occurs when a person uses an illegal drug or misuses a legal one.

Drugs. Substances that alter the function of one or more body organs.

Duodenum. The first part of the small intestine. The bile in the duodenum breaks down fats contained in food.

Empathy. When you really feel for a person who is hurt because you've experienced the same hurt.

Emphysema. A disease that affects the alveoli (air sacs) of the lungs.

Empty calories. Those foods that don't have any nutritive value.

Endocrine system. The system of the body that secretes hormones into the bloodstream as messages to the cells.

Epidermis. The outer layer of skin.

Epiglottis. A small flap of skin that prevents food from entering the trachea.

Epilepsy. A brain disorder that results from a sudden burst of nerve action.

Epithelial tissues. The tissue that covers all body surfaces inside and out of the body.

Esophagus. A passageway that carries food to the stomach.

Essential amino acids. Eight amino acids that your body does not produce naturally and must get from the foods you eat.

Excretory system. The system that provides ways for waste to be removed from the body.

Farsightedness. A condition where a person has difficulty seeing things that are close.

Fats. Concentrated source of energy that can provide twice as much energy than carbohydrates.

Fat-soluble. Vitamins that don't dissolve in water and can be stored in the body.

Fat-vs-lean body weight. (see *Body composition*).

FDA. Food and Drug Administration. The organization that tests drugs to make sure they are safe.

Fear. A concern or anxiety about something real or imagined.

Fitness. The ability of your mind and body to work together to their highest possible level.

Flatulence. Gas produced in the stomach or intestines.

Flexibility. The ability to move your joints and muscles through a full range of motion.

Follicles. The roots of your hair are secured in these small pockets.

Forgive. To release all of your desire to punish or get even with those who have hurt or offended you.

Fracture. A break in the bone.

Friendship. A social connection in which people willingly share common interests or activities.

Gallbladder. A pear-shaped sac which lies underneath the liver. Bile produced by the liver is passed to the gallbladder.

Gallstones. Pebble-like stones that are formed when the bile stored in the gallbladder hardens into small crystals.

Germs or Pathogens. Tiny particles that may be plant or animal that cause disease.

Gingivitis. A gum disease caused by a build-up of plaque and tarter on your teeth.

Goal. An achievement toward which you work. Your personal aim, purpose, or end in doing or not doing something.

Habits. A pattern of behavior established from repetition.

Halitosis. A condition that results in bad breath.

Hallucinogen. A group of drugs that cause the brain to form unreal images.

Head lice. Insects that live in the hair and look very similar to dandruff.

Healthy. A state of physical, mental, social and spiritual well-being.

Heart. The muscle that pumps blood throughout the body.

Heartburn. A discomfort that occurs when stomach acid flows back into the esophagus.

Hematoma. A condition which occurs when blood vessels are broken in an area of the body as a result of an injury.

Hemophilia. A disease in which the blood is lacking one or more of the clotting factors.

Heroin. An illegal drug that is a depressant and is extremely dangerous.

High blood pressure. (see *hypertension*).

HIV. Human Immunodeficiency Virus. The virus that causes AIDS.

Homeostasis. A balanced, stable internal environment inside the body.

Hormones. Chemicals released by the glands of the endocrine system often called "chemical messengers".

Humility. Realizing your own limitations.

Hypertension. A condition which occur when the pressure on the inside walls of the arteries becomes too high.

Hypocrites. Giving the impression that you have certain beliefs, or feelings that you really don't have. Often called being "two-faced".

Incubation period. The most infectious time of the disease.

Indigestion. A discomfort that occurs when food is not completely digested.

Infatuation. Feeling strong emotional attraction to a person of the opposite sex.

Infectious disease. An illness caused by germs that spread from one person to another.

Influences. The power of persons or things to produce effects on others.

Ingrown toenail. A nail that pushes into the skin on the side of your toe.

Inhalants. Substances whose fumes are breathed in to give the user a high-like feeling, can cause permanent brain damage.

Inhibitory effect. A result of alcohol that causes the blocking of the center of the brain that controls a person's degree of self-control and shyness.

Insulin. A hormone produced by the pancreas to control how the body uses sugar.

Interferon. A communication system between the cells to inform them to prepare to fight the virus.

Jealousy. The feeling of resentment against another for having a success or talent that you want to have.

Joints. Strands of tissue that join bones or keep organs in place.

Keratin. A hard substance that gives nails their strength.

Kidneys. Two bean-shaped organs that cleanse the blood of impurities and send it back to the bloodstream.

Kidney stones. A condition which occurs when hard stones composed primarily of calcium are developed in the kidneys.

Large intestine. The cecum, colon, rectum and anal canal. Moves waste through the body.

Leukemia. A form of cancer characterized by an uncontrolled increase in the production of white blood cells.

Lifetime sports. Activities that a person can participate in throughout a lifetime.

Liver. The largest organ in the body which produces bile that helps digest food.

Long-term goal. Something that you make specific plans to get done over a relatively long period of time.

LSD (lysergic acid diethylamide). An extremely dangerous hallucinogen.

Lung cancer. A disease that occurs when cells grow out of control and destroy the alveoli.

Lungs. Large, soft cone-shaped organs. The main organs of the respiratory system.

Lymphocytes. White blood cells that fight off germs.

MADD. Mothers Against Drunk Drivers.

Malocclusion. A condition when your upper and lower teeth don't line up properly.

Masticate. Chew thoroughly.

Mature. To grow physically, mentally, emotionally, socially and spiritually.

Medicines. Drugs that are meant to relieve pain, cure diseases, or prevent other illnesses.

Metabolic rate. The speed at which your body burns calories.

Minerals. Inorganic substances that are essential for the body.

Morphine. Highly addictive narcotics that are prescribed as pain killers.

Multiple sclerosis (MS). A disease in which the outer coating that protects some nerves is destroyed.

Muscle tissue. Tissues that provide movement to the body.

Muscular fatigue. A condition which results when a muscle or group of muscles have been overworked and are tired.

Muscular fitness. The measurement of your muscle strength and muscle endurance.

Muscular system. The group of tissue that makes body parts move.

Narcotics. A form of depressant that induces sleep or decreases feeling.

Nausea. A sickness in the stomach that is often accompanied by an involuntary impulse to vomit.

Nearsightedness. A condition where a person has difficulty seeing things that are far away.

Negative peer pressure. What you feel when others encourage you to do something that is harmful for you.

Nerve tissue. Tissues that receive and transmit impulses to various parts of the body.

Nervous system. The complex set of impulses which controls and coordinates all the body parts.

Nicotine. A colorless, oily, water-soluble, highly toxic and addictive, liquid alkaloid obtained from tobacco.

Noninfectious disease. An illness caused by heredity, the environment, and a person's lifestyle.

Nonprescription drug. "Over-the-counter" drugs that are medicines that can be sold without a doctor's written permission.

Nonverbal communication. Sharing a message without talking such as body language hand motions.

Nutrients. Substances in foods that your body needs (proteins, carbohydrates, fats, vitamins, minerals and water).

Obese. Weighing more than 20% over ideal weight.

Organ. Two or more tissues grouped together to perform a singular function.

Orthodontics. A practice where braces treat severe irregularities of the teeth.

Osteoporosis. A loss of bone tissue.

Ovaries. The glands of the female reproductive system, located inside the female body. Gradually release hormones responsible for female sex characteristics.

Overweight. Weighing more than the desired weight for age, sex, height and frame size.

Pancreas. Elongated organ that lies back of the stomach. It produces pancreatic juice that break down fats, proteins, and carbohydrates.

PCP or angel dust (phencyclidine). An extremely dangerous hallucinogen.

Periodontal disease. A more advanced gum disease.

Periodontium. The name of the bone, tissue, and gum that support your teeth.

Peripheral nervous system (PNS). The nerves that connect the CNS to other body parts.

Peristaltic movement (peristalsis). A wave-like action that moves the food down the esophagus into the stomach.

Personal identity. To know who you are in Christ.

Pharynx. Often called the throat.

Pimple. A clogged pore that has become infected and filled with pus. Pimples are the most serious type of acne.

Pinched nerve. A condition which results when a nerve is squeezed causing pain or paralysis.

Pink eye. A very contagious condition caused by a bacterial infection.

Pituitary gland. A gland located in the brain, the master gland releasing the growth hormone.

Plaque. A grainy, sticky coating that is constantly forming on your teeth.

Plasma. The liquid portion of the blood.

Platelets. The portion of the blood that helps the blood to clot.

Pneumonia. A serious illness affecting the lungs.

Positive peer pressure. What you feel when others encourage you to do something that is good for you.

Prayer. Talking to God and listening to hear what God would say to you.

Prescription drug. Drugs that are sold only with a written order from a doctor.

Pride. To think yourself better than you are, an "I don't need anyone" attitude.

Proteins. A string of amino acids used by the body to build new cells and tissues.

Pulled muscle. A condition which results when a muscle has pulled away from the bone.

RDA. Recommended Daily Allowance. An assumed percentage for the average non-pregnant adult.

Red blood cells. The portion of the blood that carries oxygen.

Regress. To go backward.

Relationship. A tie with people by blood, marriage, work, or social role.

Reputation. What people think of you.

Resident bacteria. Friendly bacteria that your body needs.

Resistance. The ability of the body to fight the invading germ.

Respect. Esteem, admiration, acceptance, or courtesy; not intruding upon or interfering with another person's rights.

Respiratory system. A group of passages that exchanges gases in order for the body to function properly.

Revenge. To get even with someone.

Saturated fat. These fats are solid at room temperature, which tend to increase blood cholesterol.

Scoliosis. A condition when the vertebral column develops an abnormal curvature so that one hip or shoulder is lower than the other.

Sebum. An oily substance that eventually clogs the pores of your skin.

Self-control. Being able to restrain your words or behaviors that might hurt you or someone else.

Self-esteem. The way you feel about yourself.

Short-term goal. Something that you make specific plans to accomplish within a relatively brief period of time.

Side effects. Any reactions to a drug other than the effect intended.

Skeletal muscle. Muscles that cause the body to move.

Skeletal system. The group of 206 bones that make up the frame of the body.

Small intestine. The location in the body where most of the digestion and absorption of nutrients occurs.

Smooth muscle. Muscles found in the digestive system and blood vessels.

Social health. Your ability to get along with different kinds of people.

Soul. A person's mind, will, and emotions.

Sprain. An injury that results when a ligament is stretched or torn at a joint.

STD. Sexually transmitted disease (venereal disease). Diseases that pass from one person to another through sexual contact.

Stimulants. Drugs that speed up the body's nervous system.

Strain. An injury that results when a muscle or group of muscles have been overworked.

Stroke. When the flow of blood to one part of the brain is severely restricted or cut off.

Sty. When one of the small glands in your eyelid gets infected and swollen. It may look like a pimple.

Subcutaneous layer. The deepest layer of skin.

Substitutions. Replacing one person or thing with another.

Symptoms. Reactions from your body (stuffy nose, sore throat), that indicate that it is trying to fight an intruder, an infection. Your body redirects its energy to fight the germ.

Tar. A thick, dark, sticky liquid that is formed when tobacco burns.

Tartar. A substance that hardens on your teeth.

Temptation. Something that allures or draws someone especially to evil.

Testes. The glands of the male reproductive system, located outside the male body. Gradually release hormones responsible for male sex characteristics.

Thyroid gland. Hormones released from the thyroid controls how fast the body metabolizes (uses) food for energy.

Tissues. Similar cells organized into specialized groups to carry out particular functions.

Tolerance. A resistance in the body to something.

Total Health. The physical, mental, social and spiritual well-being of an individual.

Trachea. A passageway that carries air to the lungs.

Tumors. A group or mass of abnormal cells.

Unsaturated fats. Usually liquid at room temperature and don't tend to raise blood cholesterol

Vaccine. Weakened or destroyed cells of a particular germ that is injected into a person to produce enough antibodies to keep a person from contracting the disease.

Vegetarian diet. A diet that typically excludes animal products.

Veins. Blood vessels that carry blood that lacks oxygen (deoxygenated blood) back to the heart.

Verbal communication. Sharing a message through words, talking.

Virus. Smaller than bacteria and attack individual cells. They are responsible for the common cold, chicken pox, measles, and AIDS.

Vitamins. Organic substances the body needs in small amounts.

Wall. A barrier between people that hinders their communication.

Water-soluble. Vitamins that dissolve in water and can pass through the body.

White blood cells. The portion of the blood that fights germs, viruses, and diseases.

Whitehead. A type of acne that is created when oil becomes trapped inside a pore.

Withdrawal. The physical disturbance that results when an individual does not consume a substance he/she is addicted to.

INDEX